Penal POPULISM AND PUBLIC OPINION

RECENT TITLES IN

STUDIES IN CRIME AND PUBLIC POLICY

Michael Tonry and Norval Morris, General Editors

Making Crime Pay: Law and Order in Contemporary American Politics
Katherine Beckett

Community Policing, Chicago Style
Wesley G. Skogan and Susan M. Hartnett

Crime Is Not the Problem: Lethal Violence in America
Franklin E. Zimring and Gordon Hawkins

Hate Crimes: Criminal Law & Identity Politics
James B. Jacobs and Kimberly Potter

Politics, Punishment, and Populism
Lord Windlesham

American Youth Violence
Franklin E. Zimring

Bad Kids: Race and the Transformation of the Juvenile Court
Barry C. Feld

Gun Violence: The Real Costs
Philip J. Cook and Jens Ludwig

Punishment, Communication, and Community
R. A. Duff

Punishment and Democracy: Three Strikes and You're Out in California
Franklin E. Zimring, Gordon Hawkins, and Sam Kamin

Restorative Justice and Responsive Regulation
John Braithwaite

Maconochie's Gentlemen: The Story of Norfolk Island & the Roots of Modern Prison Reform
Norval Morris

Can Gun Control Work?
James B. Jacobs

Penal Populism and Public Opinion: Lessons from Five Countries
Julian V. Roberts, Loretta J. Stalans, David Indermaur, and Mike Hough

Penal Populism and Public Opinion

Lessons from Five Countries

Julian V. Roberts

Loretta J. Stalans

David Indermaur

Mike Hough

OXFORD UNIVERSITY PRESS

2003

OXFORD
UNIVERSITY PRESS

Oxford New York

Auckland Bangkok Buenos Aires Cape Town Chennai
Dar es Salaam Delhi Hong Kong Istanbul Karachi Kolkata
Kuala Lumpur Madrid Melbourne Mexico City Mumbai Nairobi
São Paulo Shanghai Taipei Tokyo Toronto

Published by Oxford University Press, Inc.
198 Madison Avenue, New York, New York 10016

www.oup.com

Oxford is a registered trademark of Oxford University Press

Library of Congress Cataloging-in-Publication Data
Penal populism and public opinion : lessons from five countries /
by Julian V. Roberts . . . [et al.].
p. cm. — (Studies in crime and public policy)
Includes bibliographical references and index.
ISBN 0-19-513623-3
1. Sentences (Criminal procedure)—Public opinion—Cross-cultural studies. 2. Crime—Public opinion—Cross-cultural studies.
3. Punishment—Public opinion—Cross-cultural studies.
4. Crime in mass media—Cross-cultural studies.
5. Public opinion—Cross-cultural studies.
I. Roberts, Julian V. II. Series.
HV8708 .P46 2002
364.6'5—dc21 2002019182

9 8 7 6 5 4 3 2 1

Printed in the United States of America
on acid-free paper

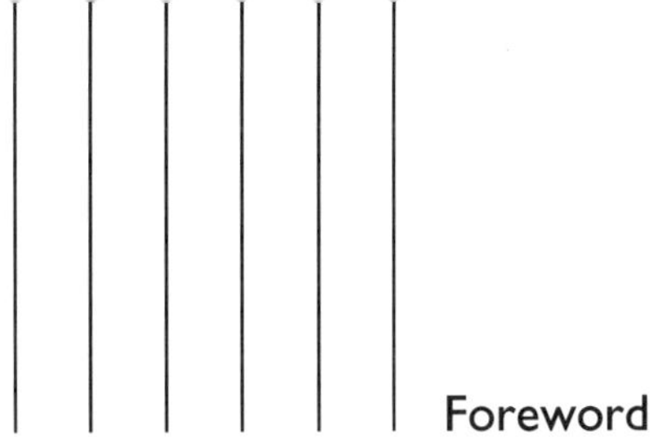

Foreword

I remember an era when the only feature of penal policy that politicians discussed was capital punishment, and even that was forgotten at election time. The increases in crime-rates—real and apparent—after World War II discredited "liberal" strategies and provided right-wing penologists and judges with new ammunition.

It was inevitable that rising rates of crime—or reported crime—would sooner or later thrust law enforcement and sentencing onto political platforms, but nobody foresaw the extent to which by the end of the century law enforcement would become a shuttlecock between parties.

This book, the product of collaboration between authors with experience in at least five jurisdictions, documents the process with an impressive collection of empirical data. Politicians and penal reformers may call the result cynical. In fact, it achieves as much realism as is scientifically possible. The science of interpreting public opinion has become much more sophisticated than it was in the days of simplistic opinion polls. For example, at last it can be said that "It is bad practice to ask people questions when it is clear that the majority lack the information necessary to make a sensible response."

This book's main theme is the interplay between politicians and voters, complicated by the oversimplifications and distortions of the news media. Hard cases make bad law, and spectacular cases make knee-jerk policy. The authors see this as a downward spiral that could descend even further. Is it a spiral which can be halted? Chapter 10 outlines expedients that may combat it. Among its suggestions is the creation of a "policy buffer"—an institution without politicians whose task it would be to advise and supply relevant information about penal proposals. None of the authors' jurisdictions has quite succeeded in imposing a brake of this kind on governments; and civil servants are not as authoritative as they used to be.

In the sixties and seventies, England had an Advisory Council on the Penal Systems, which considered ministers' ideas and reported publicly on them. Some of its reports initiated sensible reforms, but ministers (and civil servants) became impatient with the time it took and abolished it.

What is clear is that penal populism is a recipe for serious mistakes, and that all the antidotes discussed in this excellent book should be tried. It is not merely opportune, but overdue.

Institute of Criminology
University of Cambridge
Cambridge, England
April 2002

Nigel Walker

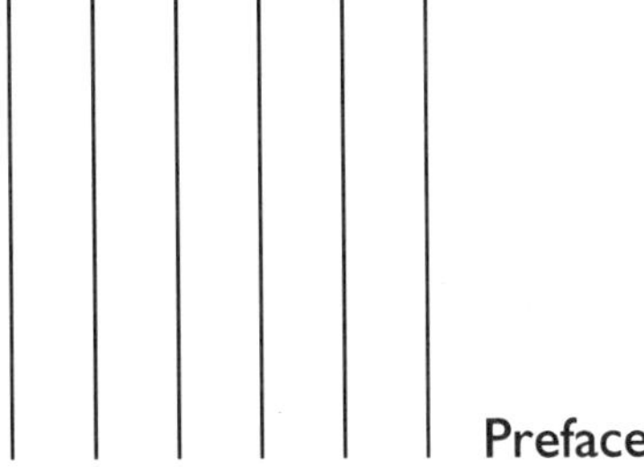

Preface

Responding to crime represents a perennial challenge to all nations, and the ways in which we respond reveal a great deal about the nature of our societies. Too often history records our responses to this challenge as a failure on both humanitarian and moral grounds. While criminal justice policies vary significantly from country to country, one theme has repeatedly emerged in recent years: All Western nations have witnessed an upsurge in both the rhetoric and practice of severe punishment for offenders; we refer to this as a rise in penal punitiveness. In the 1960s, many criminologists and penologists believed that sentencing was becoming more rational, more research-based, and more humane. The abolitionists had carried the day with respect to capital punishment; community-based sentences were gaining a foothold, and probation services were expanding. This liberal trajectory did not continue; the death penalty returned to America, most countries have adopted mandatory, punitive sentencing policies, and prison populations are on the rise again.

What is responsible for this renewed emphasis on harsh punishment and broader punitive policies? Why have we sought ever harsher ways of responding to offenders? Most important, what role has politics played in influencing penal policies in recent years? What has made severe punishment an attractive political commodity? These are some of the questions which we address in this book.

We are trying to understand an issue which cuts to the heart of a liberal democracy: the punishment of offenders. In particular, we explore one specific response to crime, which we term *penal populism*. A great deal has transpired in the field of criminal justice since the mid-1980s, and public opinion has played a pivotal role in the sentencing reforms that have been proposed or enacted in the five countries included in the present analysis. Although there are significant differences between countries and even between jurisdictions within countries, it is the important and compelling commonalities emerging in many Western countries that have led us to conduct the present inquiry. The major common theme is the policy position examined in this book: penal populism. As will be seen, penal populism is essentially a rather simple political response to a complex social problem.

Although attempts to "play the crime card" in U.S. elections go back to the 1960s (see Finckenauer, 1978), in the 1990s, politicians have more frequently turned to crime in their appeal to the public—particularly in the run-up to elections—by identifying crime problems that can be "fixed" by various sentencing reforms. Violent crime by recidivists; murders committed by juveniles; crimes by prisoners released on parole; many examples spring to mind. For each of these problems, the public is offered punitive (and simplistic) solutions (such as "three strikes" statutes, "adult" sentences for juvenile offenders, and flat-time (no parole) sentencing) that often violate fundamental sentencing principles and create more problems than they solve. For example, some "three strikes" statutes count less serious felonies as a "strike." This triggers a highly punitive outcome for the offender and violates sentencing principles such as proportionality and restraint in the use of imprisonment that are found in the case law or which have been codified in many jurisdictions.

By the time that research has demonstrated the futility of many of these "solutions" to crime, the parade has moved on, and the election is over; the "reforms," however, generally remain in place. For example, mandatory minimum sentences have been accumulating for years in four of the five countries included in this survey; seldom are any of these laws repealed. In a similar way, sentence length ranges in sentencing guidelines tend to move upward, becoming ever harsher, never more lenient. Sentencing reform guided by politics and provoked by public pressure proceeds down a one-way street of punitiveness. The irony of course is that this movement toward harsher sentencing has accelerated at a time when crime rates in most jurisdictions have been declining. This suggests one of the theses of the present volume: the drift toward punitiveness is neither exclusively nor primarily instrumental. Penal populism is more plausibly explained as an emotional response to horrific, but rare, crimes that generate intense media attention, and other less-clearly defined influences relating to the culture of punishment (cf. Garland, 1990, 2001).

Whenever most people think of crime, they also think of punishment. There is variance in the punishment preferences of the public in different countries, but punishment is generally a reflex response to offending. Neither of the two growing international movements in criminal justice, one which promotes alternative, nonpunitive or restorative responses to crime (e.g., Braithwaite, 1999; Daly, 2000), the other which emphasizes crime prevention rather than crime control through punishment, have done much to change this reality. This is true in all Western nations. The importance of public opinion is characteristic of all common law jurisdictions. With the advent of polling over the last few decades, community views have come to play an increasingly important role in the evolution of criminal justice policy, particularly in the realm of sentencing.

A principal focus of this book is on the nature of public attitudes to sentencing and the interrelationship between the views of the public and the development of sentencing policy. We explore the degree of congruence between penal policy and the views of the public. In so doing, we draw upon the results of representative opinion surveys, as well as more sophisticated research tools. The former alone cannot provide an adequate portrait of the nature of public opinion. In our experience, public opinion polls with respect to criminal justice issues are frequently constructed to generate a particular response from the public: they are seen as a means to bolster specific policies rather than as a tool to better understand community views. Politicians often commission surveys the way attorneys question witnesses: safe in the knowledge that the answer will support their position.

Politicians repeatedly cite opinion polls to demonstrate support for their criminal justice policies. In all the areas that we discuss, it is clear that law reform is seldom well-served by the automatic invocation of public views, measured by simplistic opinion surveys. One of the goals of this volume is to encourage politicians, policymakers, and criminal justice professionals to tread carefully when attempting to discern the views of the public. But outside the academic literature, the views of the public are seldom canvassed in a scientific manner. The thoughtless use of surveys can lead to spurious conclusions being drawn about the nature of community views, as we shall illustrate over the course of this book.

We shall show, by reference to systematic research, how public opinion research can easily be manipulated, and how an adequate answer to the question "What does the public think?" cannot be generated by asking the public a simple question such as "Are sentences too harsh, too lenient, or about right?" Regrettably, this is exactly the way that public opinion has been explored in many surveys over the past 20 years. This conclusion is not new; criminal justice researchers working in the area of public opinion have long been aware of the limitations on simplistic surveys as a means of sounding community views. But some politicians cling to the idea that placing a single question on an omnibus survey which poses 40 questions in half as many minutes will actually say something about the public's views about complex issues relating to sentencing and parole.

Scope of the Present Inquiry

The current volume draws together findings from five jurisdictions: the United States, the United Kingdom, Canada, Australia, and New Zealand. The goal of the book is to uncover trends which are applicable to several countries and to develop a corpus of knowledge with an international foundation. We draw attention to some important variations between countries, particularly when they say something about the legal and political culture of specific jurisdictions. We also try and establish the limits of penal populism: When are populist proposals founded upon false perceptions of the public's view? When are politicians more punitive than the public to whom they are accountable?

The commonalities in research findings are noteworthy because they represent responses to punishing offenders which transcend national boundaries. This is striking because the magnitude and nature of the crime problem varies considerably across the jurisdictions included in this survey. In addition, the criminal justice systems respond to those problems in diverse ways. The treatment of offenders convicted of murder in different jurisdictions illustrates this variability.

In America, juveniles and mentally challenged offenders convicted of murder risk execution, whereas in Canada, juveniles convicted of murder serve only a few years in prison. Offenders in the United States who are convicted of murder but not executed can be sentenced to spend the rest of their natural lives in prison; life imprisonment without parole is not a sentencing option in most other jurisdictions. In Canada, almost all offenders serving sentences for second degree murder (and sentenced to life imprisonment) will be released after 10 years in prison. In Britain, the average life prisoner spends 14 years in custody before release on parole. Another interesting difference between the countries is the extent to which the views of the public are incorporated into the sentencing and parole processes. Juries in America play an important role in determining whether an offender will be executed or imprisoned for life. In Canada, juries can reduce by up to 10 years the amount of time that an offender convicted of first degree murder must spend in prison before becoming eligible for parole. Juries in Britain have no such powers. Sentencing policy and practice in all jurisdictions is affected—directly or indirectly—by the views of the public; our goal is to generate a better understanding of those views and their effects.

Outline of Volume

Chapter 1 provides a definition of the term "penal populism," followed by an overview of crime trends and sentencing patterns in the countries included in this survey. While a detailed analysis is unnecessary, it is important for the reader to have some understanding of recent trends. Chapter 2 summarizes research on public knowledge of and attitudes toward crime and punishment. Chapter 3 provides a discussion of sentencing policies across the five countries, including the most egregious example of penal populism which has emerged in all the countries included in our survey: mandatory sentencing. Theoretical perspectives are explored in the next chapter (4), which is followed in chapter 5 by a discussion of the primary source of information for the public: the news media. We shall examine the ways in which the news media have shaped public conceptions of punishment. Chapter 6 explores the limits of penal populism, in which we review research which has addressed public reaction to unjust or excessive punishment. Chapter 7 examines an area of criminal law in which there has been considerable legislative activity in recent years: juvenile justice. Chapter 8 explores an issue that causes great public concern: the criminal justice response to sex offenders. Chapter 9 documents the role of penal populism with respect to drug offenders. In the concluding chapter (10), we address the practical questions that lie at the heart of our inquiry: How should the criminal justice system respond to the forces of penal populism? How can we remove politics from penal policy development? We shall propose some specific mechanisms and strategies with which to limit the influence of penal populism, and which may lead to more informed, research-based sentencing policies.

Acknowledgments

Although Julian Roberts was primarily responsible for bringing this volume to press, the book is a collective effort to which all the other authors contributed equally. We would like to acknowledge the assistance of the Department of Criminal Justice at Loyola University in Chicago for providing support for research assistants; Alex Berkowitz, Pamela Loose, and Allison Ulmham provided diligent research assistance. The Center for Ethics at Loyola University provided a research fellowship to Loretta Stalans to study jury nullification. We would also like to thank the following individuals whose feedback has influenced the final content of this book: Anthony Doob, Benedikt Fischer, Arie Freiberg, Jane Sprott, Don Weatherburn, and Warren Young. In addition, we express our appreciation to Oxford University Press and to the anonymous reviewers, who evaluated the proposal that gave rise to this book, as well as the final manuscript.

Loretta Stalans dedicates her work on this volume to her daughter, Maggie Stalans Yarnold, her husband, Dr. Paul Yarnold, and Dr. Harry S. Upshaw, mentor.

Finally, we would like to recognize that our primary debt is to the editor of this series, Professor Michael Tonry from the Institute of Criminology at the University of Cambridge, without whose sagacious advice and guidance this volume would have remained unwritten.

Contents

Penal Populism and Public Opinion

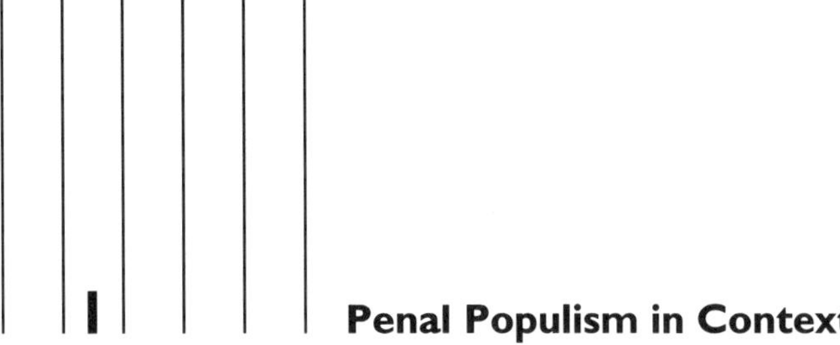

1 Penal Populism in Context

The Argument

This book addresses and explores the evolution of criminal justice policies, particularly those pertaining to the sentencing of offenders. Our sentencing policies represent the greatest intrusion into the lives of offenders and are therefore worthy of the closest scrutiny. The policy making process is complex and cannot be reduced to categories of "good" and "bad" programs or policies; nor can policymakers and politicians be assigned to categories such as "populists" and "rationalists." All policies—and the individuals responsible for them—are subject to pressures relating to the reality of electoral politics. It is these pressures, the ways in which they are managed, and their effects that are the subject of this book.

There is no escaping the fact that over the past decade, sentencing has become harsher in most Western nations, particularly the United States. As Tonry notes, "Most U.S. jurisdictions have comprehensively overhauled their sentencing laws and policies, usually to reduce officials' discretion and make penalties harsher" (2001, p. 517). Some of the harshest policies—such as the "three strikes" laws—bear the clear imprint of populism. Populism is a political response that favors popularity over other policy considerations.

Populist penal policies can arise in a number of ways. In some cases they can be a consequence of an intentional attempt to exploit public anxiety about crime and public resentment toward offenders. In other contexts they have emerged out of a desire by policy makers to respond to public opinion without having undertaken an adequate examination of the true nature of public views. Public expressions of punitiveness are taken at face value. We shall attempt to demonstrate that these (and related) policies have not arisen in response to an escalating crime problem or an increase in public punitiveness. Populist pressures cannot alone explain the shifts in penal policy that we have witnessed in recent years, but they play an important role and represent one of the few forces present, to a greater or lesser degree, in all Western nations.

We shall also demonstrate that in many areas, sentencing (and other penal) policies have been introduced that are more punitive than can be sustained by a reasonable, research-based measure of public opinion. Indeed, we shall provide illustrations in which members of the public actively subvert punitive policies, when they perceive those policies to be unfair or excessively harsh. In many areas it seems clear that policies have emerged in response to an inaccurate representation of the public response to crime.

But this volume is not an attempt to promote specific policies or to castigate the politicians and policymakers responsible for them. Rather, it is an appeal to those who control our criminal justice systems to exercise restraint with regard to policies that have unintended and disproportionate consequences on certain sectors of society. We see mandatory sentencing as a clear example of such policies. Mandatory sentencing laws affect a far wider range of offenders than is desirable and tend to affect some groups in society more than others.

This volume is also an appeal to the media to place their coverage of specific crimes and sentencing decisions within some context which news consumers may use to arrive at an informed judgment about the case reported. The book is also an attempt to convey to critical decision makers (including policymakers and politicians) a sense of where the public stands on a number of vital areas of criminal policy, including juvenile crime and drug offenders. In these areas we have attempted to build a portrait of public opinion about the issue based on in-depth research rather than simple opinion polls.

Some of these themes have been explored in recent years by other researchers. Our contribution to this literature is twofold. First, we explore the influence of penal populism on an international level, drawing examples from five jurisdictions. Second, at the end, we offer some practical suggestions with respect to containing penal populism and improving the way that criminal policy develops. Our hope is that these proposals may be of general application. We are not, ultimately, trying to divorce punishment policies from the views of the community. By paying greater attention to the consequences of specific policies and making a greater effort to understand what the *informed* public thinks, sentencing policies will be more, not less, in line with the views of the public. The policies will also be more humane, and, we hope, more effective in responding to crime.

Defining Penal Populism

The term "penal populism" (or variants on it such as "populist punitiveness"; see Bottoms, 1995) has gained considerable currency in recent years. What exactly does it mean? Populism is a value-laden term.[1] Its nuances can be drawn out by contrasting populist policies to ones which are *responsive*, on the one hand, and to those which are merely *popular* on the other. It would be naive to complain about politicians being responsive to public opinion. Such responsiveness is a central feature of representative democracy: the whole point of an electoral system is to ensure that politicians do not stray too far from the wishes of their electorate. In other words, elected politicians are always to an extent mandated; they do not, and should not, have unfettered freedom to interpret the best interests of those whom they represent. Politics is the art of the possible, and public opinion defines (in part) the limits of possibility. If responsiveness to public opinion is not, of itself undesirable, it would be equally unreasonable to attack a politician for pursuing *popular* policies. Indeed, it would be a cause for some concern if elected political parties failed consistently to have broad-based support for their policies.

Responsiveness and popularity are necessary ingredients of populism, but they are not the key ones. In our view, policies are populist if they are advanced to win votes without much regard for their effects. *Penal populists allow the electoral advantage of a policy to take precedence over its penal effectiveness.* In short, penal populism consists of the pursuit of a set of penal policies to win votes rather than to reduce crime rates or to promote justice. We are not overly concerned with what might be termed "benign" populism: politicians who pursue the right policies (effective crime policies) but for the wrong reasons (to be popular). Our concern is rather with a more malign form of penal populism: the promotion of policies which are electorally attractive, but unfair, ineffective, or at odds with a true reading of public opinion.

It is important, analytically at least, to draw a distinction between the negligent disregard for evidence about effectiveness inherent in penal populism and the sincere and thoughtful belief in effectiveness that underlies some politicians' advocacy of some harsh policies. Populism is also to be distinguished from a more defensible form of responsiveness to public opinion that is premised on the belief that the pursuit of harsh punishment will promote a greater consensus about the wrongfulness of criminal behavior (cf. Bottoms, 1995, p. 39)—an interesting hypothesis. The central tool of penal populism is imprisonment; we assume the position that while necessary, prison has been overused for decades, and with the rise of mandatory sentencing, matters have become even worse in this regard. This book does not summarize the evidence which leads us to regard the use of mandatory imprisonment as unfair and ineffective. We will make only brief remarks about the disproportionate impact of the heavy use of imprisonment on certain groups.

Race and Imprisonment

One clear result of the emphasis on imprisonment as a sanction is that racial minorities have been disproportionately affected. The "war on drugs" has contributed greatly to the harsher treatment of Black and Latino men and women in the United States, and the federal and state sentencing guidelines have failed to reduce the racial discrimination in judicial sentencing (Miller, 1996; Spohn, 2000; Tonry, 1995). For example, analysis of sentencing data for drug offenders in federal court found that both Latino and Black drug offenders received more severe sentences, received less benefit for pleading guilty, and received a significantly smaller benefit for assisting the prosecution. This racial disparity remained, even after controlling for the influence of prior criminal history and other relevant variables (Albonetti, 1997). In her review of the research on racial disparity in sentencing, Spohn and Holleran (2000) concluded that discrimination in sentencing for drug offenders is a product of "the moral panic surrounding drug use and drug-related crime, coupled with stereotypes linking racial minorities to a drug-involved lifestyle" (p. 478).

Racial discrimination, however, does not occur for all crimes and for all minorities. Studies find that minorities are sentenced more harshly than whites (with similar characteristics) if they are young and male, have more serious prior records, or come from a lower socioeconomic class (Spohn & Holleran, 2000). Bonczar and Beck (1997) noted that "at the current levels of incarceration a black male in the United States today has greater than a 1 in 4 chance of going to prison during his lifetime, while a Hispanic male has a 1 in 6 chance and a white male has a 1 in 23 chance of serving time" (p. 6). The injustice of racial disparity is also apparent in other countries. England also incarcerates blacks at a rate six times higher than whites, and incarcerates other minority races at a rate two times higher than whites (Langan & Farrington, 1998). The only large-scale Canadian study to examine racial disparities in sentencing found little evidence of sentencing discrimination against Black offenders, but differences did emerge for drug offenders, who were more likely to be denied bail and imprisoned than whites accused with comparable profiles (see Roberts and Doob, 1997).

Imprisonment and Crime Control

In addition to the question of fairness, the heavy use of imprisonment is ineffective as a crime control strategy. A considerable body of literature has shown that harsher sentencing results in only modest reductions in crime rates.[2] This is a fundamental point that fails to register with many politicians; the key to lowering crime rates lies not within the hands of judges, as the sentencing process can have only a limited impact on overall crime rates. As one of the world's leading sentencing scholars notes: "if criminal justice policy expects sentencing to perform a major preventive function, it is looking in the wrong direction" (Ashworth, 2000, p. 25).[3] Finally, it is important to note that an emphasis on imprisonment diverts resources from other crime control policies that may more effectively promote community safety (such as early intervention and other preventive measures). We shall return to the issue of resource allocation later in this volume.

Some people may find our concern about harsher penalties to be misplaced; after all, serious crime requires a rigorous response, and communities have a right to protection from predatory criminal conduct. What we show in this volume, however, is that in the name of greater community protection, harsher penalties affect a wide range of offenders. [Mandatory Sentencing]

In many cases these penalties are unjustified on grounds of dangerousness or desert. There is an additional element lost in the debates about penal policy: when harsher punishment is translated to mean mandatory terms of imprisonment, the sentencing process becomes very inflexible, and this lack of flexibility leads to a lack of justice.

Mandatory Sentencing: Catching the Wrong Fish

When most people think of harsh mandatory sentencing, they may be comforted by the thought that dangerous, violent offenders are taken off the streets and that this results in the prevention of further crimes. The image is misleading; the comfort illusory. The Canadian mandatory penalties for crimes committed with a firearm provide a good illustration of the point. These four-year minimum sentences were introduced to deter and denounce offenders who rob banks and commit other serious crimes with a gun. But an examination of the cases being caught in the new law suggests that many offenders, who do not constitute a danger, end up paying the price.

A good example is the case of Marty Morrisey, who was convicted of an offense carrying a four-year minimum sentence of imprisonment (criminal negligence causing death). Morrisey, who pleaded guilty to the crime, has no previous convictions. He is a woodsman who has had a drinking problem since he was 14. He stopped drinking for a while, but started again after the break-up of a relationship. One day, when he had been drinking heavily, and had taken some prescription drugs for depression, Marty went into the woods with a friend. At some point, while holding a loaded gun, Marty tried to wake his sleeping friend. He slipped, and the gun discharged, killing the other man.

It is reasonable to ask whether other people, in the same circumstances as Morrisey, are less likely to engage in this criminal conduct now that it carries a mandatory sentence of imprisonment. If it is hard to justify on grounds of deterrence, what about denunciation? Is Canadian society any better for using a mandatory sentence to denounce this kind of conduct?

The populist politician implicit in our definition may look like a cynical monster. In truth, the political environment is far more complicated. A minister of justice under attack from populist opposition parties may feel that there is no option but to "talk tough" in return. At any particular time, the choice may seem a stark one: lose power—and along with it the chance of making improvements to the criminal justice system—or make some small compromise with populism. The difficulty is that the relationship between political leadership and public opinion is a dynamic one: a politician who intends to respond to opinion may (consciously or unconsciously) in fact be leading it. A small compromise forms part of a continuous process in which public opinion can be inflamed and then placated. The process can become truly dysfunctional, resulting in increasing expenditure and decreasing effectiveness. Sacrificing the rationality of penal policy in order to achieve other goals in other policy arenas strikes us as a form of populism—a classic example of the ends justifying the means.

By implication, penal populism involves the exploitation of *misinformed* opinion in the pursuit of electoral advantage. Central to our argument is that informed opinion would oppose policies that had limited social utility. Penal populism stands in sharp contrast to penal policies which, on the one hand, are grounded in principles of justice and which, on the other, draw on a corpus of sentencing research. Informed opinion would draw the same conclusions from this evidence base as those responsible for penal policy.

The possibility of misreading public opinion adds a further dimension to penal populism. As we shall demonstrate, many manifestations of penal populism are premised on assessments of public opinion which are oversimplifications or incomplete in some way. No criminal justice system in our experience has adequately conveyed (or, in some countries, even attempted to convey) to the public the reality of crime trends or the facts about criminal justice policy options with respect to offending. Public opinion is therefore often based on misrepresentation and misinformation; the result is that most people subscribe to a number of misperceptions about crime and punishment. Many politicians tend to ignore this reality (if, indeed, they are themselves aware of it all).

Second, the technology for assessing the views of the community may be very flawed. At its worst, this involves generalizing from the letters to politicians to the electorate as a whole. Politicians tend to make a lot of what they hear from their specific constituents, who are seldom representative of the general population. Even when a more systematic approach to sounding the views of the community is taken, opinion can be canvased in a superficial way. Our view is that penal populism involves the frequent misreading of public opinion with respect to crime and crime control strategies. But we are not advancing an elitist argument that penal matters should be left exclusively in the hands of criminal justice professionals. On the contrary, we argue that it is essential to listen to the views of a *properly informed* public. This consultation must be thorough and involves more than simply a question on a public opinion survey (see Fishkin, 1995; Yankelovich, 1991 for a discussion of different methods of exploring public views).

Thus, attending to the *informed* views of the public is not the cause of the problem. On the contrary, it is essential that politicians should take intelligent stock of opinion. History is replete with legal reforms which failed because they were at odds with community views. It is the fatal combination of misreading public opinion and political opportunism that produces some of the punitive yet ineffective sentencing policies that have emerged in recent years. [Penal Populism: Examples from Five Countries]

To summarize, there are three essential elements to our definition of penal populism. Populist penal policies arise from one or more of the following:

- an excessive concern with the attractiveness of policies to the electorate;
- an intentional or negligent disregard for evidence of the effects of various criminal justice policies;
- a tendency to make simplistic assumptions about the nature of public opinion, based upon inappropriate methods.

Penal populism can therefore be contrasted with a more positive form of responsiveness to public attitudes, in which penal policies are developed that are consistent with (a) a careful reading of *informed* public opinion, (b) the results

Penal Populism: Examples from Five Countries

- Mandatory sentencing: over the past decade, mandatory minimum sentences of imprisonment have been introduced in four of the five countries included in this survey. "Three Strikes" sentencing provisions that mandate very severe penalties for a third "strike" are the most visible example of mandatory sentencing laws.
- Disenfranchisement: Canada and almost all states prohibit inmates from voting while serving a felony sentence or while on parole. Ten U.S. states prevent ex-offenders who have completed their sentences from voting. Four million Americans (one in 50 adults) have lost the vote as a result of a felony conviction. Well over one million African-American males are disenfranchised, a rate seven times the national average.
- Undermining judicial discretion: the ability of judges to impose just penalties has been undercut in many jurisdictions by legislation which restricts judicial discretion.
- Transfer of juveniles: young offenders accused of a wide range of crimes have been transferred to be tried in adult courts and punished in adult correctional facilities.
- Criminalizing behavior of children: proposals have been advanced and legislation adopted that have lowered the minimum age of criminal responsibility.
- Criminalizing minor forms of anti-social behavior: legislation in several countries has banned "Squeegee kids" and criminalized "nuisance" behavior.
- Shaming and stigmatizing offenders: In some Australian states, young offenders undertaking community service have been obliged to wear distinctive clothing. In the United States, "shaming" penalties have been imposed which result in the public humiliation of offenders. In addition, some U.S. states permit members of the public to access other peoples' criminal records.
- Creation of boot camps: boot camps located in the wilderness and which impose harsh conditions on young offenders have been created in several jurisdictions.
- Educational restrictions: College students in the U.S. must disclose whether they have been convicted of a drug crime; the presence of a drug crime record may mean that they will be denied financial aid to attend college.
- Judicial "accountability": a proposed law in Canada would create a data-base specifically designed to embarrass judges who impose "lenient" sentences. Every time a sentence was imposed a record would be made of the name of the judge, the sentence imposed, and the maximum sentence permitted according to the Criminal Code.
- Increasing maximum penalties: although the statutory maxima are very high in most Western nations, new, higher maxima have been introduced or proposed in several nations.

of systematic criminal justice research, and (c) well-established, consensual principles of sentencing, such as proportionality and restraint with respect to the use of imprisonment.

At this point we present some information on trends with respect to crime and punishment in the five countries examined over the course of this volume. The purpose of presenting this material is to provide some context for the penal policy developments that are discussed in subsequent chapters.

Recent Crime Trends

While criminal justice policies have varied across our countries, there has been considerable consistency with respect to the trends in official crime statistics. In general, crime rates rose steadily from the 1960s, then more sharply in the 1980s, before peaking in the early 1990s. Since then, crime statistics derived from police reports and from victimization surveys have tended to show stable or declining crime rates.

United States

Both principal sources of crime statistics in the United States (the Uniform Crime Reports and victimization surveys) reveal that over the past few years crime rates have been declining. In the most recent year for which data are available (1999), crime rates dropped 7% over the previous year. This followed several years of decreases in the crime index.

Data from the National Crime Victimization Survey (NCVS) show that the decline in the crime rate began in 1994. In that year, just over 51 violent crime victimizations per 1,000 population were recorded. This statistic declined steadily over the next few years. In 1999, the violent crime rate was 37% lower than in 1994. Some specific crimes, including the most serious assaults, showed an even more dramatic decline. The number of aggravated assaults decreased by 38% and the number of robberies declined by a similar percentage. The homicide rate dropped from over 10 incidents to 7 incidents. In 1999, the FBI recorded 16,910 homicides, a 7% decline over the previous year. The number of homicides recorded in 1999 was the lowest in 30 years.

The U.S. property crime rate shows a somewhat more variable pattern, having risen and then fallen in the late 1970s and 1980s. However, it too has declined over the past decade. The index of total crime reached a 40-year peak in 1991, when the rate was 5,898 per 100,000 inhabitants.[4] That rate declined 4% over the next year and has declined every year since then. The 1997 rate was 17% lower than the 1991 statistic.

Canada

Crime rates in Canada peaked in 1991, when the rate of police-reported crime hit 10,342 incidents per 100,000 population (Tremblay, 2000). The overall crime rate in Canada has declined each year since then, to 7,733 incidents per 100,000 population in 1999 (Tremblay, 2000). This represents a 23% decline over the seven years, not a dramatic decline, perhaps, but a clear reversal of the trend to that point. In the seven-year period *ending* in 1991, the crime rate had climbed by 23%. The crime rate recorded in 1999 was the lowest since 1978.

The violent crime rate is, of course, of greater concern to the public than the rate of all criminal incidents (cf. Zimring and Hawkins, 1999; Roberts and Stalans, 1997). In Canada, this category of crime accounts for approximately 10% of all incidents recorded by the police. The trends in violent crime rates mirror those of the overall crime picture. The peak occurred in 1991 and began to decline the following year. Over the period 1991–1999, violent crime statistics collected by the police declined by 10%. While this is less striking than the decline of total crime, the increase has also been steeper: over the seven-year period *ending* in 1991, violent crime had increased 55%. Indeed, the official violent crime rate increased by 67% over the decade of the 1980s. The homicide rate in 1999 was the lowest in almost 40 years, following a steady decline since the mid-1970s (Fedorowycz, 2000). Property crime also peaked in 1991 and declined by 26% over the period 1991–1999. In the seven years ending in 1991, property crime rates had increased by 11%.[5]

United Kingdom

The United Kingdom is served by three separate criminal justice systems, respectively covering England and Wales, Scotland, and Northern Ireland. In the interests of simplicity we present figures only for England and Wales (see Home Office, 2001c). Crime rates rose rapidly in the late 1980s and early 1990s, peaking in 1992 at 5.5 million. This increase represents a rate per 100,000 population of 10,535. Recorded crime fell successively over the following six years. Changes in both counting rules and accounting periods make it hard to provide precise comparisons since then, but there appears to have been a small increase in crime rates. Taking into account changes in counting methods, recorded crime figures have held steady, with a rise in violence offset by a fall in property crime. The 12-month period ending in September 2000 is some 20% lower than the annual figure in 1992. This yields a rate per 100,000 population of 9,784. (It can be estimated that this figure would have been 8,583 per 100,000 according to the previous counting rules.) These trends are broadly confirmed by the British Crime Survey (BCS), a victimization survey broadly comparable to the National Crime Victimization Survey in the United States. The BCS has been conducted since 1981, usually biennially and from 2000 on an annual basis (see Kershaw et al., 2000). The BCS shows that crime rose throughout the 1980s and early 1990s. It suggests that crime peaked in 1994.[6] Between 1995 and 1999, crimes measured by the BCS fell by one-quarter, a little more steeply than the fall in police figures.

Australia

Crime trends in Australia present a similar picture to other countries. A substantial rise in recorded crime throughout the 1980s continued a trend which began in the 1970s. The trend is observed in both recorded violent and property crimes. The 1990s "slowdown" or plateau observed in other countries is also clearly evident in Australia. According to police figures, most crime rates remained stable from 1993 to the end of the decade. However, robbery and assault continued to rise moderately until 1998 and then leveled off. The trend according to the available comparative figures in Australia's national victimization surveys was also fairly stable and slightly downward from 1993. Victimization survey findings suggest that the rise in violent crime is largely, if not entirely, an artifact of increased police productivity due to more reports and more diligent recording of such crime. The victimization survey findings also suggest that the growth in property crime ceased a little earlier than shown in police figures.

The plateau in Australian general crime figures is much closer temporally to that observed in England and Wales with few offenses showing a dramatic rise or fall. The plateau effect in terms of police figures is more evident with property crime than with violent crime, and it is the escalation in violent crime rates that often dominate media reports and policy concerns.

New Zealand

The trend in the overall crime rate in New Zealand shows a rapid and substantial rise from the 1960s until 1990 and then a leveling since then (Triggs, 1997). The crime rate, in fact, tripled between 1962 and 1995. As Triggs (1997) notes, this rise has not occurred at an even pace and can be linked to a variety of economic factors. The 1990s plateau in total crime is largely a function of the leveling out of the most voluminous category—property crime. The total number of property offenses still increased by 19% between 1986 and 1996, despite a period of decline between 1992 and 1994. Those offenses more susceptible to changes in policing practice such as violent offenses and "offences against justice" showed more substantial increases. The number of recorded offenses against the person doubled between 1986 and 1996, and the number of recorded offenses against justice trebled (New Zealand Ministry of Justice, 1998a).

Confirmation of these trends in police-recorded crime through comparison with the results of victimization surveys are not possible in New Zealand, as no series of such surveys is available. However, one indication that it is "police productivity" that explains the consistent rise in violent offenses is the stability of the homicide rate in that country. The homicide rate has varied little from the average of 2.12 per 100,000 from 1985 to 1998, and the rate in 1998 (1.69) was substantially lower than the rate in 1985 (2.29). The main message from a study of New Zealand's homicide rate is that it mirrors Australia's in terms of its general level and its stability, pointing to the likelihood that the increases in police-recorded violence are a function of the increasing sensitivity and capacity of the system to detect and record violent offenses.

Summary of International Crime Trends

Examination of crime trends in the five countries demonstrates that crime rates rose in the 1980s and then began to decline in the early or mid-1990s. The magnitude of the decline varies from country to country, but by 2000, all jurisdictions had experienced several years of either declining or stable crime rates.[7] The growth of penal populism has therefore not arisen as a response to a worsening crime problem. However, we acknowledge that the forces that put crime on the populist agenda would be helped by the rising (official) crime rates that peaked in the early to mid-1990s. The fact that populist policies are now out of step with the downturn in crime may reflect the fact that these forces take some time to build momentum, but importantly that they are only loosely linked with the factual evidence on crime rates.

Declining crime rates may take the steam out of the populist agenda. It certainly becomes harder for populist politicians—or certain criminal justice professionals—to demand harsher sentencing in order to show their "willingness to do something about crime." However, in our collective experience, elections still bring out the penal hawks from all political quarters; the justification for punitiveness simply shifts. The most recent example comes from the federal election in Canada held in November 2000. The right-wing party adopted the phrase "putting the *justice* back into the justice system." Thus, calls for harsher sentences in order to "do justice and to acknowledge the harm inflicted on crime victims." In this way, victims of crime have been drawn, willingly or unwillingly, into the war against crime (see Roach, 1999). In the Canadian election, all opposition parties, even the left-wing New Democratic Party promised to make sentencing tougher and to "champion changes that respect victims' rights." And this trend, it should be recalled, occurred in the country that has experienced the most protracted period of declining crime rates.

Reacting to "Good" Crime News

The picture of stable or declining crime rates is at odds with the perception of the public and populist politicians. How then do they react to statistics that disconfirm their views? First, it is important to note that among social indicators, official crime statistics provoke a unique reaction from the public. When economic statistics are published in the news media, they tend to be accepted without demur. Few people argue that the Consumer Price Index must be wrong because yesterday's trip to the supermarket cost more than the week before.

But when declining crime statistics are released, many people suddenly acquire a high degree of skepticism with respect to official crime statistics.[8] "These statistics can't be right!" is a response that we have repeatedly heard from members of the public, as well as some criminal justice professionals such as police officers. The media are presumably responsible for this close relationship between personal (but indirect) experience and perceptions of crime trends. After all, crime is a constant subject in our newspapers and on our television screens. Information about economic activity—that might give rise to a similar degree of skepticism about statistics relating to the economy—is less often conveyed by the media or is contained in less popular parts of the newspaper. Violent crime, on the other hand, makes headlines and provides material for front page stories.

There is another reason for the skepticism. Accepting the view that crime rates are decreasing is seen by many as tantamount to being satisfied with, or complacent about, the current levels of crime. Suggesting that crime is not out of control is an unpopular position, one that is often viewed with suspicion.

People who argue that crime is not increasing in severity are seen at best as being complacent about a serious social problem and at worst as excusing offenders. To express the view that crime is increasing is to assert that "I am concerned about crime and find the current levels of crime intolerable."

Rejecting Reality

Reaction to the declining crime rates has been consistent across the countries. Many politicians have refused to accept that crime rates have actually declined. On some occasions politicians simply ignore the "good news" and emphasize the volume of crime rather than changes in rates. Stuart Scheingold provides examples of this from the 1982 election campaign in the United States. Although crime rates had not been rising, crime was still an election issue (see Scheingold [1984] pp. 80–81).[9]

Politicians and the news media have been quick to seize on counterevidence. When a change in statistical procedures in England and Wales created an artificial crime surge of 14% in 1999, the media generally treated this increase as hard evidence. Academics who have pointed out the statistical reality have been labeled as being insensitive to the suffering of crime victims. This is particularly true with respect to murder statistics. In 1999, the murder rate reached a 30-year low in Canada (Tremblay, 2000). The rate of lethal violence is generally regarded as a "pure" statistic, unaffected by victims' willingness to report to the police or changes in police data-collection practices. Nevertheless, academics noting the decline have been accused of minimizing the problem of murder. In our view, informing the public about the statistical reality places the issue of crime in the proper statistical context; it does nothing to diminish the loss to the community or the harm inflicted on individual victims.

Although politicians and editorial writers found little cause to question the validity of police statistics in the 1980s (when crime rates were rising), now that rates are falling they have become increasingly critical of official sources of crime data. This phenomenon has been observed in several countries. In Canada, in 1993, data from a national victimization survey were released and attracted considerable media attention (Gartner and Doob, 1994). The survey's findings confirmed the conclusion (derived from the police statistics) that crime rates were not escalating. The reaction to the victimization survey data was predictable: Doob and Marinos note that "when the 1993 victimization survey results were released, the far right-wing and the right-wing press publicly attacked the results, Statistics Canada, and the authors of the report" (1995, p. 416). The crime statistics have often been dismissed by populist politicians as "not giving the full story." Occasionally, these individuals have sought refuge in the explanation that only a minority of crimes are reported to the police, oblivious to the fact that this limitation of crime statistics existed prior to the onset of the decline.

Another way in which the declining crime rates have been dismissed by politicians and newspaper editorials is by making comparisons over a longer period of time, thereby dismissing the recent decrease. Thus, in Canada, in 2000, when victimization surveys and police statistics had shown eight consecutive years of declining crime rates, one major national newspaper asked "So why do so many Canadians feel like crime is increasing?" under a lead editorial entitled "Inside the Crime Stats."[10] The question was then answered for the reader by the observation that "violent crime is actually up by 57% over the last 20 years." While it is certainly true that over a 20- or 30-year frame crime rates are up, should the media treat the 10% decline in violent crime over the last decade as being irrelevant?

The deep-rooted perception of constantly rising crime rates has led to (or perhaps been the consequence of) a high level of moral indignation that has manifested itself in a number of ways. The news media regularly feature stories that contribute to a siege mentality. A number of citizens' groups such as "Citizens against Crime" and "Enough is Enough"—to cite two Australian examples—have sprung up to respond to an imaginary escalation of crime rates. At the political level, "law and order" campaigns have attracted the attention of all political parties, not just those on the right wing of the political spectrum. Even some judges, who in most common law countries have typically been discreet about these issues, have made public statements about community concerns over rising crime (see New South Wales, 1996).

If crime rates have been stable or declining over the past few years, what about punishment trends? If populist penal policies are not a response to a worsening crime problem, could they represent a reaction to sentencing systems becoming progressively more lenient?

Recent Sentencing Patterns

Before presenting some information on sentencing patterns in the five countries, it is important to note that these jurisdictions have larger per capita prison populations than most other Western nations. Table 1.1 presents recent prison population statistics from a number of Western nations that confirm this observation (all figures derived from the period 1996 to 1999; see Walmsley [2000] for more information).

The following table 1.2 presents changes in the prison populations in the five countries included in this survey. As shown, all countries have experienced recent increases in their prison populations.

The statistics relating to the use of incarceration in the five jurisdictions present a more complicated picture. However, for the purposes of simplification, we focus on two indices: the *number* of admissions to custody, and the *percentage* of all convictions resulting in a term of incarceration. The first statistic is of course influenced by a number of factors, including the volume of convictions which itself reflects the number of crimes recorded by police. In light of the declining crime rates experienced in the early 1990s, it would be unsur-

Table 1.1.
Relative Prison Populations, Selected Jurisdictions

Country	Prison Population (per 100,000 population)	Country	Prison Population (per 100,000 population)
United States	645	Italy	85
New Zealand	145	Netherlands	85
United Kingdom	125	Belgium	80
Canada	125	Ireland	65
Spain	110	Sweden	60
Turkey	95	Norway	55
Australia	95	Finland	55
Switzerland	90	Greece	55
France	90	Malta	50
Germany	90	Albania	30
Austria	85		

Source: Walmsley (2000).

prising to find a comparable decline in the number of admissions to custody. And that is what has occurred in several countries. However, this clear relationship between crimes rates and prison populations does not tell us about trends in *punitiveness* per se; in order to know about trends in punishment severity, we need to examine incarceration rates, the percentage of offenders sentenced to prison rather than a community-based sanction.[11]

United States

The dramatic increase in the number of people imprisoned in the United States over the past decade is now well documented. The use of imprisonment is clearly higher in the United States than in the other four countries included in this survey (see table 1.1). Langan and Farrington (1998) conducted a systematic comparison of conviction and incarceration rates in the United States and the United Kingdom. These researchers found (a) that convicted offenders are more likely to be committed to custody in the United States, and (b) that judges

Table 1.2.
Changes in Prison Populations, Selected Jurisdictions, 1988–1998

Country	% change 1988–1998	% change 1994–1998
United States	increased 90%	increased 22%
New Zealand	increased 58%	increased 23%
Australia	increased 55%	increased 19%
England and Wales	increased 31%	increased 33%
Canada	increased 24%	increased 1%

Source: Barclay & Tavares (2000); Walmsley (2000).

impose significantly longer sentences in the United States than in England. For example, the average sentence of incarceration was nearly three years longer for murder and for assault, four years longer for rape and robbery, and two years longer for burglary in the United States. As well, offenders in the United States serve a greater proportion of their sentences in custody compared to their counterparts in the United Kingdom.

The same finding emerges from comparisons involving the imprisonment rate per 100 convictions. Since the state-level courts account for almost all (96%) of felony convictions, we shall concentrate on the state court sentencing patterns. In 1996, state courts imposed a prison sentence on 39% of all persons convicted of a felony, while a further 31% were sent to local jail (Brown and Langan, 1999). The percentage of people sentenced to imprisonment has been relatively stable over the 1990s. Sentence length statistics were also stable through the 1990s: in 1996, the average sentence length imposed by state courts was just over five years, while it was over six years at the federal level. These figures are unchanged from 1990 (see Brown and Langan, 1999).

If the proportion of sentences involving custody has not changed, the explanation for the increased prison population in America must lie in an increase in the number of convictions. The number of convictions in state and federal courts increased by 20% within the six-year period 1990–1996 (Brown and Langan, 1999). In the last two years of this interval (1994–1996), the number of convictions increased by 14%. In mid-2000, there were 1.9 million persons in federal or state prisons (Beck and Karberg, 2001).

Canada

A common misperception among criminal justice professionals in Canada is that the use of incarceration as a sanction has declined in recent years; in reality it has not. The number of admissions to custody has dropped, but this simply reflects a decrease in the number of convictions. In 1998–1999, the number of admissions to custody declined for the sixth consecutive year (Thomas, 2000). Thus, the number of admissions to custody began to decline once the number of convictions recorded started to fall. Recent data relating to the use of custody as a sanction tell a very different story, however.

Both the incarceration rate and the average sentence length imposed remained remarkably stable over the period 1985–1995. The percentage of convictions resulting in a term of custody varied little and remained in the range 30–33%. However, in the mid-1990s, the imprisonment rate rose, and sentence lengths increased dramatically. The incarceration rate increased from 32% in 1994–1995 to 37% in 1998–1999 (Roberts and Grimes, 2000). The same period also saw a more dramatic shift in the length of sentences of imprisonment. For example, sentences of two years or more increased by one-third, while the number of short sentences declined (Roberts and Grimes, 2000).

Explaining the Canadian trends with respect to imprisonment is far from easy, but some things are clear. Official sentencing policy cannot be responsible for the increase in punitiveness because at the time that sentence lengths were increasing (and crime rates declining), the government introduced a sentencing reform bill that contained two elements designed to reduce the use of incarceration.[12] One possible cause of the increase was the introduction of mandatory four-year minimum sentences of imprisonment for a number of crimes if committed with a firearm. Before these mandatory minima were enacted, the incarceration rate for these crimes was approximately 60%, and the average sentence length was about a year. As of January 1996, all such cases now result in imprisonment for at least four years.

Mandatory minimum legislation cannot be the whole story, however, since the increase in imprisonment was not restricted to offenses carrying a minimum sentence. A more likely explanation, but not one which can be empirically tested at present, is that judges have become harsher in response either to pressure from prosecutors or perhaps from judicial perception that society favors the imposition of harsher punishments. It is possible that even Canadian judges, who are more appointed and not elected (like their counterparts in the U.S.), have also been influenced by penal populism.

England and Wales

As with the crime statistics, we have restricted this description to the criminal justice system in England and Wales. The number of offenders sentenced to custodial sentences for all types of offense, including summary ones, steeply increased over the 10-year period ending in 1985, peaking at 83,000. Thereafter, the figure fell, bottoming out in 1990 at 58,000. It then showed very small increases until 1992, and much larger increases since then. In 1998, the figure was 100,600, 73% greater than in 1990.

These admission trends are mirrored by the *proportionate* use of custody statistics. The proportion of offenders sent to prison for indictable offenses (i.e., excluding the less serious summary conviction offenses) rose from 13% in 1977 to 18% in the mid-1980s. It then fell to 15% in 1990. From 1993 it rose steeply, standing at 23% in 1998. These increases in the use of custody were accompanied by longer sentences in the (superior) Crown Court. This increased use of imprisonment, coupled with longer terms of custody, has meant that the daily prison population has recently grown considerably. The number of prisoners rose from a low of 43,250 in 1991 to 65,298 by 1998—an increase of 51% (Home Office, 1999). Although custody rates have been increasing over time, the probability of being caught and convicted of a crime in England and Wales has been declining (Langan and Farrington, 1998). This suggests a shift in crime control from certainty to severity of punishment, a regrettable movement since research has clearly demonstrated the superiority of certainty over severity.

As we shall argue in a later chapter, these trends are readily explicable in terms of a policy of "penal parsimony" that was pursued until the end of 1992, with minor fluctuations, and by the clear rejection of this policy in the course of 1993. The declines in the use of custody were a reaction to legislation designed to curtail its use; the increases can largely be attributed to changes in the "sentencing climate" which occurred in the absence of significant legislation. However, the late 1990s have seen the introduction of various provisions for mandatory imprisonment, both for some very serious offenses and for burglary.

Australia and New Zealand

In both Australia and New Zealand, the incarceration rate has been increasing over the past 20 years. Over the period 1982–1998, the number of prisoners in Australia (relative to the population) rose by 55% (Carcach and Grant, 1999; see also Freiberg, 1997b; 1998). This increase was not abrupt; it reflects annual increases over the decade.[13] The imprisonment rate in New Zealand followed a comparable trajectory, increasing 46% over the decade 1987–1996.

Explaining these trends is no easier than explaining the pattern of imprisonment elsewhere. The two principal explanations are (a) an increase in punitiveness (which itself provokes further questions regarding its origins) and (b) an increase in the volume or seriousness of cases appearing before the courts. Freiberg (1999) attributes part of the increase in incarceration in Queensland to an increase in the number of cases sentenced, and the same explanation may apply to other states as well.

Statistics showing the percentage of convictions resulting in custody are not available for Australia as a whole. However, in one recent detailed analysis of the rise in prison admissions in Queensland, it was found that the courts in that state were becoming more punitive. This conclusion was based on the finding that the incarceration rate rose between 1992 and 1998 (Queensland Criminal Justice Commission, 2000). This increasing punitiveness by the courts was seen as only one factor contributing to the substantial rise in prison admissions in Queensland. Other factors included the tightening of parole and other early release programs. Similar analyses by the Crime Research Centre in Western Australia have found substantial increases from 1990 to 1997 in the proportion of cases sentenced to prison by the superior courts.

The increase in imprisonment in New Zealand can be attributed to an increase in the proportion of convictions involving violence (and hence a greater likelihood of prison). In addition, sentence lengths have increased: Speir (1999) notes that the average sentence length in New Zealand increased from 9.8 to 12.0 months over the period 1989 to 1998. Finally, changes to the parole provisions have meant that prisoners are serving a greater proportion of their sentence in custody (New Zealand Ministry of Justice, 1998b).

Conclusion

To conclude, it is clear that the increase in the use of imprisonment is not a direct response to increases in the crime rate, since several countries have seen the sharpest rise in imprisonment at a time when crime rates have been declining. Freiberg and Ross (1999) attribute the increase in Australia's imprisonment rate not to changes in the crime rate, but rather to shifting political, cultural, and social forces. The same explanation can be applied to the other countries included in this survey. Sentencing is a consequence of complex social and cultural changes that have been the subject of a considerable number of sociological inquiries (e.g., Garland, 1990; Garland, 2001; O'Malley, 1994; Pratt, 1998b). What is clear, however, is that neither the declining crime rates, nor the increase in punitiveness, have diminished public calls for harsher punishments or populist legislation, as will be seen in the next chapter. If anything, these trends have encouraged populist politicians to introduce more repressive legislation. These legislators have not been slow to respond, as will be seen in a subsequent chapter.

2 Public Opinion about Crime and Punishment

In this chapter we briefly review the principal findings from the research on public opinion, crime, and criminal justice that has accumulated over the past 30 years (for earlier reviews of this literature, see Cullen, Fisher, and Applegate, 2000; Flanagan and Longmire, 1996; Kury and Ferdinand, 1999; Roberts and Stalans, 1997; Roberts, 1992). Public views are of particular interest to the evolution of penal policy, because the argument is frequently made that the hardening of sentencing policies is a reaction to changes in public demands for harsher sentencing.[1] This is particularly true for mandatory sentencing. As we shall demonstrate, there is a remarkable convergence of findings from the countries included in this survey: most people respond to polls about sentencing trends with the same answer—sentencing is too lenient.

However, we must add two qualifications to this generalization. First, most people have little accurate idea of the actual severity of the courts, and tend to assume that judges are very lenient. Second, there is also a significant body of research, using subjects from many countries, that demonstrates that the poll result to which we have just referred fails to capture the subtleties and flexibility of public attitudes toward the sentencing of offenders. Reconciling these two bodies of literature (single-question polls and research involving more "informed" subjects) and conveying the results of the academic research to a broader public is one of the strategies for responding to penal populism to which we shall return in the final chapter of this volume.

Calls for harsher sentencing may themselves be a reaction to public perceptions that sentencing is getting more lenient, or that the problem of crime is spiraling out of control. It is as important, therefore, to know about public knowledge as it is to understand public opinion. We begin with public perceptions of trends in crime rates.

Perceptions of Crime Trends

The recent statistics relating to crime rates and sentencing trends documented in the previous chapter contradict the views of the public. When asked about crime trends, most people think that crime rates have been escalating, regardless of when the question is posed. For example, in 1974, 85% of the Canadian public fully believed that crime rates were increasing (Roberts, 1994); in 1999,

83% of respondents to a national survey believed that crime was stable or increasing, although rates had declined for seven consecutive years (Besserer & Trainor, 2000). In the United Kingdom, the 1996 and 1998 sweeps of the British Crime Survey (BCS) revealed that most people believed crimes rates had been increasing over the previous two years, when in fact there had been a decline in crime rates[2] (Mattinson and Mirrlees-Black, 2000). Similar misperceptions exist for juvenile crime patterns.

The most recent American survey found that over half the polled public thought that there was "more crime in the U.S. than a year ago," although as we have seen, crime rates actually fell across the country over the previous year (Maguire and Pastore, 2000). Five consecutive surveys conducted in Ohio found that almost four out of five residents believed that crime rates were increasing when in fact they were stable (Knowles, 1987). Whether crime rates are up, down, or stable, most people seem to think that things are worse than the year before. It might be argued that the public are right to think that crime rates are up, if the time frame under consideration is 30 years. Crime rates in the five countries included in this survey are considerably higher than they were in the 1960s; however, the surveys to which we are referring have framed the question carefully in terms of the previous year.

Public estimates of trends for specific offenses are no more accurate. Surveys conducted in Canada and Australia found that 70% of Australians and 80% of Canadians believed that the murder rate had increased, when in fact it had declined significantly in Canada and remained stable in Australia (Roberts, 1994; Indermaur, 1987). When people are asked to identify the specific offenses that they think are increasing fastest, they tend to cite the more serious offenses or offenses which have been in the news, regardless of whether they have actually been growing more frequent (see Roberts, 1995).

These findings with respect to public misperceptions of crime trends are also important because they are related to public attitudes toward, and confidence in, the judiciary and the sentencing process. Thus, Mattinson and Mirrlees-Black analysed data from the 2000 BCS and found that respondents who thought that crime rates were increasing were the individuals with the least confidence in the justice system (Mattinson and Mirrlees-Black, 2001). Although polls show that people see responding to crime as a general responsibility shared by many agencies, it is clear that some people see crime as the exclusive responsibility of the justice system, and increasing crime rates are perceived as evidence that the system is failing.

Salience of Crime as a Social Problem

Another question that has been repeatedly addressed to the American public concerns the salience of crime as "the most important problem" facing the country. Responses to this question also reveal the dissociation between public views and crime statistics. Until the latter part of 1993, no poll had shown more than 5% of the U.S. public naming crime as the most important problem. As

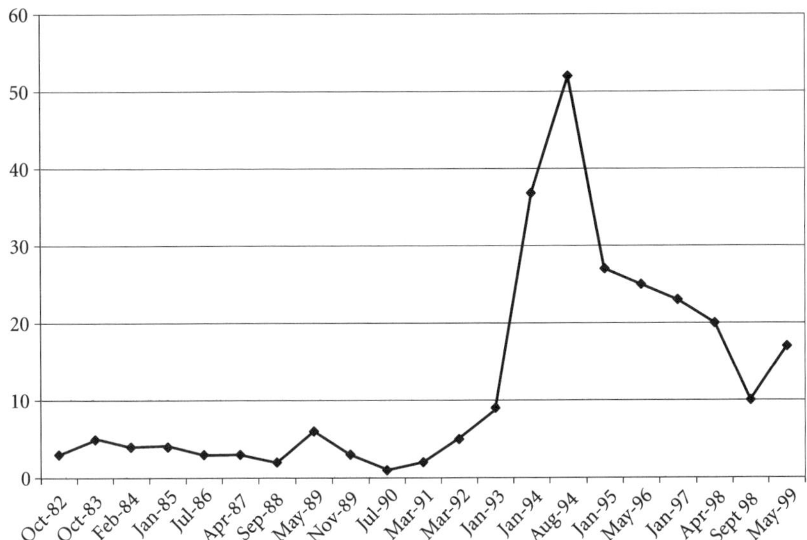

Figure 2.1.
Percentage of Americans Identifying Crime as Most Important Problem Facing the Nation
Source: Sourcebook of Criminal Justice Statistics (2002).

can be seen in figure 2.1, the percentage had been very stable for many years, even while the crime rate was escalating. In 1994 and 1995 however, this percentage spiked upward to a high of 31% in 1995. At this point, crime rates in the United States were declining. This pattern of responses suggests that as with perceptions of crime trends, public concerns about crime as a problem are being influenced by forces other than the actual volume of offending.

When asked to estimate the proportion of crime that involves violence, the public are equally at odds with reality. This question has been asked repeatedly on surveys conducted in several of the countries included in the present analysis; the results have generally been consistent. The percentage of the public overestimating the amount of crime involving violence (and by a significant amount) was 73% in Australia, 74% in Canada, and 77% in England and Wales (Roberts and Stalans, 1997). The most recent data on this issue from the 1998 BCS reveal that approximately four-fifths of the public estimate that 30% or more of recorded crime involves violence. In reality, violent crime accounts for approximately 10% of crimes recorded by the police (Mattinson and Mirrlees-Black, 2000). [Increasing Crime Rates]

These trends in public opinion are important for they provide the context to understanding public reaction to populist proposals in the area of criminal justice. Punitive sentencing policies are likely to appeal to a public concerned with rising crime rates; many people believe that harsher sentencing, particularly more (and longer) prison sentences, will reduce the incidence of crime.

Increasing Crime Rates: Media Hype?

It might be argued that the question about crime rates generates a thoughtless "off the top of one's head" reaction and that when provided with an alternate explanation of why the misperception may exist, members of the public will be more accurate. This does not appear to be the case. A direct test of this hypothesis comes from a Canadian poll, in which people were asked the following question: "Some people say that crime rates are not really increasing and that it's mainly dramatic crime stories in the media that are affecting people. Others say that crime is really getting worse. Which do you believe?" At the time that the survey was conducted, crime rates across the country had been declining for six consecutive years, and the murder rate had fallen to a 30-year low. Nevertheless, after hearing this question, four out of five respondents replied that there had been a real increase (Focus Canada, 1998).

Knowledge of Sentencing and Corrections

As with crime rates, public misperceptions of the sentencing process and sentencing trends abound. This finding has emerged from representative surveys conducted in several countries over the past two decades (see Mattinson and Mirrlees-Black, 2000; Hough and Roberts, 1998; Roberts and Stalans, 1997; Indermaur, 1990). As Cullen, Fisher, and Applegate note in their review of public opinion and punishment, "people's understanding of sentencing severity and options is restricted and distorted" (2000, p. 3)

Improving public awareness of the sentencing process is therefore a clear priority and has been for some time. Sentencing is, of course, not the only criminal justice issue for which public knowledge levels are low. A recent public survey conducted by the American Bar Association found that over one-third of Americans were unaware that a defendant is innocent until proven guilty—perhaps the most basic fact of criminal procedure and of the pillars of our judicial system (American Bar Association, 1999; see Roberts and Stalans, 1997, for a review of the literature relating to public knowledge of criminal justice). [Public Knowledge of Punishment Trends]

Attitudes to Sentencing

The volume of empirical research on public attitudes toward sentencing (and parole) has increased dramatically over the past 30 years.[3] The majority of the research has been conducted in the United States, Canada, and the United Kingdom, but we now have a clearer idea of where the public stands in all Western nations on the critical criminal justice issues of our time (for other jurisdictions, see e.g., Kury and Ferdinand, 1999). In chapter 7, we shall describe

Public Knowledge of Punishment Trends: Some Representative Findings

Surveys have been conducted on public knowledge of punishment trends. We summarize some of these findings here. Several selection criteria have been applied. First, we include only representative, large-scale surveys of the public. Second, we include surveys conducted in at least two countries. Third, we include only issues in which the views of the public have been compared to verifiable statistics, in other words, questions to which there is a "right" and "wrong answer." The public

- have little accurate knowledge of statutory sentencing; few people, for example, know which offenses carry a minimum penalty or have any idea of the severity of these mandatory minima;
- know little about the many sentencing alternatives (such as probation and community service) and focus exclusively on imprisonment when thinking about sentencing;
- underestimate the severity of maximum penalties;

The public also

- underestimate the severity of sentencing practices (e.g., the incarceration rate for specific offenses);
- underestimate the severity of prison life (e.g., many people assume prisoners are routinely provided with televisions, computers, etc.);
- overestimate the percentage of offenders released on parole;
- overestimate the proportion of prison terms served in the community on parole;
- overestimate the percentage of parolees who will reoffend while on parole

(Sources: Mattinson & Mirrlees-Black, 2000; Hough & Roberts, 1998; Doob & Roberts, 1988; Roberts, 1994; Indermaur, 1987).

and explore the extent of public knowledge and the nature of public attitudes to specific topics such as youth justice. In this chapter, we summarize trends with respect to public opinion and sentence severity.

Public opinion is, of course, a nebulous concept and many writers have attempted to capture its essence. For the present purposes, we are concerned with the views of the public on two levels. First, there is the representation of public views captured by large-scale opinion polls, best represented by questions such as *"In your opinion, are sentences too harsh, too lenient, or about right?"* This question, or variants on it, has been posed in our five countries repeatedly for the past 40 years. We shall turn to the findings from those polls shortly. It is important to note the limitations on such a question as a measure of the public mood toward punishing offenders. As has been pointed out elsewhere, a single poll fails to do justice to the complexity of sentencing; no one would consider addressing a question of such simplicity to criminal justice professionals. Their responses would be complex and generate many other questions, such as "What kinds of offenses?" and "What kinds of offenders?" In addition, criminal justice professionals would constitute an *informed* sample, whereas the public are (unfairly) asked to make a decision without an adequate amount of information about the issue.

Why then do we discuss public responses to simplistic questions? The reason for paying attention to poll data is twofold: First, repeated testing gives some idea of historical trends with respect to the views of the public. The measuring device may be imperfect, but its imperfections have been apparent to us for many years. Tracking public responses to this question therefore tells us something about fluctuations in the public mood. The second and perhaps more important reason for presenting these statistics is their importance to penal policy.

When politicians want to know what the public thinks about juvenile crime, the death penalty, the future of parole, or any other criminal justice issue, they seldom conduct a systematic search of the scholarly literature. They are far more likely to turn to one of the many national polling companies and commission a quick poll or place a question on an omnibus survey which addresses many issues.[4] This is a curious strategy in many respects, because original polling is expensive, and if it adopts the form that we have described, quite limited in what it reveals about public attitudes.

One example of the relationship between public opinion and sentencing policy comes from Australia and relates to the mandatory sentencing laws in the Northern Territory. The link between public views and the sentencing provisions was made crystal clear by Prime Minister Burke when he stated that "he was not surprised at the overwhelming support [Australians] have shown for the introduction of mandatory sentencing laws in their state" (Burke, 2000). He added that "the poll figures justify the government's decision to stand firm against a campaign to scrap the Territory's laws." And concluded that "the public want sentencing to reflect community attitudes." The poll to which the minister referred was, in fact, an unrepresentative (and unscientific) newspaper "survey," in which interested readers were asked to express their views on the issue.

A much better reading of public attitudes toward an issue such as the death penalty can be obtained from a careful literature review, with qualitative and possibly quantitative features such as a meta-analysis. But since this is almost never done, public opinion surveys have acquired, and will continue to possess, great importance as a weathervane for politicians. Finally, opinion polls are also frequently misused; questions are constructed to ensure a particular response from respondents. We have witnessed numerous examples of this tendency in recent years. [Leading Questions: The Misuse of Surveys]

Unlike the cycles in crime trends and the complexities associated with determining how sentencing patterns vary across different jurisdictions, the picture with respect to public opinion is much clearer and more consistent. In all jurisdictions included in this volume, the vast majority of the public express the view that sentences are too lenient, and this has been the case for many years now. In addition, this finding emerges from large-scale quantitative surveys such as the National Crime and Justice Survey in America (see Cullen et al., 2000; Flanagan and Longmire, 1996), as well as from smaller-scale focus group re-

Leading Questions: The Misuse of Public Opinion Surveys

If the question is asked in an inappropriate way, public support for any policy can be guaranteed. One of the worst examples of a question designed to elicit a particular response comes from New Zealand. In 1999, a referendum was held in that country, and one of the questions asked was the following: "Should there be a reform of our justice system placing greater emphasis on the needs of victims, providing restitution and compensation for them and imposing minimum sentences and hard labour for all serious offenders?" Clearly, it is impossible, in the minds of New Zealand's legislators, to be in favor of improving services for victims and yet opposed to mandatory sentencing. Not surprisingly, over 90% of citizens who responded to the referendum voted affirmatively.

The second example comes from Canada. A public opinion survey was commissioned by a Member of Parliament who had sponsored a bill that would make life sentences consecutive. The survey was ostensibly to determine whether her proposals were consistent with the views of the public. The wording used demonstrates how public opinion surveys can be manipulated to support a populist proposal. Question: "The maximum prison sentence that one is required to serve is a maximum of 25 years before becoming eligible for parole, regardless of how many crimes are committed. Do you believe that a person convicted of several murders should be required to serve 25-year sentences for each person murdered one after the other before becoming eligible for parole?" Not surprisingly, given this wording and the amount of information, this question generated near unanimity: nine respondents out of 10 responded affirmatively. It is hard to imagine any other outcome to a survey question constructed in this way.

But was it a fair test of public attitudes toward the issue? The wording does not provide any information about the distinction between concurrent and consecutive sentences or the purpose for having concurrent sentencing. Respondents are not informed that since the average age of a life prisoner is 39 years, two consecutive terms of 25 years without parole effectively amounts to a natural life sentence, something that the Canadian Parliament rejected when it reformed the sentencing arrangements for offenders convicted of murder.

search involving in-depth discussions with a handful of participants (e.g., Hough, 1996).

United States

As noted, the historical record is more complete in the United States than elsewhere. The statistics show that the overwhelming proportion of Americans express the view that sentences are too lenient. The percentage of respondents endorsing the view that the courts are too lenient has not fallen below 70% or risen above 85% between 1971 and 1998 (see Cullen et al. 2000, figure 2; Maguire and Pastore, 1999; Roberts, 1992, figure 1). It is interesting that public attitudes to sentencing have stayed so stable at a time when there have been many changes to sentencing policies, including the introduction of punitive mandatory sentencing policies such as "three strikes" (see Tonry, 1995, for a review). Thus, just as perceptions of crime trends tend to be independent of changes in crime rates, perceptions of sentencing severity seem to be unaffected by changes in the severity of the system. A similar pattern emerges for American attitudes to the death penalty. For the past 25 years, the percentage of the public supporting the execution of offenders has been quite stable; in 1976, 66% of the public expressed support for capital punishment, and when this question was posed in 2000, exactly the same percentage expressed this view, with little variation over the intervening years (Maguire and Pastore, 2000).

Canada

The Canadian survey data on public attitudes to sentencing tell essentially the same story. In 1999, a survey revealed that 69% of the public believed that sentences were too lenient. The percentage expressing this view has changed little over the past 25 years: in 1974, 66% believed sentences were too lenient (see Roberts and Doob, 1989, table 1). While the changes in sentencing practice and policy have been less striking in Canada, a major reform did occur in 1996. This reform was designed to make sentencing more rational, and more consistent, and to improve public confidence in the courts. However, the percentage of the public expressing the view that sentences were too lenient remained between 61% and 69% over the period 1990–1999. And, although sentencing patterns became harsher in the mid-1990s (Roberts and Grimes, 2000), this had no effect on public perceptions of judicial leniency. Public perceptions appear to be independent of statutory reforms or the practice of the courts.

United Kingdom

The trends in British public perceptions of judicial leniency show a similar pattern. In 1987, 71% of the polled public believed that sentences were too lenient (Dowds, 1994) and, as noted, the latest poll found 74% of the polled public held this view (Home Office, 2001a). Tracking over time the percentage of the British public who believe the courts are too lenient produces the same relatively flat line that can be seen in the American response to this question (Dowds, 1994). Over this period, a number of sentencing reforms were introduced, and the number of people in prison rose strikingly, without any perceptible effect on the views of the public. These statistics relate to the sentencing of adult offenders, but similar trends exist for juveniles. The 1998 BCS found that over three-quarters of respondents believed that the courts were too lenient when dealing with juvenile offenders (Mattinson and Mirrlees-Black, 2000). Clearly, Britons' perceptions of sentence severity have little to do with actual trends in punitiveness.

In light of these trends, it is not surprising that most people have quite negative perceptions of the individuals responsible for sentencing. Data from the British Crime Survey make this point. Almost half the sample expressed the view that judges were "very out of touch with what ordinary people think." Less than one respondent in five held the opinion that judges were in touch with society (Hough and Roberts, 1998). And further, judges were given the lowest ratings of any criminal justice profession: only 20% of the sample rated judges as doing a good job, while two-thirds held this view of the police (Hough and Roberts, 1998). These findings from 1996 replicate earlier administrations of the BCS and have been replicated in subsequent sweeps of the survey (see Hough, 1998; Mattinson and Mirrlees-Black, 2000; 2001). Public ratings of juvenile courts are also very negative: almost half the public gave these courts poor or very poor ratings (Mattinson and Mirrlees-Black, 2000).

Australia

Fewer public opinion surveys have been conducted in Australia and New Zealand. However, when the question about sentence severity has been posed, the results have been consistent with other jurisdictions. For example, Indermaur reports that when a sample of Australians were asked about sentence severity, fully 80% of respondents stated that sentences were not severe enough (Indermaur, 1987).

While these findings suggest that the public are most dissatisfied with sentencing trends and favor harsher sentencing, it is important to recall the limitations of the survey method (see also Cullen et al., 2000). Research has clearly demonstrated that

- people answer a general question respond punitively because they have the worst kinds of offenders and the most serious crimes in mind;
- people recall particularly lenient sentences and do not consider whether the crimes and sentences that come to mind are representative of most cases;
- people fail to consider the alternatives to incarceration;
- people fail to consider the limitations on the sentencing process to affect crime rates.

In order to arrive at a more complete picture of public attitudes to sentencing, we therefore need to turn to other kinds of research.

Research Involving Informed Subjects

Against this picture of a steadfastly dissatisfied (and apparently punitive) public must be set the scholarly research that has accumulated over the past 20 years in several countries. This research reveals another, less punitive side to the public. Studies conducted in many countries and contexts have documented that the public is less punitive than these polls (and many politicians) suggest. This research has been summarized elsewhere, but it is worth illustrating the point by a few paradigmatic examples. (Chapter 6 provides examples of jurors acquitting legally guilty defendants in order to spare the offender overly harsh punishment due to the existence of mandatory sentences.)

The importance of information to public attitudes has emerged repeatedly in the research literature. An early study conducted in Canada compared the responses to sentencing of two groups of people. One group read a newspaper account of a sentencing decision involving a case of assault. The second group was given a summary of the court documents. After reading one of the materials, both groups were asked what they thought of the sentence that had been imposed. Since participants were randomly assigned to condition, we can be sure that any differences between groups were due to level of information (whether they read the news account or the court documents), and not other factors. The results, which were subsequently replicated, told a compelling story. Consistent with the polls on the subject of sentencing, 63% of the "media" group thought that the sentence imposed was too lenient; they had assimilated this view from the interpretation provided by the newspaper. In contrast, over half the people that had read the summary of court documents expressed the view that the sentence was too harsh (see Doob and Roberts, 1988).

John Doble has conducted a series of studies in the United States that approach the role of information from another perspective (e.g., Doble and Klein, 1989; Doble, Immerwahr, and Richardson, 1991). In a typical study, a group of subjects is asked to sentence an offender. This is close to the mental exercise that people go through when they read about a case in the papers or hear about a crime that has yet to result in a sentencing hearing. We think of a sentence, drawing on our limited knowledge of the sentencing options of which we are aware. Imprisonment usually comes first to mind, and it is therefore not surprising that under these conditions, significant proportions of the public favor incarceration.

However, Doble and his associates then provide respondents with a list of the alternative punishments available to a sentencing judge in that individual's state, and the result is that support for incarceration falls significantly. This occurs even for serious crimes of violence. For example, in one demonstration of this effect, over four-fifths of respondents initially favored the incarceration of a defendant convicted, for the second time, of armed burglary. However, once the alternative punishments became salient, they proved to be more popular with subjects, as support for incarcerating the offender dropped from 83% to 46% (Doble and Klein, 1989, p. 37).

This kind of study has been replicated in other countries (e.g., Hough and Roberts, 1999, in the United Kingdom; Sanders and Roberts, 2000, in Canada), and the result has been the same; when subjects are reminded (or informed, if they were unaware) of alternatives to imprisonment, these dispositions attract more public support than would be expected in light of the responses to general questions about sentence severity.

There are at least two British demonstrations of the importance of providing respondents with context and a reasonable amount of information. The so-called Deliberative Poll is an example (see Fishkin, 1995). The idea behind this concept is to marry the advantages of a representative survey with qualitative research, such as Focus groups. Indeed, the Deliberative Poll can be considered a large-scale, representative Focus Group. A representative survey is conducted of the public, and attitudes measured. A sample of the public is subsequently invited to attend the Deliberative weekend. They are brought to a university setting for a weekend of deliberation on issues of crime and justice. The experience involves presentations by academics, criminal justice professionals, offenders, and victims. At the conclusion of the weekend, attitudes toward many criminal justice issues including sentencing are measured. The people who attended the weekend of lectures represent a sample of informed public opinion.

Results from the British Deliberative Poll on criminal justice demonstrated that people's opinion about a number of sentencing-related issues had shifted significantly as a result of the experience. For example, before the weekend, 57% of the sample endorsed the goal of "sending more offenders to prison"; this declined to 38% after the weekend's events. For some other issues, however, there was little or no change in public attitudes.

This kind of attitude measurement (and attitude change) has attracted a number of critics, and for a number of reasons (not the least of which is the expense of conducting the entire poll) deliberative polling is unlikely to be a useful general tool for measuring public opinion or changing public attitudes.

The second, more recent British example comes from the recent Home Office review of sentencing in England and Wales (Home Office, 2001a). As part of its research activities, the Review conducted several public opinion studies. One of these involved an "Informed Public" study. A subsample of respondents to the main representative survey were given additional information about sentencing by one of three means: a booklet, a seminar, or a video presentation. Regardless of the mode of communication, public knowledge scores rose. For example, the proportion of participants responding accurately to seven or more questions rose from 0 to 48% in the video presentation group (see Home Office, 2001a, appendix 5).

Both of these techniques for sounding public opinion, the Deliberative Poll and the Home Office "Informed Public" study are susceptible to the same criticism: the direction and strength of any shift in attitudes is likely to reflect the nature of the information provided. If the presentations in the Deliberative Poll are not balanced, the activity may become an exercise in propaganda. This means that the technique is not impervious to manipulation. In addition, unlike the wording of a standard poll, the information conveyed to the participants is not necessarily preserved for an objective observer to evaluate. It is important therefore, if these more sophisticated methods of surveying public opinion are to proliferate and retain their scientific credibility, that the materials provided to the respondents be accessible to the research consumer, who will then be able to evaluate the extent to which they contained objective information about the issue.

Comparing Public and Courts

The final body of research, which has generated findings which qualify the position that the public is quite punitive, involves studies that have compared the sentencing preferences of the public to actual sentencing patterns. It is hard to make comparisons between public "sentences" and those imposed by judges on actual offenders, as members of the public almost never have as much information as the judge about the offense and the offender. Nevertheless, the results from comparative studies of this kind typically reveal fairly close sentencing patterns, although for some crimes the public tend to be significantly harsher than judicial practice (see Roberts and Stalans, 1997, for a review).

The 1996 and 1998 administrations of the British Crime Survey provide a good illustration of this general finding. Respondents were asked to consider the sentence that is appropriate for an offender convicted of burglary. The offender was described as having previous convictions for the same offense. A case of this kind would result in a fairly lengthy period of custody. In fact, the description was based on an actual case in which the offender had been sentenced to three years imprisonment.

The public response was, if anything, less punitive. Approximately half the sample on both administrations of the survey favored the imposition of a community-based sentence, and of those who endorsed incarceration, the median sentence was 12 months (for comparable findings, see Hough, 1992; Mattinson and Mirrlees-Black, 2000; Hough and Roberts, 1998). The most popular sentencing option was ordering financial compensation.

A nationwide survey of the Australian public generated similar findings. A random sample of the public was asked what the appropriate sentence was in 13 cases (see Walker, Collins, and Wilson, 1987). The public "sentences" were then compared to judicial practice and the researchers concluded that "the average response shows broad agreement with typical court decisions including a tendency to punish violent offenders by way of prison sentences and to punish property offenders with non-custodial penalties" (Walker, Collins, and Wilson, 1987, p. 2).[5] A Canadian study came to the same conclusions, with respect to sentencing preferences for juveniles. [Public Sentencing Preferences]

International Comparisons with Respect to Public Sentencing Preferences

The International Crime Victimization Survey provides additional insight into public sentencing preferences in specific cases. In the 1996 administration of this survey, representative samples of respondents in all five countries were asked to recommend a sentence for a 21-year-old offender, who had a prior conviction for burglary and had stolen a television set from a home (see Mayhew and White, 1997). Table 2.1 presents the percentage of respondents in each country who recommended imprisoning the offender.

Approximately half of the respondents in the United States and England recommended prison, but even in these two countries about half the sample favored a community-based sentence such as a community service order (Mayhew and White, 1998). Respondents in Australia and New Zealand were even less willing to recommend a prison sentence, preferring community service orders instead.

Why are U.S. respondents more punitive than respondents in other coun-

Public Sentencing Preferences for Juvenile Offenders

The 1999 version of Canada's National Victimization Survey provides a good illustration of the concordance between the sentencing preferences of the public and the practice of the courts. These data pertain to young offenders. Respondents were given scenarios to read and were asked to impose a sentence; these public sentencing decisions were then compared to the practice of the courts. When asked to sentence an offender convicted of burglary for the second time, 55% of the public favored imprisonment; in reality, 50% of youth court offenders with this profile were imprisoned. If the offense was the offender's first conviction, public support for incarceration dropped to 21%; the comparable statistic for the courts was 17%. For a first-time offender convicted of assault, 19% of the public favored imprisonment, somewhat higher than the 11% rate derived from youth courts. The only offense/offender combination that generated a significant discrepancy between courts and public was for the repeat offender convicted of assault: 54% of the public chose imprisonment; the actual incarceration rate for an offender with this profile was 11% (Source: Tufts and Roberts, 2002). These results lend an important qualification to the surveys that routinely find that members of the public are very dissatisfied with youth court sentencing and want harsher sentences for juvenile offenders (see also Roberts and Doob, 1989).

tries? It is unclear whether the higher levels of punitiveness of U.S. respondents reflect, or influence, the harsher criminal justice system in that country. If populist justice is a cause, rather than an effect of public punitiveness, this constitutes an additional adverse effect of populism. The more punitive climate in the United States may inflate public levels of punitiveness. Calling for the greater use of community-based sanctions is clearly out of step with the dominant ethos of punitiveness toward offenders.[6] The constant emphasis on imprisonment—in the form of political speeches, reform proposals, and mandatory sentencing laws—may further strengthen the association between *crime* and *prison*. The result is that custody becomes the normative response and community-based sentencing the exception. In this way, the punitive climate "normalizes" prison as a response to crime. The question moves from "what kind of sentence?" to "how much time?" If this tendency is stronger in some countries, it may manifest itself in the results of surveys measuring the views of the public.

Table 2.1.
Percentage of Respondents Recommending Prison for Recidivist Burglar

United States	England and Wales	Canada	Australia	New Zealand
56%	49%	43%	34%	25%

Source: Mayhew and White (1997).

Finally, a considerable body of research indicates that the American and Canadian public believe that government resources should be spent more on early intervention and prevention efforts than on incarcerating offenders (Cullen et al., 1998; Doob, 2000; Moon et al., 2000). In surveys conducted in several jurisdictions, the majority of the public supported "after school" programs, Head Start and Big Brother/Sister programs, counseling for abused children, parental training classes, and other programs that attempt to intervene in the life of children that may be at high risk for delinquency or later criminal behavior (Cullen et al., 1998). Moreover, the majority of the public support rehabilitating juvenile delinquents as the most important goal (Moon et al., 2000; Sundt, Cullen, Applegate, and Turner, 1998). In general, there is still substantial support for the rehabilitation of offenders.

Survey studies also now document public support for intermediate community-based sanctions such as electronic monitoring, more intensive supervision probation, and boot camps for youths (Elrod & Brown, 1996; Senese, 1992; Higgins & Snyder, 1996; Payne & Gainey, 1999; Reichel & Gauthier, 1990; Turner, Cullen, Sundt, and Applegate, 1997). The Canadian public also prefer community-based alternatives for adult offenders rather than building more prisons (Doob, 2000). Support for family group conferences or restorative justice also is quite high for cases that involve theft from businesses (Doob, 2000). The public, however, are skeptical of standard probation that requires offenders to visit the probation department only once a month; few respondents believe this is an appropriate sanction for offenders that commit violent crimes or serious property crimes (Turner et al., 1997).

To summarize, there appears to be a clear disjuncture between the results of general opinion polls and the findings from more refined public opinion research. Ironically, the former appear to carry far more weight with politicians and policymakers. The portrait of public views of sentencing that emerges from the more sophisticated research suggests that public support for harsh sentencing is less solid than many politicians appear to believe. Evidence from many studies suggest that the public favor alternative measures and that support for rehabilitation remains strong (e.g., Applegate, Cullen, and Fisher, 1997).

The challenge then, to those who favor a more reasoned use of public opinion research, is to bridge the gap between the research published in academic journals and those who shape and determine sentencing policy. We shall return to this challenge in the concluding chapter of this volume.

3 Recent Penal Policy Developments

This chapter explores developments in our five jurisdictions over the last two or three decades. These case studies show how public opinion has played different roles in the formation of criminal policy in different countries at different times, although commonalities do emerge. For example, the tendency toward populist punitiveness is common to all countries. Within this picture, however, as will be seen, there are important variations between jurisdictions. Inevitably, our case studies are impressionistic. There is rarely a clear audit trail which leads to the factors that politicians and practitioners have taken into account in shaping and executing criminal policy. Populist politicians are unlikely to admit that they advocated or endorsed a policy merely because of the votes that it would attract. Whatever the actual political motivation underlying a particular policy, the public debate is almost always in terms of its social utility as a way of preventing crime. We begin with the United States, where the influence of penal populism has emerged most clearly.

United States

Over the past three decades, many changes have occurred to the sentencing systems at the state and federal levels. In 1975, all states as well as the federal system relied primarily on an indeterminate sentencing system that accorded judges wide discretion with respect to sentencing and gave parole boards virtually unchecked discretion regarding the release of prisoners (Tonry & Hatlesad, 1997). All jurisdictions placed great emphasis on the philosophy of tailoring sentences to reflect offenders' characteristics. This strategy represented an attempt to achieve the rehabilitation of the offender. That uniform response to sentencing has disappeared; in the year 2000, there is no common philosophy or common sentencing practices across jurisdictions in America (Tonry, 1999). All states, however, have adopted statutes requiring mandatory minimum prison sentences for certain violent, drug, and property offenders.[1] The result has been increased sentence lengths (and numbers of admissions to custody) for a wide range of offenses. This, in turn, has led to overcrowded prisons across the country.

Despite many legislative changes regarding specific crimes, 30 states still rely primarily on an indeterminate sentencing system which incorporates parole release (Tonry, 1999). Fourteen states have eliminated early release at the discretion of a parole board for all offenders, and many more states have substantially reduced "goodtime" credits, by which prisoners may earn their early release (Ditton and Wilson, 1999). Some jurisdictions have attempted to structure sentencing through the use of presumptive or voluntary sentencing guidelines. Several states have made a conscious effort to avoid populist punitive policies by requiring legislators to consider the impact of a law on criminal justice resources.

For example, before approving legislation, Louisiana legislators must consider an impact statement on how a mandatory sentencing bill would affect jury trials, plea bargaining, overcrowding in prisons, and the corrections budget (DiMascio, 1997). In stark contrast to the federal sentencing guidelines, eight states have adopted "front-end resource matching"; the resources required for the implementation of a sentencing law must be approved *before* the sentencing law is enacted.[2] This focus on resource matching may create more rational sentencing and allow legislators some breathing space in which to resist intense public pressure arising from high-profile cases (see Frase, 1995, p. 179). These efforts, however, are infrequent, and policies reflecting penal populism still carry the day more often than not in contemporary America.

Over the last 25 years, most sentencing reforms in the United States have been guided by punitive populism. The entanglement of politics and media creates an environment encouraging politicians to offer quick solutions for the most serious crimes. In this environment, penal populism can provoke highly punitive policies that reflect a posture of outrage more than a rational consideration of the policy options to offending. Many politicians believe that policies such as "zero tolerance," "war on drugs," and "three strikes and you're out" truly reflect the public will. Several states have enacted punitive policies that appease or appeal to the public's moral outrage and fear of crime. These include the following: longer mandatory minimum prison terms; three- and two-strikes-and-you're-out recidivist sentencing premiums; statutory transfers of juveniles accused to adult court; truth in sentencing (flat time sentencing) statutes; zero tolerance of violence/drugs in schools; mandatory sex offender registration, and "sexual predator" laws. Public outrage or fear is often cited as a justification for harsh and largely ineffective policies and sometimes provides the impetus to enact such policies. The relationship between public opinion and penal policies will be explored in the remainder of this section on the United States.

Sentencing reforms in the mid-1970s and early 1980s across the United States began on what could be considered a rational basis. By the mid-1970s, conservatives and liberals alike were critical of the indeterminate sentencing system. Conservatives believed it gave judges too much discretion and allowed judges to be excessively lenient with criminals. Influenced by the findings from academic research, Liberals became disillusioned with the ineffectiveness of rehabilitation and were concerned about jurisdictional, racial, and gender-based disparity in sentencing.[3] Moreover, the emphasis in sentencing on consideration of the offender's background produced unwarranted and unjust differences in sentences for offenders who had committed offenses of comparable seriousness. In short, both poles of the political spectrum called for changes in sentencing laws, albeit for quite different reasons. Sentencing reform efforts thus were initially grounded in rationality. However, concern for adopting reforms consistent with the public's view was always present and was particularly true at the federal level.

Federal Sentencing Guidelines

In 1984, Congress enacted the Sentencing Reform Act of 1984, which created the U.S. Sentencing Commission. This commission is a bipartisan independent agency with a mandate to draft presumptive sentencing guidelines for the federal system. When setting sentence ranges for each offense, the commission was specifically enjoined to develop sentencing guidelines consistent with the public's view. The commission examined past sentencing practices and held public hearings across the country. The views of the public and other constituent groups played a pivotal role in the creation of the federal guidelines (see Rossi & Berk, 1997). Guided by the results from a national survey of the public's sentences for different federal cases, the commission created guidelines that were generally consistent with the public's view of punishment (Rossi & Berk, 1997).

For some offenses, the punishments proscribed by the guidelines are harsher than public opinion would impose. One such discrepancy illustrates the unstable foundation of populist concerns. When the sentencing guidelines were being drafted, public and news media attention focused on sensational cases of carjackings, extortion, and bribery. The publicity and subsequent public concern surrounding these incidents may have influenced the commission's eventual decision regarding the appropriate level of punishment for these crimes (Rossi & Berk, 1997). Once the intense media attention had subsided, it became clear that the public's view of appropriate punishment for these crimes was less punitive than the commission guideline, which had been created at the height of the publicity (see discussion in Rossi & Berk, 1997).

"Three Strikes" Sentencing Policies

As several writers have noted, the most clear-cut example of a punitive policy enacted more for its popular appeal than for its efficacy as a crime control strategy is the "three strikes" legislation. Twenty-four states and the federal government have by now enacted "new" three strike laws. Although the meaning (and consequences for the offender) of each "strike" varies from state to state, all such statutes define violent felonies as a triggering crime, and a few states also count other, less serious crimes as strikes. Some states have actually passed "two strikes" legislation. Twelve states impose mandatory life imprisonment with no possibility of parole on offenders who make the third strike. The other jurisdictions impose "flat time" (i.e., no parole) prison terms that vary in length from 25 to 40 years. Although politicians touted these policies as representing a novel approach to crime control, most states already had repeat or habitual offender statutes. The new "three strike" laws in most states are expected to have very limited impact because the repeat violent offenders targeted were already receiving long sentences. States that include offenders other than violent offenders and also have two strike laws are expected to increase prison terms and swell prison populations (Clark, Austin, & Henry, 1997).

Clear Limits to Public Support for Recidivist Sentencing Premiums

These statutes were enacted in the wake of intense media publicity to cases in which repeat violent offenders had committed another violent crime. The laws in some states reflect a very direct link to popular appeal. For example, in at least two states, proclamation of the statute was preceded by a referendum which generated widespread public support (Clark et al., 1997). Truth in sentencing laws require violent offenders to serve at least 85% of their prison sentence before becoming eligible for early release. The Sentencing Reform Act of 1984 abolished parole boards and enacted this truth in sentencing law in the federal system. The law has the support of the public, who prefer to see offenders serving the entire sentence imposed by the judge. The federal system then provided incentive grants to states that enacted the truth in sentencing law. By 2000, 30 states and the District of Columbia had enacted such legislation. These laws have dramatically increased the amount of prison time served for violent offenses. In 1996, violent offenders across state systems were serving approximately half of their sentence or about 45 months in prison. With truth in sentencing laws, the average time served will substantially increase to about 89 months.[4]

In the 1990s, violent and repeat juvenile offenders became the object of intense media attention and public concern. The media publicity surrounding sensational violent crimes committed by juvenile offenders also stimulated debate among legislators. The response from legislatures was not slow in coming. Soon after such tragedies occurred, several states changed the waiver provisions regulating the transfer of juvenile accused to adult court. This was one of several ways in which states have increased the severity of juvenile penalties, as well as changed the system in other ways, to hold juveniles more accountable. (Chapter 7 provides a more detailed description of how public opinion relates to statutes regulating the sentencing of juvenile offenders.)

Similarly, penal populism has directed public attention to the most serious sexual offenders, "sexual predators," and jurisdictions have increased the duration of incarceration for these offenders, as well as created indefinite confinement through the civil system. These laws, however, target only a very small percentage of all sex offenders, and many sex offenders, especially those who violate family members, remain on standard or specialized sex offender probation programs. The public's demand to know who is living among them has also resulted in most states adopting statutes requiring sex offenders to register with their local police departments. (Chapter 8 explores this issue in greater detail.)

The winds of populism have affected sentencing policy in America in other ways as well. The United States has generally lagged further behind in creating restorative community-based justice programs for less serious drug and property offenders. In addition, the development and implementation of intermediate sanctions for violent and repeat juvenile offenders has suffered from underfunding. Intermediate sanctions include community service orders, day fines, day reporting centers, home confinement, intensive supervision probation programs, and boot camps. Most intermediate sanction programs are created by local innovators rather than state policymakers. Thus, there are no standardized policies for the vast majority of offenders who commit less serious property and drug offenses that could be sanctioned with community-based intermediate programs.

Punitive mandatory minimum sentences have dramatically increased the number of property offenders who are imprisoned. Zimring and Hawkins (1992, p. 39) note that the population of incarcerated burglars grew more than three times faster than the population of convicted robbers. Punitive policies have also increased the length of time served for violent offenders who are imprisoned, but have not affected the risk of imprisonment for a violent crime (Block, 1996). In part, the risk of imprisonment has remained constant because violent offenders represent a much smaller proportion of the prison population than before populist laws were enacted (Zimring and Hawkins, 1992). Whereas other countries have had some success in targeting violent offenders for imprisonment and diverting other offenders to community-based sanctions, the state and federal systems in the United States have changed the prison population to include a higher percentage of less serious offenders and a lower percentage of violent offenders.

Canada

Penal populism has exercised a more muted influence on policy development in Canada. Indeed, the federal government, which has exclusive responsibility for criminal law reform,[5] has pursued a policy of restraint in terms of the use of imprisonment (although there are some exceptions to this observation). Several provincial governments, however, have kept continual pressure on the government to introduce tougher legislation in a number of areas.

Penal Populism at the Provincial Level

These provincial governments have called for a wide range of punitive policies, including three strikes laws, tougher sentences for young offenders, laws that

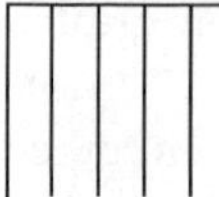

Penal Populism in Ontario

When the Conservative government in Canada's largest province took office in 1997, it vowed to "do something about crime" and rapidly cast about for possible targets. The first manifestation of the government's crackdown on crime came in the form of a bill called the Safe Streets Act. The bill contains provisions aimed at responding to those twin scourges of urban society: street beggars and Squeegee kids. According to the law, soliciting is defined as requesting money (or other "thing of value") using the "spoken, written or printed word or gesture." In other words, silently holding out your hand to someone is considered soliciting under this legislation. Soliciting is legal; the bill simply creates an offense of soliciting in an aggressive manner. What is an "aggressive manner"? The bill helpfully defines the circumstances that may be considered aggressive. One of these is simply that a person who solicits "while intoxicated by alcohol" is deemed to be soliciting in an aggressive manner (section 2 (3) (5). Thus, silently holding out your hand for money after having had a few drinks has become an offense in Ontario. Some, perhaps many, people who beg also have substance abuse problems. They are subject to criminal penalties as a result of this bill. Consider a person almost passed out from intoxication and lying on the ground. He silently raises his hand to a person striding past; that is defined as soliciting in an aggressive manner. Or consider a college student staggering out of a bar late at night and who decides to ask a passing motorist for a ride back to his residence. He's in double trouble. First, the act states that no person while on the roadway "shall solicit a ride." Second, he's guilty of aggressive solicitation, since (a) he's intoxicated and (b) he's asking for a "thing of value" (a ride home). And let's be realistic about panhandling in the midst of a Canadian winter: If you had to beg in midwinter, wouldn't you have a few drinks first? A first conviction under the act carries a fine of up to $500; a second conviction carries a maximum penalty of six months imprisonment. The Squeegee provisions in the act are equally draconian.

criminalize "Squeegee kids," and the creation of a wide range of minimum sentences, to name but a few. [Penal Populism in Ontario]

Harsher Prison Conditions and Recidivism

In May 2000, the Ontario government decided to take a stand on prison conditions in the province. The provincial minister responsible for Ontario's prisons announced a series of changes to the correctional system that would make prison life significantly harsher and would curtail the possibility of parole. The justification advanced by the government was that prisons had become too easy, and that this was responsible for the high rate of recidivism among ex-inmates. Not surprisingly, no evidence was ever offered to support the dubious proposition that making prison conditions harsher will reduce the reoffending rate. The government was eager to contrast its new policies with the correctional stance taken by the federal government, which has responsibility for penitentiaries housing inmates serving terms of two years or longer.

Taking a tough stand on prison conditions, particularly when the message is directed as much against the federal government as for the punitive policies themselves, carries a double pay-off for the provincial governments in Canada: the public are reassured (a) that offenders will receive harsher treatment, and (b) that the province is also standing up to the federal government, always a popular message in Canada's fractious federation. The political motive emerges clearly: the provincial governments have nothing to lose in calling for such draconian measures since they are not responsible for criminal law reform; these measures therefore prove useful in provincial election campaigns. Despite this pressure, the federal government has generally held its ground with respect to criminal justice policy. As will be seen, with a few specific exceptions, the reforms eventually introduced did not result in harsher sentencing.

Sentencing Reform

Concern over the problems of sentencing, accompanied by awareness of the reform movement sweeping the United States, led the government to create a Sentencing commission in 1984. Three years later, that Commission published a report advocating a desert-oriented model of sentencing, which included the principle of restraint in the use of incarceration as a sanction.[6] The government spent a number of years considering the reform options and eventually introduced reform legislation which became law in 1996. By American standards, the reforms were relatively modest. They included the creation of a statutory statement of purpose and principle, as well as a new (for Canada at least) alternative to imprisonment called a conditional sentence of imprisonment (see Roberts and Cole, 1999). The statement of purpose included injunctions to judges to exercise restraint when contemplating the imposition of a term of custody.[7]

These reforms have (so far) failed to achieve significant reductions in the use of custody. Indeed, as noted in chapter 1, Canada has witnessed an increase in the use and length of terms of imprisonment. Still, the Canadian reforms are not consistent with penal populism, for as noted, polls conducted over the period 1984–1999 have repeatedly found that Canadians favored harsher sentencing. The influence of penal populism was not totally absent; it emerged in several areas, and we shall briefly consider two: the sentencing of offenders convicted of serious crimes involving firearms and private member bills relating to criminal justice.

Mandatory Minimum Penalties

The area in which the hand of penal populism can be seen most clearly concerns the creation of mandatory minimum terms of imprisonment. Until 1995, the Canadian *Criminal Code* contained only a handful of mandatory minimum penalties. One reason for this was recognition by Commissions of Inquiry that minimum penalties can be unfair and can violate principles of proportionality and restraint (e.g., Canadian Sentencing Commission, 1987). Also, the best research evidence suggests that they achieve little in the way of crime prevention (see, e.g., Tonry, 1995). Indeed, a study commissioned by the federal government in Canada found that the existing mandatory penalties in the *Code* had failed to achieve their goals (Meredith, Steinke, and Palmer, 1994).

Nevertheless, Parliament proclaimed a bill in 1996 that created more mandatory minimum sentences than any previous bill in Canada's history (Crutcher, 2001). This legislation was in part a reaction to a high-profile tragedy, the mass murder of a number of women at a college in Montreal. The Firearms Act created a mandatory sentence of at least four years imprisonment for a number of serious crimes if the offense was committed with a firearm. The minimum penalties attracted little criticism in the course of parliamentary debate. Indeed, it was suggested by some parliamentarians that four years was insufficient, and that an eight-year minimum term would be more appropriate (see Crutcher, 2001).

Some of the offenses affected by the new mandatory penalties account for significant numbers of cases. For example, approximately 5,000 convictions for robbery are recorded every year, many involving a firearm (Roberts, 2000). After January 1, 1996, any case of robbery involving a firearm would result in a term of imprisonment of at least four years.[8] The following year another mandatory minimum sentence of five years was added for aggravated procuring and at the time of writing, several other mandatory penalties are envisaged for a number of crimes. If history is any guide, there is little chance that in the future any of these mandatory minima will be repealed (see discussion in Crutcher, 2001).

Private Member Bills Relating to Criminal Justice

Canada has recently seen a dramatic increase in the number of private member bills pertaining to criminal justice (Campbell, 1999). In one six-month period (fall 1999–spring 2000), over 30 criminal justice bills were introduced or reintroduced in Parliament. Almost all the bills are punitive in some nature, and several call for the reinstatement of capital punishment. The following list includes some of the changes proposed as part of these bills.

- Introduction of a new maximum penalty of life imprisonment for causing death while attempting to evade arrest;
- criminalization of consensual activity involving 16-year-olds;
- creation of a mandatory minimum "two strike" term of imprisonment for burglary;
- lowering age of criminal responsibility from 12 to 10 years of age;
- introduction of postsentencing detention: prisoners could be designated dangerous offenders *after* having been imprisoned for years;
- creation of mandatory, consecutive sentence of imprisonment for using a stolen vehicle;
- creation of mandatory life sentences for 15 offenses, including piracy;
- introduction of legislation to prevent judges from imposing a community-based sentence in cases of violent or drug offenses;

- reinstatement of death penalty;
- abolition of early parole hearings for prisoners serving life for murder;
- abolition of parole for life prisoners;
- introduction of mandatory penalty of four years imprisonment for auto theft;
- introduction of life sentence maximum penalty for "people smuggling."

As noted earlier, most have little chance of proceeding beyond second reading, but they nevertheless create pressure on the government, along with legislation proposed by opposition parties, to adopt a populist position. Perhaps the clearest example of a private member's bill with populist origins was Bill C-251.

Consecutive Terms of Life Imprisonment

Bill C-251 would provide judges with the power[9] to order an offender convicted of two or more murders to serve multiple periods of parole ineligibility consecutively. Thus, an offender convicted of two counts of first degree murder could be ordered to serve 50 years in prison before becoming eligible for parole. Since the average age of a life prisoner is 39, this bill thereby effectively creates a "natural life" penalty for certain offenders convicted of murder. This has occurred despite the fact that life imprisonment without parole was not advocated as a possible penalty in the debates surrounding the sentencing arrangements for offenders convicted of murder, but it has arrived (if the bill passes) by means of the back door.[10]

Review of the parliamentary debates surrounding this bill show that while many members spoke to the resolution on both sides, little discussion related the content of the bill to the statutory statement of the purpose and principles of sentencing. No member of the government, including the minister of justice, pointed out the inconsistencies between the proposed bill and the statement of sentencing purpose and principle that this same government had introduced just a few years ago.

Although criminal justice officials detailed the serious implications of this bill in terms of sentencing and correctional policy and practice, the political will to oppose such a populist bill was absent. In fact, most members of the government, including the federal minister of justice, who bears the responsibility of introducing legislation relating to sentencing, were absent from the House of Commons when the critical vote was taken. In this way they spared themselves from being labeled as someone who opposed a bill that would get tough on offenders convicted of multiple murders or sexual assaults.

Finally, as is the case in other countries, reform proposals became more punitive as election day approached. The 1997 federal election produced many populist proposals. [Populist Policies at Election Time]

Populist Policies at Election Time

Nothing hardens the penal policies of political parties quite like an election campaign, and Canada is no exception. In the 1997 federal election, all opposition parties, except the left-leaning New Democratic Party, wheeled out a number of reform proposals that shared several characteristics: they were very punitive, would have been very expensive to implement, and would have minimal or no impact on the magnitude of the crime problem. The proposals included

- abolishing parole;
- introducing two-strike sentencing legislation for all crimes of violence;
- introducing legislation that would hold parents responsible for criminal acts of their children;
- abolishing jury reviews of parole eligibility dates for life prisoners;
- increasing the severity of mandatory penalties for impaired driving, even though the incidence of impaired driving reached a 17-year low at the time, and notwithstanding the fact that impaired driving already carries mandatory penalties;
- lowering the age of criminal responsibility from 12 to 8 years of age;
- increasing the severity of existing mandatory sentences of imprisonment.

United Kingdom

In this case study we have focused on developments in England and Wales, making only passing reference to Scotland and Northern Ireland, which have separate criminal justice systems. Below we have identified three separate periods.

1979–1992: Prison as an Expensive Way of Making Bad People Worse

The Conservative Party defeated Labour in the general election of 1979 and remained in power until 1997. A striking paradox is that for 13 of these 18 years, the "party of law and order"—as it presented itself at elections—actually pursued penal policies of liberal reform. These policies emphasised the use of diversion of young offenders from the criminal process, reductions in the use of imprisonment, and increased regulation of police powers. These developments are all the more surprising when one considers two factors. First, whether measured by police statistics or crime surveys, crime was rising quite rapidly throughout this period (cf. Kershaw et al., 2000).

Second, the strongly neoclassical flavor of the government's rhetoric about crime implies a preference for deterrence and retributive justice rather than diversion from punishment. For example, Conservative politicians consistently resisted any argument that crime might arise as a response to adverse social conditions and represented offending itself as a moral failure to exercise one's personal responsibilities. (It was of particular importance to them to undermine any causal linkage between unemployment—which was rising steeply—and crime. The main rhetorical device here was to argue that it was a "slur on the unemployed" to suggest any link between joblessness and crime.)

Sentencing policy in this period was implemented through the 1982, 1988, and 1991 Criminal Justice Acts. The first two largely comprised provisions to reduce the use of custody for young offenders. The 1991 Act was a more far-reaching piece of legislation which set out a framework for the principles of sentencing, on the one hand, and explicitly discouraged sentencers from sending either young or adult offenders to prison. The sentencing framework was a hybrid one (cf. Von Hirsch, 1993), combining principles of proportionality in sentencing with the utilitarian goal of rehabilitation.

The act introduced a narrow desert-based system according to which the severity of punishments imposed had to be proportional primarily to the offense rather than to the broader culpability of offenders, taking into account their reactions to previous punishment (Ashworth, 1995).[11] The freedom of judges to sentence according to the offender's previous criminal record was more explicitly circumscribed than previously—ruling out, for example, the possibility of imprisonment for persistent petty offending. This is in sharp contrast to the "three strikes" and similar recidivist legislation in the United States, whereby previous convictions were the primary determinant of the weight of punishment for specified offenses (see Roberts, 1997).

The act also contained a provision that required sentencers to take account of offenders' means in imposing fines. The aim was to ensure proportionality between the offense and the impact of the fine on the offender. The so-called Unit Fine system required the sentencer to fine in units, which were then translated into a cash amount using a formula which incorporated the offender's income. The legislation was introduced in October 1992, with dramatic effects on the prison population, which dropped by more than 10% within the first three months. Whatever sentencers' personal views about the legislation—and these were decidedly mixed—sentencing practices had responded to the philosophy underlying the new act.

What impelled a radically conservative administration to pursue penal policies more generally associated with the politics of the center-left? Throughout this period, public opinion continued to support the imposition of harsher sentences. Why did the government turn its back on public opinion—or at least the opinion of their supporters as they perceived it to be—at a time of rising crime? Part of the explanation is to be found in the strategic alliances struck between two successive Home Secretaries (William Whitelaw and Douglas Hurd) and their senior civil servants. Both Whitelaw and Hurd were liberally minded, and they were powerfully placed within the Conservative Party, even if they represented a patrician political tradition which was in decline. Their civil servants—who in the 1980s exercised more autonomy than was to be the case a decade later—also played a significant part in pressing for policies of decarceration. Ministers and their officials both subscribed to the view that imprisonment was simply an expensive way of making bad people rather worse (cf. Home Office, 1990a). A different set of individuals might have created a quite different set of policies.

However, this is only part of the story. Equally or more important, the policies constrained the rising costs of the criminal justice system; and they were politically uncontested. While in opposition, Labour politicians in the 1980s found it hard to take issue with the unexpectedly liberal Tory penal policies. So long as the Conservatives succeeded in maintaining their "law and order" mantle, there was no immediate pressure to change.

1993–1996: Prison Works

Pressure to change arrived abruptly, only three months after the implementation of the 1991 Criminal Justice Act. Several factors combined to trigger a newspaper campaign led by the *Daily Mail*, attacking the government's penal policies. Two highly publicized murders occurred in early 1993: a young child, James Bulger, was killed by two boys not yet in their teens, and a teenage boy was shot dead in Manchester. In addition, the press focused on a series of erratic sentencing decisions, prompted either by the new legislative requirement on sentencers to ignore previous convictions or by quirks in the application of the Unit Fine's formula. (One case achieved particular notoriety: an offender was fined £1,200 for a litter offense involving a single packet of potato chips, as a result of the court following an obtusely literal interpretation of the Unit Fine guidelines.) Finally, several sentencers and senior police officers spoke out against the new legislation. The result was that the media constructed a convincing picture of a crime problem spiraling out of control, while out-of-touch liberal do-gooders wrecked the criminal justice system.

In the face of this attack, the liberal policies sank beyond recovery. Successive Home secretaries showed no sign of sacrificing their careers on the altar of rational criminal policy. By July 1993, a new Criminal Justice Bill was enacted to amend the 1991 Criminal Justice Act. The legislative changes were rather minor; the Unit Fine system was dismantled and sentencers were once again permitted to take into account an offender's criminal record in passing sentence. However their symbolic impact was significant, signaling a break with the penal parsimony that had characterized much of the previous 13 years. The whole climate of sentencing opinion shifted in the direction of severity to a much greater degree than these two changes would suggest (cf. Ashworth and Hough, 1996).

A further cabinet reshuffle resulted in the appointment of Michael Howard to Home Secretary. From October 1993 onward, he pursued a policy which advocated greater use of imprisonment, under the slogan "Prison works." He successfully mined a broad seam of public opinion that supported harsher sentencing. The sentencing climate changed dramatically, and the prison population grew by 50% over the following four years. Astonishingly, this shift occurred in the absence of any significant change either in sentencing legislation or in the volume of criminal cases being processed by the courts. Sentencers simply used imprisonment more often, and when they did so, they passed longer sentences.

What underlay this abrupt reversal of penal policy? One argument is that public tolerance for liberal penal policy was increasingly strained in the face of rising crime, and that politicians simply had to respond to this public anger. Another is that politicians were responding to the demonstrable failure of the previous penal regime. The most economical explanation, however, is that the Conservatives lost their monopoly as the party of law and order. In 1992, the shadow Home Secretary, Tony Blair, announced New Labour policy on crime as "Tough on crime, tough on the causes of crime." This clever slogan was to capture the public's imagination and indeed was subsequently adopted by politicians in many other countries as well, including Canada and Australia. New Labour talked a new penal rhetoric which stressed the blighting costs of crime and the need for firm and decisive action to tackle it. Penal parsimony now looked—not only to politicians but also to the conservative press—to be an electoral liability.

For the remainder of the Conservative administration, public opinion was as central in the formation of penal policy as it had previously been marginal. Ministers articulated—at least within the Home Office—the need to place some "clear blue water" between their policies and those of the opposition. Movement could occur in only one direction. Populist punitiveness had arrived in Britain, in the sense that perceived public acceptability was now a central criterion for assessing the value of a penal policy. By 1996, the government had implemented or announced a raft of tough[12] new policy initiatives (cf. Home Office, 1996), including

- "three strikes" prison sentences for crimes of drug trafficking and burglary;
- "two strikes" automatic life sentences for serious violent and sex offenders;
- tougher enforcement of community penalties;
- introduction of limits on a suspect's right to remain silent during questioning by police;
- increase in length of maximum detention sentences for young offenders aged 15–17;
- creation of a Secure Training Order for 12–14 year olds.

These changes may well have consolidated the reputation of the Home Secretary as a "penal hawk," but they are unlikely to have affected public confidence in the justice system, if the experience of mandatory imprisonment for burglars is any guide. [Public Opinion and Mandatory Sentencing]

1997–2001: Tough on Crime, Tough on the Causes of Crime

New Labour won the 1997 election with a substantial majority. Since then, there has been a substantial legislative program intended to

Public Opinion and Mandatory Sentencing: Findings from the British Crime Survey

The mandatory sentences of imprisonment were introduced to send a strong deterrent and denunciatory message to society; the evidence is that they passed unnoticed. The 2000 British Crime Survey asked members of the public whether they were aware of the mandatory three-year sentence of imprisonment for repeat burglars; less than one-quarter of respondents had heard about the mandatory sentence. So much for general deterrence. More tellingly, respondents were then asked if their confidence in the criminal justice system had changed as a result of hearing about this new, tough sentence. Only 18% of respondents stated that they had a lot more confidence in the system as a result of learning about the sentence; most people responded that their level of confidence would not change. So much for promoting public confidence by making sentencing tougher. These results are consistent with findings from other jurisdictions: the public are generally unaware of the offenses that carry a mandatory sentence of imprisonment (Roberts, 2003).

- establish more effective crime reduction partnerships at local level;
- broaden the range of sentencing options open to the courts to deal with drug-related crime, sexual offenses, and various forms of "anti-social behavior";
- hasten the certainty and celerity of action in relation to youth crime;
- streamline the administration of justice.

Some of these provisions have a popular—even populist—appeal, while others carry the hallmark of rational, evidence-based criminal law policy. It is hard to assess precisely to what extent penal policy is now shaped with an eye to its popular appeal. There are ample signs—even if submerged—of the dynamic which led to a period of intense populist competition between Conservative and Labour politicians in the mid-1990s. Intermittently, policies are announced whose only discernible rationale is their appeal to those sections of the public favoring decisive and punitive action against crime. Examples include the activation of "three strikes" mandatory sentences for burglary—enacted but not implemented by the previous government—and proposals to deny bail to any person arrested who has tested positive for various illicit drugs. (Both these initiatives were "surprise announcements," made with minimal consultation with departmental officials and practitioners; the drug-testing proposals substantially revised in the course of legislation.)

By the spring of 2000, the political landscape showed signs of change. The electorate's early enthusiasm for New Labour began to wane. Although Conservative politicians had initially failed to mount any effective challenge to Labour's economic and social policies, they began to attack the government in ways that resonated well with growing public dissatisfaction. Two events helped to ensure that law and order provided one of the focal points of attack.

The first arose from the trial of a farmer, Tony Martin, who had shot and killed a burglar in his home. [The Norfolk Farmer]

Martin was convicted of murder and received a life sentence. The popular press successfully engendered a sense of public outrage at the perceived severity of the sentence; politicians were adept in linking the specifics of the case with a general (but inaccurate) view that rural crime was spiraling out of control. The government was unable to take up any position that effectively countered these attacks.

The second event arose from the participation of England in the European Nations Football Championship, in which English fans (but not the English football team) played a significant part. The government was far slower than opposition politicians to denounce the behavior of the fans. When it did respond, with legislative proposals, they were clearly designed to eradicate the impression that the government was complacent with respect to football thugs. The Football Disorder Bill would have granted police the authority to confiscate the passports of people who had never been convicted of an offense and would have permitted the detention of persons for 24 hours while the police made "further inquiries." Several of these proposals were changed as a result of amendments proposed by the opposition.

These developments left the government discomfited with respect to criminal justice policy, as was demonstrated by the leak of a confidential internal briefing paper from the prime minister. In the document, Tony Blair expressed the view that New Labour was vulnerable in several areas of social policy, in-

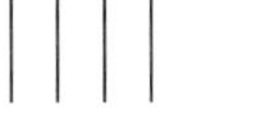

The Norfolk Farmer

Martin was a farmer living a reclusive life in an isolated part of the English countryside. Preoccupied—even obsessed—by crime, he attributed local crime problems to gypsies, denounced the lack of effective policing, and advocated the use of extreme forms of protection, including the use of firearms. In 1999, Martin answered his own call to arms. Having disturbed three young burglars in his house late at night, he shot at them, killing one 16-year-old boy and injuring another. Coverage of his trial dominated the news media for weeks. In the course of the trial, it became clear that Martin had booby-trapped the farm and slept, fully dressed, with a shotgun at his side. In addition, he had previously lost his licence for the shotgun, having already shot at trespassers. The jury rejected defense arguments that Martin had acted out of self-defense and found him guilty of murder, resulting in the imposition of the mandatory life sentence.

Martin's case was then taken up by a well-known publicist, who argued that the farmer had been the victim of a grave injustice. The tabloid press followed this line of argument. Purportedly rising rates of rural crime and lack of an effective police response provided the context for the story. The criminal justice system was portrayed as inflexible and unjust. On this occasion, the sentencing system was condemned for the incarceration of the "true" victim, Tony Martin. The case was pivotal in reframing the debate about the future direction of penal policy in the United Kingdom. It was ironic that the core of the media coverage concerned excessive severity, while portraying the government as directionless and soft on crime.

cluding law and order. The document displayed considerable sensitivity to the views of the public with respect to law and order. The memo discussed police initiatives to respond to crime and added that "as ever [i.e., the government] we are lacking a tough public message along with the strategy" (quoted in the *Weekly Guardian*, July 23–26, 2000). The government subsequently cast about for fresh policy initiatives that would be seen as tough and decisive with respect to law and order.

The first of these initiatives was floated in June 2000 and misfired badly. The proposal involved the imposition of on-the-spot fines for public drunkenness. The image used to present the plan consisted of "lager louts" being frog-marched by police officers to bank machines, where they would be obliged to withdraw money to pay the fine. The suggestion appeared risible to many commentators; most critically, however, it was quickly dismissed by senior police officers, who obviously had not been consulted about the proposal. This incident served to undermine the government's credibility with respect to criminal justice.

The "Name and Shame" Campaign

A striking development in the United Kingdom unfolded as this book was nearing completion. It concerned the murder of a young girl, Sarah Payne, by a pedophile. One tabloid newspaper took it upon itself to launch a campaign against all pedophiles. The newspaper published the names, addresses, and photographs of convicted pedophiles. The newspaper also claimed to have massive public support for the campaign. A poll was commissioned which found that 80% of the public supported "Sarah's law" for which the newspaper was campaigning. What the *News of the World* did not mention was that just over half of the British public also thought that the "Name and Shame" campaign was wrong, and a further 11% were undecided. [Sarah's Law]

In addition, the question used to gauge support for "Sarah's law" was most leading: "The Sarah's law campaign wants to introduce a new law in Britain that would ensure every parent's right to controlled access to information about individuals in their neighbourhood who may pose a risk to their children. The campaign is endorsed by the NSPCC, the Association of Chief Police Officers and the Association of Chief Officers of Probation. Do you support the introduction of Sarah's law?"

The Conservative leader quickly swooped on the issue as well, advocating the imposition of life terms for pedophiles (Hague, 2000).[13] This case illustrates the weaknesses of a populist response to a tragedy of this nature. Surely, an event of this magnitude calls for an appropriate mourning of the lost life, followed by a careful scrutiny of the circumstances giving rise to the crime: Was it preventable, and if so, what policy or legislative changes are necessary to prevent or reduce the probability of a repetition?

The last issue that arises from the UK experience is an example of how penal populism can backfire when politicians misjudge the mood of the public

"Sarah's Law"—Tabloid Campaigning in Britain

In mid-summer 2000, an eight-year-old girl, Sarah Payne, disappeared as she walked a short distance back to her grandparents' home. Eventually, her body was discovered. She had been murdered following a sexual assault. The whole nation mourned the young victim and shared the anguish of her parents.

Four weeks after Sarah's disappearance, a tabloid newspaper, *News of the World*, launched a campaign for the introduction of "Sarah's Law," with the support of her parents. The campaign was inspired by the introduction of "Megan's Law," following the murder of seven-year-old Megan Kanka in New Jersey in 1994; this and similar legislation in other U.S. states provided for greater public access to registers of known sex offenders. The Sarah's Law campaign called for

- greater public access to sex offender registers;
- more stringent registration requirements;
- heavier punishment for failure to comply with these requirements;
- fuller court powers to prevent offenders from contacting victims;
- more rigorous conditions of supervision of sex offenders following release on parole;
- greater powers of preventive detention.

The campaign also called for a form of "truth in sentencing," whereby all life sentences would mean imprisonment for life without any possibility of parole (*News of the World*, August 6, 2000, p. 5.) It mobilized support—or apparent support—from various senior criminal justice figures and from opposition politicians, particularly the leader of the opposition.

The unique feature of the campaign was not its agenda, but the means by which the proposals were pursued. The newspaper promised to "name and shame" 50 convicted pedophile offenders each week, by publishing their names, addresses, and photographs. Predictably, public anger about the murder was focused on the offenders thus identified. Several were attacked and there were also cases of misidentification: five families with no connections to sex offenders were driven from their homes. The home of a pediatrician was vandalized by a group of vigilantes whose moral outrage exceeded their levels of literacy (*Guardian*, August 30, 2000). A wave of violent demonstrations, attributed by the police to the campaign, occurred in the course of which cars were torched and police vans attacked. The newspaper eventually suspended the naming and shaming program, on the condition that the government review the legislation—something that was in fact already in progress.

Newspaper readers were given very limited information indeed by which they could assess the prevalence of crimes of this sort and the risks that children run of being targeted by a pedophile predator. The consensus of informed opinion was that the British registration arrangements worked at least as effectively as those introduced under "Megan's Law" and related U.S. initiatives. Undoubtedly, however, the campaign put the government in a difficult spot. Failure to respond would look inept and complacent; equally, however, if they responded with tough measures, they would look merely reactive: the newspaper and opposition politicians would undoubtedly garner all the credit for forcing action. In any event, they managed to hold to the line that rushed legislation was bad legislation, and that they would review the legislation as planned. Without doubt, however, the campaign has served to compound public frustration about the criminal justice system and has simultaneously constrained politicians' ability to locate strategies that genuinely minimize the risk of predatory pedophile crime. At the time of writing, the offender had recently been convicted, and it emerged that he had a previous conviction for sexually assaulting a young girl. The Home Secretary was still reviewing whether changes were needed to the system for registering convicted sex offenders.

in assuming that any punitive proposal in terms of responding to crime will prove popular. In the wake of this episode—and similar ones in other areas of social policy—media commentators became much readier to attribute populist motives to politicians; and politicians were equally quick to accuse their opponents of "playing to the gallery." The gains in popularity that the Conservatives had achieved a few months earlier appeared to have been largely dissipated. [Zero Tolerance for Cannabis in Britain]

Sentencing in England and Wales is about to be reformed once again in 2002. Following a review of the sentencing process, the Home Office has released a report which calls for sweeping changes to the sentencing and parole arrangements (Home Office, 2001a). The proposed reforms were designed,

Zero Tolerance for Cannabis in Britain—Misjudging the Public Mood

The main opposition party since 1997, the Conservative Party began to cast around in 2000 for new social policies whose toughness might attract broad-based public support in the forthcoming election. As part of this package, the opposition spokesman for home affairs, Ann Widdecombe, announced a "zero tolerance" policy on cannabis at the party's annual conference. She called for "zero tolerance" of the offense of cannabis possession, proposing a fixed penalty fine of 100 pounds ($150) for the first offence and tougher sentences for persistent offenders. She suggested that the most common way of dealing with the offense, a formal police warning (usually called a caution), should no longer be allowed.

The proposal was immediately condemned by the police as unworkable, and the press greeted the proposal with derision. Worse still, seven of her senior colleagues admitted smoking cannabis. (As is conventional in such confessions, the majority denied deriving any pleasure, although two subsequent admissions by senior Tories more bravely referred to "agreeable" and "mellow" experiences.) In the face of this criticism, Widdecombe backtracked. She said that her proposal had been misunderstood, and that she had never intended the police to stop issuing informal warnings, as opposed to formal cautions. The party leader, William Hague, announced that the policy would be reconsidered, after further consultation. (Perhaps the most surprising thing about this episode was the failure to consult either with the police or with other party colleagues before its announcement.)

At first sight, this provides an example of a political party keen to find popular support for tough policies, but failing to accurately read the popular mood. Certainly, subsequent polls showed widespread support for relaxing current legislation. For example, a Mori poll for the *Mail* (Sunday, October 15, 2000) found that 58% favored decriminalization of personal use; 49% opposed the proposal for fixed penalty fines, against 38% in support. However, it could equally well be seen as a consequence of a power struggle within the Conservative Party. The failure to consult within the shadow cabinet could be seen as a strategy to ambush the liberal wing of the party leadership, by using the party conference as an opportunity to secure grass-roots support for zero tolerance of cannabis before the liberals could express their objections.

At the time of this writing, the Home Secretary had recently announced his intention of reviewing the cannabis legislation, with a view to downgrading the status of the offense of possession to that of a non-arrestable offense.

among other things, to bolster public confidence in the criminal justice system, and public opinion clearly guided the Review team's deliberations. This is clear from the report which states that "the Review's assessment of public views on how sentencing should operate has informed its recommendations for a new framework" (Home Office, 2001a, p. ii).

Australia

In Australia, despite sentencing policy being a matter of state responsibility, all levels of government have attempted to exploit the issue for political advantage. For example, prior to the 1998 federal election in Australia, the incumbent prime minister made crime and punishment an election issue by adopting a pro-punishment line. Howard adopted a typically critical position (suggesting he was speaking for the people), accusing judges and others of being "soft" on crime. In the lead up to the 2001 election, both parties "got tough" on illegal immigrants. By denying entry to a boatload of asylum seekers, the prime minister was able to "snatch victory from the jaws of impeding defeat" at the polls. Following what appeared to be a groundswell of opinion for the hard line stand Labour backed legislative reform to restrict access by refugees to Australia and its courts.

At the state level, the position over the last decade has been one of successive "reform" or compromise influenced by populist forces working through both government and opposition. Every state and territory in Australia reformed its sentencing legislation at least once between 1988 and 1998. These reforms typically were announced with great fanfare, often in the heat of an election campaign and always against a gathering storm of public indignation and excited media coverage. The consequence has been significant increases in the size of the prison population. The dawn of this new era of populism can probably be best located at the 1988 New South Wales (NSW) state election marked, as it was, by a punishment "bidding war" and a promise of tough new penalties. The Sentencing Act (1988) introduced as part of this election campaign established Truth in Sentencing (abolition of remission), which effectively inflated the prison population by a considerable margin.[14] The act also introduced higher maximum sentences including a "natural life" sentence.

Hogg and Brown (1998, pp. 38–39) note that the NSW minister leading much of this reform matched his stated desire to "put value back in punishment" with a ready acceptance of deteriorating prison conditions and the plight of prisoners suffering the consequences of overcrowded, underserviced prisons. The same pattern was observed in Western Australia, which saw rapid rises in its prison population through the late 1990s. This increase in prison populations precipitated by populist legislation led to overcrowded and underserviced prisons; the result was a major prison riot in 1998. Although the report into the riot identified overcrowding and underservicing as causes, the minister for justice had already taken a public stance of blaming prisoners for the riot and even expressed the view that they were lucky that they had not been shot. Such a cavalier disregard of government responsibility for the care of prisoners seems to be now increasingly excused by simplistic portrayals of "us" against "them."

The split between different levels of government in Australia engendered by the politicization of punishment is also reflected in the split between different arms of government. The traditional "separation of powers" between the parliament, the executive, and the judiciary that is a hallmark of the Westminster system of government appeared to be breaking down at the close of the century in Australia. The 1990s saw increasing public criticism from populist politicians regarding the courts, tribunals, and individual judges.

In the 1990s, the lesson learned by all political parties was that "law and order" works as a political tool. In much the same way as seen in the United Kingdom, the Labour Party—traditionally adopting a more socially sensitive and humane approach—jettisoned any links to positions that could be seen or accused of being soft on crime. In both Western Australia and New South Wales, the British slogan "Tough on crime, tough on the causes of crime" was adopted with much enthusiasm. Labour did everything it could to prove that it would be even tougher on crime than its opponents.

Mandatory Sentencing

The phenomenon of Labour trying too hard to throw off the accusation that they are "soft" on crime is observed in Australia in the 1990s. It is demonstrated, for example, by its introduction of one of the first mandatory sentencing bills in Australia. This was introduced by the Labour government in Western Australia in 1992. The Crime (Serious and Repeat Offenders) Sentencing Act 1992 (WA) was introduced to target and incapacitate a presumed core of recidivist juvenile offenders. The manner in which this was drafted and the events which precipitated it serve as an archetypal example of populist legislation.

The general background from the late 80s to the early 90s in Western Australia was one of growing disdain for rehabilitation and intolerance of juvenile crime. The push toward a simplistic view of offenders and the effectiveness of punishment was to a considerable extent fueled by a popular "talk back" radio commentator, culminating in a rally before Parliament House in August 1991. The rally attracted 20,000 people and provided powerful "copy" in a debate now largely in the hands of the media. The tinderbox was primed and simply awaiting the spark. The spark is typically a case involving an archetypal (middle-class innocent) victim, offender (lower-class recidivist), and a terrible crime (such as the Polly Klaas case in California). Just such a case provided the spark to the tinderbox in Western Australia in late 1991.

On Christmas day 1991, a young family was driving home after visiting relatives. The family comprised the father, mother (heavily pregnant with her second child), and young child. Their vehicle was hit by a young aboriginal offender in a stolen car who was being pursued by police.[15] The resulting crash killed all members of the family except the father. The offender was a 14-year-old with a lengthy criminal record. Media coverage was intense and included pictures of the crash scene strewn with Christmas presents.

The Christmas and New Year's period in Australia is typically a festive time with many social occasions. The premier of the state was away and the crisis ensuing from the Christmas day tragedy was borne by the acting premier and his cabinet. On the sixth of January, the acting premier announced that "Western Australia's hard core juvenile criminals will be subject to the toughest laws in Australia under measures approved by State Cabinet today." Further details promised mandatory minimum terms of imprisonment for repeat juvenile offenders, particularly for offenses involving violence. Despite serious flaws now evident in the proposed strategy designed to achieve selective incapacitation, the legislation was introduced in Parliament. The proposed act was largely unworkable. Recognizing the limitations of the legislation, the Labour Party attached a "sunset clause," which effectively terminated the legislation after two years (in 1994).

Despite the flaws in the legislation and its ineffectiveness in reducing crime (Harding, 1995), the Crime (Serious and Repeat Offenders) Sentencing Act 1992 (WA) served a distinct political purpose and stands out now as an early example of populist sentencing legislation. The same problems with California's Three Strikes Law have now been well documented (see Austin, Clark, Hardyman, and Henry, 1999), as have the political benefits of passing the law (see Rubin, 1999).

Western Australia ended the decade also in controversy about populist sentencing legislation. The attorney general was pushing for a sentencing matrix (numerical sentencing guidelines restricting judicial discretion) and introduced a bill to Parliament against the wishes of, and indeed without consulting, the judiciary (see Morgan, 1999).

Three Strikes Laws Arrive in Australia

Mandatory sentencing through the latter part of the 1990s was most often characterized by variants of the three strikes laws. Not only was the "tough and unforgiving" American stance hailed by all manner of Australian politicians looking for instant popularity, the use of such a foreign sporting analogy[16] heightened the drive not only for snappy sound bites but also for something new and highly punitive. The fact that these laws are directly imported from America is likely part of the appeal. Many Australians believe that their culture is being systematically Americanized and part of the underlying process here is a belief that populist and tough justice has to be better in the "new world order," just as American economic systems set the pace in the global marketplace.

Three strikes laws introduced in Australia in the 1990s have resulted in the same sort of penal absurdities and reversals of proportionality observed in the United States: relatively trivial offenses triggering lengthy prison terms. The Northern Territory (NT), well-known as a frontier and renegade jurisdiction with Australia's highest rates of crime and imprisonment, introduced one strike laws mandatory imprisonment for first time property offenders.[17] In a statement introducing this legislation, the Northern Territory attorney general stated that "I believe it is the rightful role of the parliament to reflect the concerns of the community. And who doubts that Territorians want harsher penalties for those who continue to abuse the rights of others?[18] In the general enthusiasm for punishment, the Northern Territory government also passed a number of provisions creating punitive work orders and requiring distinctive clothing to be worn by offenders while in public and carrying out the order. This mirrors other moves around Australia for more visible and vibrant displays of punishment including boot camps (another Americanism, attractive because it is distinctly American and punitive)[19] and shaming ceremonies.

Western Australia also introduced a version of three strikes sentencing with its Criminal Code Amendment Act (No 2, 1996). The law was introduced to deal with the specific problem of home burglary that was (and remains) a major concern in Western Australia. The law provided for a mandatory term of 12 months imprisonment on the third strike of a home burglary conviction or appearance.

By the end of the 1990s, the Australian mandatory sentencing laws in place in Western Australia and the Northern Territory had led to calls for repeal from human rights groups (and others). Receiving no support from populist state governments, these groups activated mechanisms available at the federal level. An overview of the mandatory sentencing laws and their effect on Australia's international human rights obligations was completed by the Australian Human Rights and Equal Opportunity Commission in August 1999. The Green's senator (Bob Brown) introduced a bill into federal parliament seeking to overturn the state laws on the grounds that they contravened Australia's international human rights obligations.[20] Senator Brown made the point that the mandatory sentencing laws were based on misinformation in the community about juvenile crime. The government and the public perceived a "juvenile crime wave" where none existed.

It was also argued that mandatory sentences contravened Australia's obligations under the United Nations Convention on the Rights of the Child (CROC). There are a number of principles and articles which appear to be contravened by mandatory sentencing, but the most direct is 37b which states that "Detention of children must only be used as a last resort and for the shortest possible time." Article 40(4) also refers to the sentence being proportionate to the crime. By the end of 1999, a number of disproportionate sentences had already accumulated in the Northern Territory.[21]

The problems with the NT's mandatory sentencing laws drew intense national interest following the suicide of a 15-year-old aboriginal boy in a Darwin detention center in February 2000. The boy had stolen some stationery worth only a few dollars. The NT laws mandate 28 days in prison for a second property offense committed by a juvenile. The boy was from a remote area, had recently lost relatives, and just prior to the suicide had been disciplined for not washing his dishes. In responding to calls to repeal the laws, the state premier continued to justify the laws as being enacted after community pressure, thus shifting responsibility away from government to the community.

Although the Western Australia and Northern Territory mandatory sentencing laws represent the worst of Australian populist penal policy, every other state has been affected to a greater or a lesser extent by penal populism. In Queensland, the Penalties and Sentences Act introduced in 1992 led to sharp rises in the rates of imprisonment. This effect was mainly the result of the curtailment of parole and remission. The act increased the minimum period to be served by persons convicted of a violent offense before becoming eligible for remission or parole from 50 to 80 %. The influence of punitive populism has always been strong in the state dubbed the "deep north" and calls for tougher penalties have always been heard. Legislation was introduced in 1997 which excluded the operation of the common principle that imprisonment should be viewed as the sanction of last resort, where the person being sentenced was seen as a serious offender. The effect of these provisions likely explains a very rapid rise in Queensland's imprisonment rate—which accelerated to become the highest of any state by 1998.

Victoria remains Australasia's Netherlands, with rates of imprisonment now even lower than that country. However, a new conservative government in Victoria came into power in 1992 and within six months had introduced legislation increasing sentences for sexual and violent offenders. Freiberg and Ross (1999, p. 212) note that it is highly ironic that these punitive policies were implemented as crime rates were declining, a finding repeated in other countries. However, the changes in the Victorian legislation, ostensibly quite similar to those in Queensland, did not result in the sharp rises in imprisonment observed in the latter state (Freiberg, 1998).

An analysis of the severity in penalties in New South Wales (Baker, 1998) indicates that the courts in that state were hardening throughout the 1990s, delivering harsher penalties for a range of crimes. As discussed earlier in this section, populist "bidding wars" at the end of the 1980s had seen the introduction of "truth in sentencing" in that state leading to an increase in the prison population.

The key shifts in Australia in the 1990s, as evidenced in the statements of the politicians introducing and promoting populist sentencing legislation, have been toward protection and punishment and away from social reform and rehabilitation. This reflected a sea change in the way society was viewed by the media, politicians, and the public. Australia's vision of social order and social justice was increasingly coming to resemble America's.

New Zealand

Increasing public concern about crime provides the essential background to sentencing policy in New Zealand, as it does elsewhere in the English speaking world. However, the effect of this concern has been much more muted, at least so far, with little in the way of mandatory sentencing legislation introduced from Parliament to direct sentencing policy.[22] Despite this, two major legislative reforms aimed at increasing the use of custody for violent offenders were introduced (in 1985 and 1993). Legislatively, the main development came in 1985 with the Criminal Justice Act, which sought to distinguish violent and sexual offenders from other offenders and apply much more rigorous sentences to this group. This legislation and the substantial amendments in 1993 were brought about to reflect public and political concern with violent crime. It is the increasingly severe sentences for violent offenses over the last decade in New Zealand that largely explain the escalating imprisonment rates in that country.[23] These reforms and other forces were responsible for the rapid rise in New Zealand's prison population.

New Zealand has also experienced the populist penal policy sparked by highly sensational specific cases. What occurred in New Zealand in late 1996 fits well the "tinderbox and spark" model. In March 1986, a sex offender with a long history was released from prison. Just five weeks later he committed an atrocious crime involving sexual violence. The resulting media coverage of this awful crime generated considerable pressure on the government. Ultimately, this led to the scope of preventive detention being expanded (in 1987) and an increase in the use of this sentence by the courts (Meek, 1995). The measures seem to be triggered by this case but also constituted a response to a crisis of confidence around "law and order" at that time. As Meek notes: "These events must be seen in the context of rising public concern about violent crime and a government which was vulnerable on the issue of law and order as it approached an election year" (1995, p. 236).

There were, however, very bright signs at the beginning of the 1990s with the promotion through the (then) Minister for Justice (and later Prime Minister) Geoffrey Palmer, who promoted crime prevention as an alternative to policing and punishment as the most important response to crime. The "Safer Communities Council Pilot Scheme" was established in 1990 and led into the establishment of a well-organized and comprehensive crime prevention system that remains in place. Notwithstanding these positive developments, the general political focus was, as in Australia, toward more severe sentencing. The legislative reforms directly affecting sentencing were clearly the expression of concerns about crime and a perception that a stronger stand needed to be taken against violence. This punitive populism did not abate but actually accelerated. In the run-up to the 1999 election in New Zealand, the prime minister announced a seven-step plan to get tough on crime. The seven steps focused on policing and punishment. Sentences for burglars and particularly violent offenders were to be increased and longer nonparole periods made mandatory (Bradley, 1999). The rhetoric from New Zealand politicians therefore echoed what was happening on the world stage, if perhaps delayed by a decade.

Populism in penal policy had certainly reached the distant shores of New Zealand by the end of the 1990s, clearly marked by the inclusion of a "referendum on punishment" at the time of the 1999 general election. The referendum question clearly reflected the essence of the sentiment underlying populist punitiveness. The question was: "Should there be a reform of our justice system placing greater emphasis on the needs of victims, providing restitution and compensation for them and imposing minimum sentences and hard labour for all serious offenders?" Over 90% of New Zealand voters responded in the affirmative, displaying the mood of the electorate and/or the power of this rather leading question. The fact that such a referendum question could be posed represents something of a victory for populist punitiveness and speaks volumes about the political mood in New Zealand at the end of the 1990s.

The changes in New Zealand reflect a number of forces. Although increases in severity are largely attributable to the increase in the severity of the penal response to violent offenders (both in terms of the length of sentence and curtailment of parole), it is also true that other forces are at work which have resulted in a much larger number of violent offenders coming before the courts. The growing sensitivity to violent crime has led to a much larger number of such offenses coming to the attention of the police and being prosecuted. Brown and Young (2000) also note that the severity of sentences has increased for offenders convicted of serious property offenses. It is interesting to reflect that these changes may all have occurred during a time when the actual rate of violence in the country remained stable. The victimization survey data in New Zealand available at present are insufficient to test this hypothesis, but if the underlying trends in crime are similar to Australia or the United States, what is occurring in New Zealand is reflective of a rapid increase in the reaction to violence rather than a real increase in violence.[24]

Conclusion

This review of recent penal policy developments in our five countries reveals both uniformity and diversity in responding to crime. Examples of penal populism can be found in all countries, although they seem more common and more likely to have originated in the United States. [Penal Modeling]

The mechanism by which populist solutions emerge seems common; it frequently involves the occurrence of a high-profile tragedy. Legislation frequently follows on the heels of such incidents. Criminal law reform tends to be episodic and shaped by populist forces, including opposition politicians and populist news media. In addition, populist politicians tend to exploit these incidents by advocating ever-harsher responses to crime and raising the possibility

Penal Modeling: The Americanization of Punishment

The United States generally provides the most extreme forms of populist punitiveness. Furthermore, most of the developments in populist penal policy in other nations have followed (and in many instances simply copied) earlier developments in the United States. This may happen either because a model has been provided and/or American products (especially cultural products) are constantly being "downloaded" in other English-speaking countries.

The question of cross-cultural comparisons in punitiveness has been raised in few previous studies; theorizing about comparative differences has been even more limited. Leslie Wilkins (1991) proposed a theory linking values in a society with the degree of punitiveness. Wilkins suggests that explanations of different incarceration rates are a function of what he calls "values packages." These packages determine not only crime and justice policy but also a range of other government choices including economic policy. In this analysis, the United States is seen as a "high stakes" society, where "good" behavior is rewarded with very high financial rewards and bad behavior with correspondingly extremely negative consequences (long imprisonment, death penalty). Thus, the underlying "engine" of public attitudes to punishment derives from a world view that is fatalistic and accepting of extreme consequences for individual choice. Other countries in the "American" cultural empire approximate the European model of moderated outcomes aimed at dampening the relative effects on individuals of social structure. Wilkins' work is relevant to the present analysis as it provides some indication of the differences between the five countries. Although the present interest has been with the transmission and similarity in populist values, a natural sequel would be to assume such similarities would dominate but to locate important areas of resistance and difference.

Tonry (1999) deals with the issue directly in noting that humane and cost-effective sentencing strategies developed in Europe are rarely adopted in the United States. In this respect, penal reforms proceed down a one-way street. However, the American-developed populist sentencing strategies have been copied (albeit in milder forms) in most other English-speaking countries. There appears then to be a divide between the English-speaking world, dominated by the United States and continental European countries. Part of the explanation for this Tonry notes lies in the political structures in the United States which offer virtually no protection from populist decision-making; judges, for example, are mostly elected rather than appointed. European countries, by contrast, focus on developing robust and extensive policy-making infrastructure so that careers and hierarchies of power can develop independently of popularity-based politics.

that the tragedy could have been prevented, had the government adopted such measures in the first place.

In subsequent chapters, we shall examine the principal areas in which populist justice has emerged (either in the form of proposed or actual reforms). In the next chapter, however, we explore explanations for the rise of punitive penal policies.

4 Explaining the Rise of Punitive Penal Policies

The previous chapter has documented a consistent trend toward punitive penal policies in the United States, Canada, Britain, and Australia. Although the scale and nature of the punitive policies vary across the English-speaking world, the direction over the last 20 years of the twentieth century is unmistakable. This chapter assesses some possible explanations for this phenomenon. Our primary concern is with the decision at the political level to promote punitive penal policies.

The first explanation of harsh criminal policy that would come to the mind of most people is that tough penal policies are an inevitable response to increasing crime rates. There are many public displays of anger in response to rising crime, and this may seem to be sufficient to provide the driving force behind punitive penal policies. Reasonable as this sounds, the crime trends and the literature that has accumulated on public opinion, as discussed in chapter 1, undermine such a straightforward interpretation. There is a consensus in the literature that trends in public punitiveness simply do not correspond closely with rises in crime rates. As we shall see, the pressure of public opinion by itself is not sufficient to explain the rise of punitive policies. Political opportunities present themselves in many ways when the public is misinformed and receptive to direction on punishment policy.

We begin our discussion with the two most common and competing views of the ascendancy of punitive penal policy. The first and the most simple is that the rise of these policies simply reflects a public desire for harsher sentencing. The second is that the policies are promoted with a view of exploiting public emotions on crime. We then examine two other possible explanations. One relates to the level of misinformation, myths, and mistaken beliefs that underpin both public opinion and government policy. The final view concerns the effect that diffuse anxieties brought on by social and economic changes have had on government actions.

We think it important to investigate the forces that influence political decisions to promote punitive penal policy. However, one must guard again *over*interpretation. Few decisions are carefully planned and thought through. While increasingly punitive policies may be a product of political exploitation or mood shifts in the community, politicians are often much more reactive, responding to short-term crises prompted by high profile crimes and media campaigns. The power of these forces appears to be increasing with the growing importance of the media in political debates. This more prosaic perspective seeks the roots of populist crime policy not in deep ideological commitments, but rather in responses to media coverage of individual crimes. The chapter concludes with a discussion of these more immediate influences and then advances a model that incorporates all the relevant influences shaping the drift toward more punitive and populist criminal justice policies.

Democracy at Work

The simplest explanation of the growth of punitive penal policy is that sentencing in industrialized democracies went through a period of excessively lenient sentencing in the 1960s and 1970s. This undermined the deterrent value of sentencing which in turn resulted in rising crime rates. Higher crime rates then fed public discontent and thus provided the pressure for criminal justice reform. Following the work of Katherine Beckett (1997), we refer to this first type of explanation of rising punitiveness as the "Democracy at Work" thesis—defined here as a process in which public views become more punitive and politicians then respond to this shift in opinion. There are other possibilities that are also consistent with the Democracy at Work thesis. One is that the electoral process ensures that those politicians who find themselves in office themselves share the views and policy preferences of their electorates.

The Democracy at Work explanation argues that politicians follow rather than lead public opinion. According to this view, politicians backing tougher penal policies are often merely reflecting public wishes. It is this image of representative politics at work that provides the most legitimate basis for the enactment of punitive penal policies. The question of the viability or the quality of the policies may be debatable, and there may be questions about the view of democracy that imagines government actions can be, or should be, simply the enactment of public opinion. However, the Democracy at Work thesis asserts that the groundswell of opinion in favor of the harsh treatment of offenders begins in public reactions to their own experiences or perceptions of the efficacy of current penal policy.

Clearly, there have been occasions where tougher penal regimes have been introduced exactly as described by the Democracy at Work thesis. Sometimes sentencing levels have proved unacceptable to the public and politicians have responded to public concern. However, this thesis needs substantial qualification. The clearest evidence calling its assumptions into question comes from the United States. As we have seen earlier, public attitudes to sentencing have been broadly stable for the last 20 years in the United States. Those fluctuations that *have* occurred are better explained as a consequence of policy initiatives than as a cause. Beckett's (1997) analysis of American penal and drugs policy suggests that public concern about these issues is unrelated to crime trends or drug use but is closely linked with political initiatives and media coverage of these initiatives. In the case of crime, there was a consistent upward trend in violent crime over the decades that she examines. However, public concern about crime "spiked" in 1969 and again in 1971, following a number of anti-crime initiatives and the attendant press coverage. Public concern about drugs followed government initiatives; the sharpest increase was in 1990, following a period of intense government activity in the "War against Drugs."

A more accurate indicator of the level of crime in the United States is the measure provided by the National Crime Victimization Survey (NCVS). According to the results of this survey, crime rates have not increased since 1973. The NCVS figures show that the level of violent crime has remained unchanged, while the level of property crime has actually decreased. Although there is some debate about how to interpret the disparity between official figures and victimization survey findings, most scholars agree that the activities of state agencies has had a significant impact on driving up the proportion of total crime that is captured in official figures, thus contributing to the perception that crime has increased.

The vast majority of the public derive their information about crime and punishment from the media, who are almost entirely reliant on political actors for information. The power to shape public opinion is thus shared between the media and political parties and (to a lesser degree) by lobby groups that are able to get media time. And there is evidence that despite the statistical record, most people in that latter part of the twentieth century believed that they were living in times of unprecedented crime rates. Indeed, Garland (2000) argues that it is not so much that fluctuations in crime rates have driven public opinion and political initiatives, but the growing perception and belief that crime is rampant and impervious to traditional remedies.

In Britain, as noted in chapter 3, a kind of "penal arms race" was triggered between the two main political parties, not by any obvious surge in public concern about crime, but by a decision taken by Labour to challenge the Conservatives' claim to be "the party of law and order." Labour thereby eliminated an electoral advantage long held by the Conservatives. The Democracy at Work thesis predicts a simple linear progression, consisting of growing public concern leading to a public desire for harsher punishment and a political response involving punitive policies. However, this sequence did not emerge in either the United Kingdom or the United States; a much more complex interactive process developed, in which politicians simultaneously shaped and responded to opinion.

Another problem for the Democracy at Work thesis is that the clear correlation that may be expected between perceived risk of victimization and calls for tougher punishment is missing. For example, in the United States, African Americans are most at risk in terms of victimization, but they are not always the most punitive group. In fact, it is those least at risk—white males in rural areas—who are most punitive and most supportive of tough crime policies. This suggests that the energy for punitiveness has more to do with issues of entitlement, control, outrage, and anger than fear of criminal victimization.[1]

Studies of policymakers suggest that they conceptualize public opinion loosely and creatively, looking for possibilities to support policies that serve certain interests.[2] The specifics of public opinion are less important than the perception that a policy is, or can be, popular. Politicians thus build on the observation that public opinion is malleable—it can be shaped and molded to conform to strategic needs and interests. This is not to say that public opinion can be manufactured or that it can be endlessly repackaged. Public sentiments, mood, and likely reaction are fairly broad and can be manipulated in such a way that certain reactions can be predicted from particular political initiatives. But public sensibilities and views create a bounded space within which it is safe to devise and develop themes. It is hard for policy initiatives to go outside the bounds of public acceptability, but this still leaves much space for creativity in packaging and selling policies. In this process of devising popular policy, the news media and special interest groups become crucial agents that help frame and construct not only the meaning of the policy but also the direction of public opinion.

With respect to its political importance, public opinion is better characterized in terms of more general reactions such as responsiveness and mood. Although there may be discernable sets or dispositions toward certain elements such as "criminals" and "punishment," attitudes to policies aimed at offenders and dealing with crime are fairly plastic and will depend on the kind of information that is presented, the way it is presented, and the cogency of the arguments presented. The implication is that public opinion is unlikely to determine political positions on crime, unless it is harnessed by lobby groups, media organizations, or political parties themselves.

The view that public opinion "drives" penal policy would appear to be overly simplistic. We need to examine the *interactions* between politicians' promotion of penal policies and public attitudes to crime and punishment. While the Democracy at Work thesis views the nature of the interaction as a fairly simple one-way drive from public frustration through to political action, there is now mounting evidence that politicians are not passive participants in the process but see certain advantages in shaping public opinion.

Penal Populism

The Democracy at Work thesis proposes that politicians have been properly responsive to public concern about crime by putting into place the more robust responses to offending which people want. An alternative perspective is that politicians have been populist in advocating these tougher policies. "Penal populism"—a term equivalent to Bottoms's (1995) "populist punitiveness"—is defined here as a punishment policy developed primarily for its anticipated popularity.[3] Penal policy is particularly susceptible to populism, because there is a great deal of public concern about crime, and low levels of public knowledge about sentencing practice, sentencing effectiveness, and sentencing equity. This combination of concern and lack of knowledge can present politicians with the temptation to promote policies which promote electoral advantage without doing much about crime. The more wilful that such politicians are in their disregard of the evidence about effectiveness and equity, the more we are inclined to regard them as penal populists.

One of the defining characteristics of populism is the exclusion of elite or institutional input from crime policy development. Penal populism involves a wilful disregard of evidence or knowledge, and this knowledge is accumulated and held, typically, by those who work within, or are closely involved with, the criminal justice system. Sometimes the process of discrediting elite input can be explicit. For example, when two Australian jurisdictions introduced mandatory sentencing, the public controversy became very heated. At one point, the attorney general—a political appointee—in one jurisdiction went so far as to accuse the courts of being corrupt, leading to a public showdown with the chief justice. In the end, the politicians won. Australian governments argued that mandatory sentencing was "effective" *because* it was popular.

The difference between the Democracy at Work thesis and penal populism is a subtle one, to do with the intentions underlying political initiatives.[4] How does one differentiate between sincere penal hawks—elected, no doubt, on their record of tough-mindedness—and Machiavellian populists who ensure that whatever policies they pursue, they never expose themselves to the charge of being "soft on crime."[5] Hard evidence about intentions is rarely forthcoming, and one is often driven to make inferences on the basis of the timing and context of political announcements and on the consistency of political position—or lack of it. Sometimes those involved in the policy process offer informed accounts of the factors taken into account in reaching policy decisions.

The nature of populist solutions to crime has meant that penal populism has been associated most often with the political right. However, we have also observed throughout the English-speaking world that political actors on the center-left have sometimes adopted populist positions on crime and punishment, lest they lose their whole campaign over this issue. For example, the Democrats in the United States and Labour in the United Kingdom and Australia have understood the importance of adopting tough policies on crime and punishment to rob their opposition of a winning edge in this domain.[6] The fact that it is possible to adopt a tough stance on sentencing without necessarily threatening the rest of the political platform means that political actors across the spectrum have shown themselves to be open to the seductions of penal populism.

The competitive nature of electoral politics means that emotional topics such as crime and punishment are often targeted in negative campaigning. Politicians' sense of vulnerability to such campaigning encourages an interest in penal populism: being seen to be *soft on crime* is now widely regarded as a serious political liability.[7] The way that this anxiety has penetrated the minds of key political decision makers cannot be underestimated and appears to be responsible for the decision to pass the "three strikes" law in California.

Penal populism may also be pursued to deflect attention from policy arenas that are causing a party or government damage. A metaphorical "war against crime" can be as electorally valuable as a Gulf War or a Falklands War—either in distracting interest from other policy issues in relation to which politicians feel vulnerable or in legitimizing broader policy aims. Populist solutions to crime problems typically portray offending as the result of wilfully anti-social decision-making in ways which negate the role of social exclusion in creating crime.

Populism is, of course, a pejorative term. Many would see the attribution by academics and elites of populism to punitive policies as unfairly impugning the motives of the politicians involved. They might regard the response as a predictable one, given that anti-elitism is often intertwined with punitive penal agendas. They might argue that "populist" is simply a term of abuse thrown by liberal thinkers at those who favor tougher policies—in much the same way that "liberal" itself is becoming a new political insult. However, the phenomenon deserves more subtle analysis.

By definition, the populist impulse is free of ideology. A populist penal agenda emerges not from a set of political beliefs about the nature of people and society but from the preferences of political "consumers"—the electorate. We have noted an increasing tendency for politicians on the center-left as well as the right to pursue populist penal agendas. The dynamics of populism provide one part of the explanation for the rise of punitive policies in the late twentieth century. However, other factors also need to be taken into account in explaining the precise shape taken by penal populism over the last three decades.

The rise of the New Right and the demise of liberalism from the late 1970s signaled a broad movement in politics away from endorsement of the liberal agenda to a more individualistic and divisive view of society. A growing sense of pessimism about many aspects of society developed and a growing punitiveness, especially as a political force, can be seen as part of this general decline of optimism.[8] As will be discussed below, the source of this mood-change is to be found in the wide range of social fears and insecurities besetting the middle class in the last quarter of the twentieth century.

While the growing tendency to political populism may have interacted with a shift in political and public mood, this does not explain the precise way in which problems of crime and punishment have been subject to media and political "framing."[9] We also need to consider the ways in which lack of public and political knowledge have contributed to the process.

Misinformed Democracy

Our third hypothesis for the increase in punitive penal policies explains penal policy as a function of both the misinformation provided to the public and misreading of public opinion by politicians. The Democracy at Work thesis presumes that politicians are enacting the will of the people, but it is hard to know whether they are able to "read" public opinion accurately, or whether public opinion is properly informed about the issues. However much one might value political responsiveness to public opinion, it would be hard to justify a policy based on a misreading of public opinion or on public opinion that was demonstrably misinformed. There is persuasive evidence both that opinion is misinformed, and that it is misread.

Public misinformation relating to penal policy can take various forms. First, people may have limited knowledge about the nature of the crime problem which penal policies aim to address. Leaving aside the inherent difficulties associated with measuring crime, the task of effectively communicating crime trends to the general public is one that has been poorly handled in the five countries we examine. All exhibit similar patterns: a long upward trend in the postwar period, followed more recently by stable or declining crime rates. Yet, as we have discussed in chapter 2, most people think the upward trend has continued.[10] Second, people are poorly informed about the criminal process in general and in particular about the severity of sentences imposed. If it is hard to ensure that people have an accurate understanding of crime trends, it is that much harder to communicate how the courts deal with the diversity of crimes and offenders.

Third, the ways in which opinion has been assessed are systematically misleading. There is the inevitable sampling bias in the impressions that politicians draw from feedback from their constituents or from calls to talkback radio programs. We would not argue that public frustration about crime and punishment is entirely illusory—a function of poor and misleading measurement techniques. However, current methods of measuring opinion serve to *overstate* the degree of anger and frustration that undoubtedly exists. Even those media editors and journalists who aim simply to reflect the views of their readers and viewers will then exaggerate the extent of public dissatisfaction; those people who draw their views largely from the media will share the indignation they see around them.

If policymakers are misinformed about public opinion, this is likely to limit the range of policy options that they are willing to consider. For example, Riley and Rose (1980) found that it was individuals' and agencies' perceptions of what the public would tolerate that gave rise to harsher penal policies. Governments may thus turn their backs on more constructive penal options in the mistaken belief that the public would not tolerate such policies. Thus, a key determinant of punitive policies may be the misreading of public punitiveness by politicians and officials alike.

Late Modern Anxieties

So far we have considered how the rise in punitive penal policies can be explained in terms of interactions between public attitudes and knowledge about crime and the political response to public attitudes and knowledge. We have touched only briefly on broader changes in the public mood that might shape or condition attitudes specifically to crime and punishment.

One seam of theorizing concerns the way in which social and technological change has left us bereft of traditional certainties and sources of trust. This set of changes can be referred to collectively as the transformations of "modern" industrial society into "late modernity."[11] Punitive public opinion and punitive penal policy may be considered together as responses to the complexities brought on by this rapid social change.

The focus here is on the convergence of social, cultural, economic, technological, and ecological change to create unparalleled levels of uncertainty and increasing public skepticism about the ability of national states to regulate change through the political process. In these circumstances, the wide-ranging insecurities which people feel in the face of rapid social change may be translated into concerns about the risks of crime and about threats to personal safety. Broader public anxieties create an environment in which the "criminology of the other"—to use Garland's (2000) expression—can flourish; problems of social welfare become problems of social control, and the means of control include stereotyping and social exclusion. Garland argues that the new middle-class concerns about crime have been significantly affected by three social developments within the last quarter of the twentieth century: changing lifestyles and the incorporation of "risk management" as a routine aspect of life; perceptions of increasing social disorder in the form of incivilities; and the influence of the mass media. For example, crime provides endless visual opportunities for television. As television came more and more to provide the window to the world, crime has been brought ever closer to the lives of the public. While in the past middle-class citizens were largely insulated from dealing with crime, they now had to process images on a daily basis. Television thus has sensitized the public to crime in the way that graphic images from Vietnam sensitized Americans to war.

The general perception is that crime rates are high and a matter for concern and action. Through these factors a "crime complex"[12] develops that includes a pervading consciousness and concern for crime in the media, popular culture, and the social environment. The relentless belief that the present represents a time of unprecedented danger is likely to be endorsed by many people because it provides some legitimacy for the diffuse social and economic threats that they experience. However, a consequence of this belief is that punishment policy is then seen as a kind of solution as well as a reinforcement of essential values.[13]

If the fears of late modernity emerge from a sense of citizen disempowerment, they are exacerbated by wider social and economic developments that effectively disempower the nation state. As the power of the state is being eroded, the argument goes, governments find their capacity for effective action increasingly curtailed; at the same time, they find themselves under increasing pressure from an ever more skeptical electorate to pursue policies which have the *appearance* of tough, decisive action. Offering tough action against convenient enemies has great political appeal; it offers politicians a respite from the complexity of diffuse global threats over which they have very limited control. Thus, an electorate characterized by increasing anxieties about social order and a government seeking attractive policies is a combination that gives rise to punitive penal policies. This creates a mood of receptivity to policies that exclude and punish any group that might reasonably be implicated as a source of public insecurity.

This understanding emerges in many explanations of late twentieth century punitive penal policy. For example, in seeking to explain public opinion with respect to the "three strikes" laws, Tyler and Boeckmann (1997, p. 240) found that it was the desire for actions that reassert community commitment to social and moral values that was most important. It is the concern for moral cohesion, they argue, that underlies support for strong expressive laws. Weisberg (1999) similarly explains how penal policy can be used to soothe a much wider and unrelated social malaise: "Many economists tell us that the true source of social anxiety for this iconic voter is the decline in real wages over the last two decades, but, given the difficulty we all have in understanding economic forces, the death penalty oath becomes a wonderful way for a politician to express empathy toward those so concerned with the perceived breakdown in social order" (p. 66).

Intolerance of social problems has risen in step with the rapid growth in expectations regarding control (reflected in physical safety and security). The idea here of an evolution in attitude and sentiment that reflects both structural changes and a response to various aspects associated with the liberal period, such as "defining deviance down," emerges in a number of writings.[14] The state is increasingly seen as responsible for the provision and maintenance of security and blamed for events that signify its failure. The needs and expectations of the "law-abiding" majority emerge as urgent and demanding in the new globalized and mobile world. Rather than provide social reform, the state is looked on to provide effective containment of social threats.

Integrating the Four Explanations

We have proposed that the development of punitive penal policies over the last three decades can be understood to a limited extent as the properly responsive political reaction to public anxieties about rising crime. However, we have also suggested that to derive an adequate explanation of the evolution of punitive policies several other factors must be taken into account: the increasingly populist tendency in late twentieth-century democracies; lack of public knowledge about crime and punishment; and public uncertainties resulting from rapid social change. The four types or levels of explanation are, of course, not mutually exclusive but reflect different ways of seeing the relationship between public opinion and punitive sentencing policy.

In examining the similarities and differences between the four types of explanations we can see that in many ways they are complementary. Even the distinction between the Democracy at Work thesis and populism may be seen as a difference of emphasis rather than an "either-or" choice. One way to understand the interrelation of these factors is to see them as providing relevant explanations at different levels of specificity in terms of the political decision relevant to penal policy. The choice of which level or focus to take largely depends on the particular interest. All the factors raised are important and relevant to understanding the ascendancy of punitive penal policy. One way to understand their interrelation is to consider their distance from the crucial decision to endorse punitive penal policies. The levels of explanation can be seen as falling on a continuum from the proximal—those concerned with the political decision making—to the distal—those factors such as late modern anxieties that provide the general social conditions in which the political decision making occurs. This helps us understand that these types of explanations are not so much competing as complementary and points us in the direction of a more complex understanding of the interrelation of political, economic, and social forces.

Practical Political Factors Influencing Crime Policy Formulation

Penal policy in the English-speaking world is not the outcome of a well-reasoned, highly planned, and strategic process that some people imagine. In an ideal world, the best available evidence would be brought to bear on the question. This evidence would include costs to all the individuals involved, costs to the state, and the outcomes in terms of public safety and the principles of justice. Options would be carefully weighed, and policies adopted that would each contribute to an overall crime and justice strategy. This would be the sort of rational, evidence-led policy to which many aspire.

There are now many firsthand accounts of the way penal policy and crime policy in general is formulated in the English-speaking world. These show how far reality falls far short of the ideal of rationality. Sentencing policy is often formed in haste as a result of competing interests played out against a background of media pressure and the force of public opinion.

It is illustrative to examine in some depth how one of the most well-known examples of populist penal policy was actually formed. Discussing the mood behind the passing of the three strikes legislation in California, Rubin notes that

> staff members informed us that the political pressure for increased sentences and harsher punishments was overwhelming all other considerations. The recently-enacted three-strikes-law had "sailed through both houses of the legislature faster than any statute we've even seen" they said. Even legislators who were centrally concerned with the state's ever-worsening financial situation had not dared to raise objections against this enormously expensive piece of legislation. There was a palpable sense, at this first meeting, that rational policy analysis, focussing on costs, on effectiveness, or on other alternatives, had been ground into the dust by the juggernaut of public concern about crime. The source of this heightened public concern was somewhat difficult for the legislative and administrative staff to fathom, since there had been no corresponding increase in the crime rate. Their best guess was that it stemmed from the "democratization" of crime—the increasing occurrence of crime, especially violent crime, in "nice" urban neighbourhoods. (Rubin, 1999, p. 15)

Rubin's succinct description of the environment in which the most notable form of populist legislation was forged suggests that politicians are enacting what they believe (rightly or wrongly) is the will or the sentiment of the people. Politicians themselves are in no doubt of the groundswell in favor of punitive laws, however misguided the public is and irrespective of the cause of the hostility. There is then the unmistakable political reality whereby politicians find themselves swept along by the "juggernaut" of media/opinion which they or other politicians may have helped to create. In this environment, sacrifices on the issue of crime and punishment may seem like a small price to pay to those on the Left fighting conservative-populist assaults.

Understanding how punitive penal policy is formulated clearly requires a good grasp of the factors that are deemed relevant by decision makers in the policy bureau and party rooms of both government and opposition. Rock (1986, p. 387) notes that the business of making policy is governed by its own grammar and inner logic. It is considerably more complicated than simply being the result of intrusive outside forces. Although grand theories provide the background to understanding populist crime policy, a comprehensive understanding of such legislation should highlight the rapid way in which it is typically formulated. It is this "on-the-run" quality as much as any underlying ideology or clever political strategy that results in all the hard work and deeper analyses from criminal justice specialists being unceremoniously discarded. Usually the legislation is a response to a triggering event that (through coverage in the mass media) provokes widespread public distress and anger.

To summarize, in addition to the four levels of explanation we discussed earlier, it appears that the processes governing the adoption of a penal policy are dominated by short-term factors and are often "crisis driven." Crises facilitated by the media seem to drive the need for displays of action and strength most readily transmitted in the form of "getting tough" on crime. In appreciating the importance of these very proximal factors, we can now reformulate the understanding articulated earlier of the interrelationship between the various factors. We observe different levels of influence in dynamic interaction which are drawn in figure 4.1

The model drawn in figure 4.1 bears many similarities to the integrative conflict model of crime legislation and policy developed by Castellano and McGarrell (1991). In that model, at the most proximal level to "crime legislation and policy" are the kind of immediate political processes such as the nuances of personalities, political contingencies, triggering events, and pressure groups. The possibilities at this level are shaped according to Castellano and McGarrell's

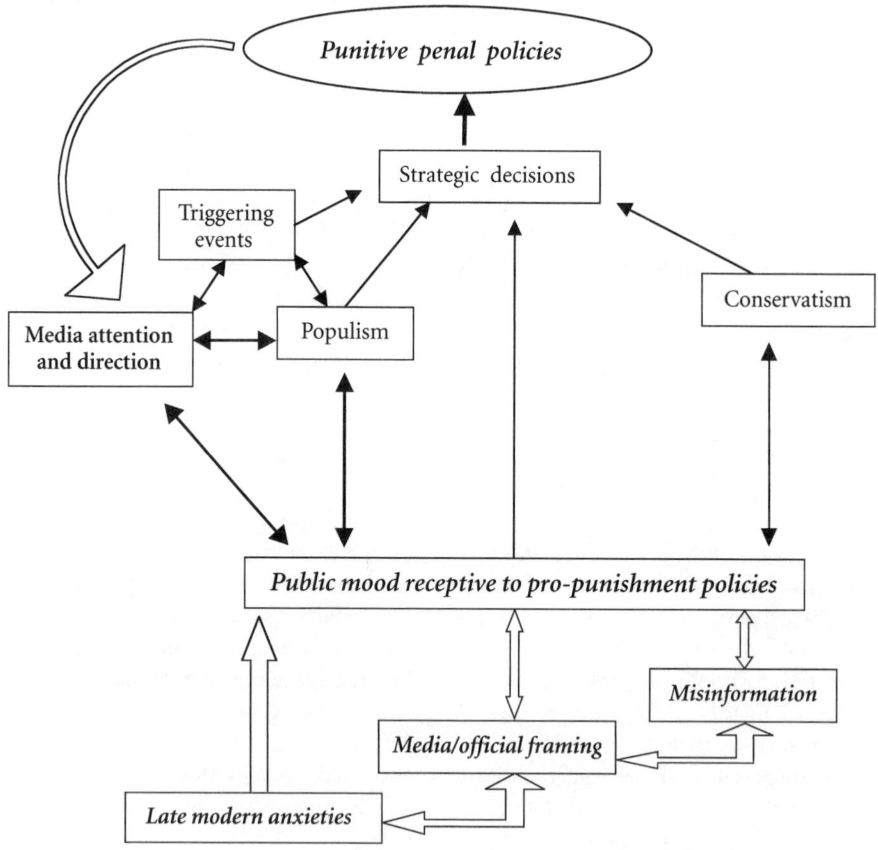

Figure 4.1.
Various Factors and Level of Influence Precipitating Punitive Penal Policies

model by the second level: public opinion (as it is understood by the political participants), the media, and what is known of "the facts" of crime. This second level in turn is a function of a third level: the structural and cultural conditions that shape not only the volume of crime that exists but also our attitudes toward the problem. This third level corresponds to all the forces that have been discussed under the headings of "late modern anxieties" and "misinformed democracy."

These models both point to two fundamental sites of influence on the generation of penal policy. At the distant or distal level are the underlying structural, cultural, global, and temporal factors which provide for the "mood" of the times. At the proximal level are the political decisions that generate punitive penal policy. It is to this more proximal site that most of our attention is drawn because it is here that responsibilities for effective penal policy lie. Between these two basic levels of influence is the dynamic and powerfully conditioning force of the media—framing not only reality to feed late modern anxieties but also telling stories about how to think about the remedies to these anxieties and what political actors are doing or failing to do in "making things better."

In understanding the susceptibility to triggering events and populist policies, it is worthwhile noting that there may exist inherent weaknesses in this regard within political arrangements in the English-speaking world. Savelsberg (1994, 1999) and Zedner (1995) point out that the same developments in punitive penal policies have not emerged in Germany, despite that country sharing many of the same social changes discussed in relation to the English-speaking world.[15] Savelsberg's thesis concerns how "knowledge" is created and institutionalized. The model sketched in figure 4.1 describes a process of knowledge creation—a relatively closed system that cycles through perception, action, and reaction. Germany has been able to achieve a much lower imprisonment rate than the United States partly because the institutions which feed and sustain key points in the knowledge production process are more complex and less subject to commercial and single interest groups. Shifts in direction and ideologically driven policies are more likely to find quick ascendancy in the United States because there are less barriers to the formulation and transmission of such impulses—either at the sphere of general perceptions or within political and legal institutions. Some examples of these differences illustrate the vulnerability of the United States to capture by ideas and impulses those that drive penal populism:

- greater emphasis on the individual politician rather than the political party;
- greater prominence of the media;
- a tradition of single-issue pressure groups.

These features of the American political landscape interact to minimize the chances that information is rigorously assembled, carefully analyzed, and rationally employed in policy-development. Issues hit the headlines with little notice and are simplified and sensationalized. Politicians are forced into crisis management and are required to respond rapidly and instinctively, with a view to their personal ratings in the polls.

Penal policy in all the countries of the English-speaking world is subject to the same process because of their similar reliance on personality-based politics combined with a plurality of inputs. In contrast, political structures in Germany incorporate more institutions and procedures to reduce the degree to which policies are seen to be the result of personalities. These structures offer the prospect of some protection from pressures to develop policy "on the run" and more generally political opportunists seeking to employ a populist strategy.

The way knowledge is constructed also brings us back to the question of why it is punitive responses that are favored as a response to the threat of crime. This has very much to do with the framing of the problem, which is restricted and shaped by underlying cultural beliefs and values. It is not difficult to frame problems of crime and punishment in ways that draw on fundamental American values of individualism. Wilkins and Pease (1987) have suggested that embracing the beliefs that each individual's fate is their own responsibility and that inequality is natural provides an excellent base for believing in the value of harsh punishments.

To endorse the legitimacy of such a belief naturally implies that offenders have created their own position in society and deserve to suffer the consequences. Such a view naturally endorses the need for severe punishments.

This vision of society is related to values such as individualism, competition, the notion that society represents endless opportunities from which individuals make their choices and take their chances. Most important, it suggests that it is the assumption of the deterrent power of punishment which underlies the faith that most Americans repose in punishment. Perhaps this helps to explain why, as Tonry observes, "the force of punitivist populism seems nowhere to be as powerful and as monolithic as in the United States" (2001, p. 518). This view of society can be contrasted with the conditions favored by most European countries which moderate both excesses of wealth, poverty, and punishment. Increasing inequality in most of the English-speaking world and an endorsement of the "American" values may lead not only to economic growth but also to the American predilection for punishment.[16]

Conclusion

In this chapter we have explored a range of possible causes of the ascendancy of punitive penal policies in the last two decades of the twentieth century across the English-speaking world. Our analysis has taken us from the very broad and diffuse social and economic changes creating anxieties and resentments in the growing middle class to the peculiarities of political maneuvering in the context of an ever more dominating media. It is clear that a range of complex forces is at work, some structural and global, others local. It appears that the forces at work that exist in all our countries find their most extreme manifestation in the United States.

Understanding the causes of rising punitiveness in public policy provides the basis for actions that may counter the drift or descent toward a void of meaning in such policies. There are some things that are clearly beyond the reach or influence of reformers. However, the model proposed in this chapter allows us to locate some possible sites of influence in terms of the construction of "knowledge" and also in political decision making. Some basic actions will be helpful. For example, providing more information on crime and punishment that is more accessible to the media, the public, and politicians; more accountability in government; and more strategic mobilizations of interest groups around the time of triggering events. These directions will be considered in depth in the final chapter of the book.

The focus on explaining rising punitiveness at the end of the twentieth century clearly revolves around the broad social anxieties besetting the middle class in this period. As we have seen, politicians' views of public opinion are derived largely from media framing. But the media have their own interests and are governed by distinct imperatives. The capture of politics by the media serves a number of distinct interests, many of them commercial. The influence of the media cannot be overstated, and the reasons why this should be of concern are explored in the next chapter.

5 The Influence of the Media

No exploration of penal populism would be complete without a discussion of media influences on the public. It is not only information about crime that is transmitted by the media but also suggestions about how to understand, view, and respond to crime; the media play a central role in shaping mainstream views of crime and justice. It will be argued in this chapter that the media treatment of crime contributes in a number of ways to a distorted view of crime and the utility of punishment. For example, the way that crime is portrayed in the news media suggests that crime is more prevalent, more threatening, and also that more punishment is required in response. The entertainment media have also been found to influence public perceptions of the perceived effectiveness of punishment.

Most of the literature on media effects and the politics of crime and justice comes from the United States. Although there are some notable contributions within our five countries,[1] these also draw on the voluminous literature from the United States and conform to the general thrust of the findings from that country. Since the findings are consistent across jurisdictions, rather than looking at each country individually, the principal ways in which the media influence penal populism will be outlined.

In this chapter the focus is on the ways that media treatment of crime supports the belief in the value of punishment as a response to crime. Media coverage of crime appears to promote penal populism in three principal ways. First, through devoting so much media time to violent crime, punishment is seen as both appropriate and necessary. Second, the media influence politicians directly through their framing of the issues of crime and punishment. Third, and in the context of this book, most important, the media provide a communication platform that favors certain types of policy response. It is this last process that particularly lends itself to the emergence of policies colored by populist punitiveness.

In the first part of this chapter, we examine public perceptions of crime, including the influence of the news and entertainment media. Then we explore the way that media influence punishment policy and the way that media treatment of crime promotes populist penal policies.

Media Influences on Public Perceptions of Crime

The overrepresentation of violent crime in the media and the public dependence on the news media have been by now well documented.[2] However, selecting which types of crime to cover is only one part of the process of "constructing" crime. Another mechanism is "framing," which refers to the way that crime events are presented to the public. Presenting crime events as particular episodes rather than as part of a theme has been shown to engender individualistic attributions of responsibility.[3] Episodic presentation encourages the view that crime is the result of individual deviance rather than wider social problems. Episodic framing is much more amenable to television formats, and thus television crime news has the potential to promote the thinking that crime has to do with problem people and not problematic systems.

When discussing the effects of the media on perceptions of crime, both news media and entertainment media are important, even though the boundaries between these categories is often indistinct (and becoming less so with the rise of reality television and "infotainment"). Reality TV will be discussed below as a form of entertainment media. Howitt (1998) outlines three approaches to media treatments of crime. First came the search for media "effects" on the audience. The second (functionalist) approach asked not so much what impact the media have on the audience, but the way the audience uses the media. The third approach starts from the position that the media constitute a major cultural institution that serves to reinforce and support existing social arrangements and interests. Each of these approaches are manifest in the studies we examine in this chapter.

The functionalist approach asserts that although the news media are of primary importance in providing citizens with their perceptions of the "reality" of crime, this perception is highly influenced by public interests. However, these interests are shaped by exposure to entertainment media. And so it would be artificial and unhelpful to exclude exposure to entertainment crime from our consideration of the influences on public perceptions.

The News Media

A great deal of research has explored the way that crime is represented by the news media.[4] Reiner (1997) notes the concern from the Left with the way in which the media shape public opinion about crime and punishment. In particular, Hall (1979) described how media treatment of crime paved the way for a "law and order" society. Reiner (1997), Ericson (1991), and Sparks (1992), among others, have criticized the view that the media represent a singular force for promoting dominant conservative ideologies. These authors argue that the media cannot be seen in isolation but rather as the product of intense conflict between various agents about what to focus on, how it should be viewed, and what it means. The result, particularly in the tabloid and broadcast media, is a simplification of the crime problem and an emphasis on law enforcement solutions. These characteristics of the media support more conservative approaches to crime and penal policy. It is possible, for example, that the very form of the media presentation may implicitly favor the preferences embraced by conservative ideologies to view crime as a matter of aberrant individual action requiring a punitive response.

Perhaps the most important way in which the media can influence public perceptions is through the shaping of beliefs about the volume of crime. A number of studies have demonstrated that the picture of crime that appears in crime news differs dramatically from trends seen in either police reports or victimization surveys.[5] The news media focus primarily on stories about dramatic, unusual, and violent crime. It is not surprising, therefore, that studies of public perceptions of crime similarly reveal a picture of crime that not only is primarily concerned with these types of crime but also actually overestimates their prevalence and the chances of victimization.[6] These findings support the view that the media have a distorting effect on public perceptions of crime.[7] Rather than following trends in the actual crime rate, public concerns reflect the amount and type of crime depicted in the media.

A number of studies have documented the increased coverage of crime in recent years. Estimates of the size of the increase vary, depending on the measure of media coverage and the period under study. For example, Chiricos, Eschholz, and Gertz (1997) found a 400% increase in crime stories between June and November 1993.[8] This sharp increase preceded a similar increase in U.S. public concern about crime, as measured by the proportion of the population nominating crime as the foremost problem in the nation.

The Center for Media and Public Affairs[9] analysis of ABC, CBS, and NBC major news programs between 1990 and 1999 of 10 possible major topics provides us with an indication of the increase in exposure through the 1990s, particularly for the peak period for populist penal policy—the mid-1990s. The analysis found that crime rose sharply as the most popular topic in 1993 and fell away from that position after 1997. Crime was the top story in four years (1993–1997), second most common story in two years (1999 and 1996), and the third most common topic in 1992 and 1998. In its report on the year 2000, the Center notes that there was a dramatic drop in crime news carried by the major networks,[10] falling 39% from 1999. This suggests that the prominence of crime news stories increased markedly but may have peaked in the mid-1990s. In summary, it appears that the amount of media-crime exposure increased substantially through the 1990s in the United States, despite the official crime rates falling or remaining stable.

Apart from distorting public perceptions about the amount of crime, the other major level of distortion is in regard to the nature of the crime problem. We have already noted that violent crime is overrepresented in all media. The actual degree of overrepresentation increases as we move from quality broadsheet to tabloid and television.[11] Content analyses also find that compared to "real time" offenders, those reported in the media are older, and media depictions of crime also emphasize stranger-to-stranger offending, involving victims that tend to be white, female, and affluent. News stories are obviously conditioned by audience interest in crimes that shock and concern. They perhaps tell us more about audience sensibilities than the facts of crime. Most crimes actually involve poorer younger people committing offenses against similarly disadvantaged people in their own families and communities.

The primary purpose of crime news is not to provide a comprehensive and "statistically correct" picture of crime. This can be taken as the starting point for our consideration of the how the news media may influence sentencing policy. The next logical question and the one that has animated many of the studies of media and crime is: "What is the purpose of crime news?" There is wide agreement that although the media are not attempting to convey accurate information about crime or the risks of victimization, media coverage of crime is guided by certain imperatives and does serve a number of distinct interests.

Some scholars (e.g., Ericson, Baranek, and Chan, 1991) examine how media representations are governed by media forms and have the effect of reinforcing "order." Others (e.g., Katz, 1987) see in the construction of crime news the packaging of a product that satisfies a desire to engage emotionally with important events in their world. Katz (1987) views crime news consumers as engaging not in dispassionate analysis but precisely the opposite—passionate engagement for the purposes of exercising moral sentiment. According to this view, people seek crime news looking for an opportunity to be shocked and outraged. The public access the media for distinct purposes and the role of the media is to anticipate these interests. These interests are largely moral and emotional; they are not fact-based and do not involve a search for a solution to crime. The wide appeal of such "moral" engagement is attested to by both the style and the popularity of the tabloid media.

A number of researchers examining the construction of crime news have been struck by the operation of certain constraints and imperatives behind the fast-paced news production process. As Garland (2000, p. 363) notes: "media representations undoubtedly give shape and emotional inflection to our experience of crime, and do so in a way that is largely dictated by the structure and values of the media rather than the phenomenon it represents." Researchers such as Ericson et al. (1987, 1989, 1991) have focused on how the nature of a particular news medium and the particular audience shaped the decisions by journalists and editors. It appears that the decision-making environment in the newsroom mirrors the heady pace in the policy bureau discussed in the previous chapter. Under this pressure the resulting "news" or "policy" is governed as much by decisions based on fear of what to avoid as what is being attempted. It is neither possible, nor necessary, here to examine these proximal level influences on crime news in any detail. However, it is worthwhile noting that the central issue of news is highlighting the new or unusual—that which does not fit with the existing order or expectation.

One way to view the audience-media relationship is that the media are employed to capture relevant deviations and new developments that do not fall into some expected order. These events are then subject to classification and control, resulting in the reinforcement of the existing order. The Ericson group estimated that stories about deviance and control (broadly defined) accounted for half or more of all news stories of major Toronto news outlets. Beckett and Sasson (2000) also point out that because the criminal justice system has a never-ending supply of stories of deviance and control they are an easy fit for a busy media.

Studies of media processes are helpful in revealing what motivates key media operatives and the implications at a very general level. However, in tracing the connections between media exposure and populist punitiveness, we need also to briefly discuss the debate about television news and the fear of crime. This debate has continued over at least two decades with many relationships and processes being proposed and counterproposed. Despite the heated debate, Chiricos, Padgett, and Gertz (2000) note that only five published studies since 1976 and prior to their study actually examined the link through empirical research.

In their own study, Chiricos et al., (2000) found that exposure to TV crime news did relate to an increase in fear independent of the influence of other predictors, including crime rates and victim experience. However, they also found that the effects of local TV crime news "overwhelm" the effect of national TV news, suggesting that the closer crime news is to the experience of viewers the more likely it is to incite fear. Chiricos et al. (2000) also found that both realism and relevance were important in understanding the effects of local crime TV news on fear of crime. Those living in high crime areas or who have had recent crime experiences or perceive the news accounts as realistic were most affected by local TV crime news. The authors interpret these findings in line with the resonance hypothesis, noting that the fear of crime was thus increased among some of the most vulnerable groups in the community.

If media exposure is under some conditions related to fear of crime, it is not surprising to find a number of studies which link media exposure to punitiveness. For example, O'Connell and Whelan (1996) found that a reliance on the news media tends to facilitate a hardening of attitudes to crime and punishment. There are a number of reasons to suspect that those who are more fearful, insecure, and punitive may be heavier users of the media.

How may increased fear of crime affect attitudes to punishment? Increased levels of fear have been correlated with increased punitiveness in a number of studies. The link may be through the mediating emotion of frustration. This was suggested by D'Anjou and colleagues (1978) in their theory of punitiveness which built on the frustration aggression hypothesis.[12] Indeed, the link between fear, insecurity, and the desire to punish is probably the most common thread running through psychological studies of punishment from the Frankfurt school in the 1940s and 1950s, psychoanalytic perspectives, and social psychological perspectives.

Some researchers (e.g., Iyengar, 1991) have examined the effects of the way crime news is presented—as episodes rather than as themes—which have the effect of depicting them as aberrant events, which are the result of "mad or bad" individuals. A thematic style of presentation, on the other hand, would invite a deeper analysis of the social and structural causes of the crime and perhaps be the starting point for alternative responses. The focus on violent crime means that most concerns about crime can be read as concerns of violent crime. A number of studies have found that most people are indeed thinking of a violent crime when asked general questions about crime.[13] This means that policy based on either undifferentiated public opinion or more directly on media treatment will be inspired by images of violent crime. However, these policies often affect nonviolent offenders. For example, the rising prison populations in the United States are mainly the result of an influx of nonviolent offenders (Blumstein and Beck, 1999).

The extent to which crime news can be seen as being part of a hegemony that legitimates and reinforces current social arrangements is contentious. For example, Barlow, Barlow, and Chiricos (1995) examined crime news articles in *Time* magazine in the postwar period and found that crime news worked to support dominant constructs, greatly overemphasizing violent crime and negative images of offenders. This concern that media constructions of crime have the power to amplify the power of the authoritarian state and engender a "law and order" society has a long history.[14] However, the concern about which political ideologies are served by media exposures are shared by many scholars in a range of fields.

It is clear that the various imperatives and constraints governing the output of the media ensure that the accurate portrayal of crime or the criminal justice system is low on the list of media priorities. Furthermore, it is the operation of these imperatives, considerations, or constraints that results in the particular complexion of crime news displayed in the media. It is therefore important to understand that if public policy is based on public opinion, that opinion is conditioned by media output. Of course, public opinion is not entirely the product of the media; this suggests the media have an entirely free hand to construct opinion about crime and punishment. Media operatives are subject to the constraints and demands of their industry in competing for public attention. However, in the way that they respond to these demands, certain implicit "rules" have developed and it is useful to understand these. The rules are important not only because of their effect on public opinion, but also (as we shall see in the next section) because media depictions fulfill a more direct role in setting the public agenda and structuring debates on crime and punishment. It is useful, therefore, to consider some of these rules, values, or imperatives and their effects on perceptions of crime.

Entertainment Media

Although crime news clearly has the potential to place crime high on the social agenda, there is a more subtle influence on citizens' beliefs and values about crime and punishment that comes from the extensive use of crime in the entertainment media. Crime has always been experienced through its entertainment function. We must therefore consider not only the growth in crime entertainment media but also the increasing access to particular media forms such as television and the increasing amount of detail (the degree of crime) in entertainment crime. These factors may have increased the "reach" and influence of entertainment crime into the hearts and minds of the populace.[15]

Many studies have attempted to document the effects of exposure to entertainment crime. The best known is the work associated with Gerbner and his content analyses of violent crime on television in the United States.[16] The general results of the studies of the cultivation analysis scholars is that—in the United States at least—heavy viewers of television were more likely than light viewers to overestimate the extent of violent crime and be fearful and concerned about crime. Gerbner and colleagues argue that because of the media distortions of the prevalence of violent crime, a misinformed and more fearful view of the world is "cultivated." The "cultivation hypothesis" suggests that exposure to entertainment media, particularly television, engenders a view of the world as a "mean and scary place" (Signorelli, 1990).[17]

Gerbner's conclusions have been subject to heavy criticism, largely on two grounds. First, it has been argued that asserting a link between exposure to television and fear of crime requires considerably more sophistication than incorporated in the studies. Because both "fear" and "exposure" are quite subjective, and there are so many other aspects of respondents' experience which must be considered in this relationship, it is argued that the link has not been demonstrated. However, Reiner (1997) points out that the amount of violence shown on television in the United States is considerably greater than in the United Kingdom, and this is likely to hold for the other countries surveyed in this book. Thus, although the direction of the effect in each of our five countries may be similar, the magnitude may be much greater in the United States and this may relate to the higher levels of punitiveness in that country. Comparative studies of media exposure and effects on public perceptions, difficult as they are, would be very useful to explore these possible differences.[18]

The second criticism of the cultivation analysis research is more general but at the same time gets to the heart of a common complaint against "cultivation analysis." This criticism concerns an objection about how to conceptualize the study of the media and its relations. The assertions of Gerbner and his associates are seen as reflecting an outdated approach looking for media "effects." This understanding of the relationship of the media and its audience is seen as insufficient to capture its highly interactive nature. Maintaining that television "causes" fear seems to not only rob people of agency but also seems to suggest that the view of reality shown on television was developed independently of audience interest. For example, Sparks (1992) takes the debate about the effects of media crime to a deeper level to reveal the extant tensions in modern life. He rejects simple notions that the media "causes" fear of crime and questions whether fear of crime can ever be labeled "unreasonable." Sparks is interested in examining the moral, cultural, and symbolic meanings of the ascendance of media crime. Although Sparks rejects the concept of simple effects, he does not deny that the way that crime and punishment is discussed in the media "contribute to the setting of parameters on what rhetorics, political postures and policies we are inclined to believe or accept" (p. 161).

Whether or not exposure to entertainment crime increases fear of crime, the central issue of concern for us is what effect such exposure has on attitudes to punishment. This question has been addressed by a number of researchers. For example, Fabianic (1997) found that depictions of homicide on television favored crime-fighting policies over other approaches to the problem and also emphasized explanations that focused on individual causation. Beckett and Sasson (2000) analyzed the range of entertainment crime shows on US television—mostly the police drama format—and found that these favored the view that "hard working" police must not only catch clever "crooks," but they must also battle against a system that favors the defendant. These scripts may be popular partly because they resonate with the archetypal American image common in the latter part of the twentieth century of a well-meaning individual struggling against a harsh, uncaring, and hostile bureaucracy.[19] Such loaded messages clearly pave the way for populist initiatives buttressed by the claim that the system is too lenient.

Surette (1994, pp. 147–148) discusses the use by the entertainment crime media of the image of the predator-criminal and the damaging effects this has on the possibilities and direction of crime policy:

> The most basic effects of the predator icon are to generate fear, degrade social networks, increase reliance on the media, and foster social isolation and polarization. We abandon society and its real problems to the media. When all external causes of crime are rejected, individual punishment emerges as the only logical social response to crime while criminology is demoted from a quest for understanding to the pragmatic task of crime detection. Offenders are stereotyped as monolithic, pathological, and violent; crime is analysed from a simplistic prey-predator paradigm; and crime policy is fixated in a punitive defensive posture (Kappeler et al., 1993).

Reality TV

Although traditional forms of entertainment crime media have provided a good base for populist punitiveness, there is now a more harmful form which holds great potential for further distorting public perceptions and promoting law enforcement solutions. This is the new hybrid of news and entertainment is known as reality TV. Reality crime TV, which has emerged as a staple TV media form over the last two decades, purports to provide a close up look at the "front line" of crime. Reality crime TV is made possible by allowing program producers special access to ride along with the police in their operations. Program producers then select the most sensational footage to create a crime story. However, they tend to include footage that depicts the police acting well and offenders acting badly. In this way "reality" TV works as a major form of advertising for a pro-enforcement agenda and reinforces beliefs about the need for vigorous enforcement.

The levels of distortion in reality crime TV programs have been documented by many researchers (e.g. Kooistra, Mahoney, and Westervelt, 1998; Doyle, 1998; and Carmody, 1998). Reality crime programs reinforce prevailing views about crime, criminals, and victims (Cavender and Fishman, 1998 pp. 7–8). By featuring stories about white victims and nonwhite offenders, a racial bias is introduced (Kooistra, Mahoney, and Westervelt [1998]) and, not surprisingly, U.S. audiences overestimate the prevalence of crime and the proportion committed by African Americans (Oliver and Armstrong, 1998).

By providing images of crime scenes, reality crime TV promotes itself as a source of insights into crime. However, investigations into the nature of reality crime TV reveal that it is highly selective and uses the same principles governing the production of entertainment crime to create archetypal pictures of law enforcement operating heroically against popular social enemies.[20] One of the attractions for the reality crime TV audience is a sense of personal empowerment through identifying with the "cops."[21]

Although we have examined the contributions of crime news and entertainment crime separately, this distinction can sometimes be misleading. People in the real world are exposed to a continuous melange of crime images on a continuum from the "real to the fictional." What evidence there is suggests that the continuum of exposure for each individual will be different. However, those who are mainly informed by "high brow" media are exposed to rather less crime and those exposed to "low brow" media and television get more crime and a more distorted picture of crime (Reiner, 1997). These distinctions are important in calculating the effect of media exposure for the politics of punishment. It is precisely those sectors of the population likely to be experiencing insecurity who are most exposed to crime media. The extent and nature of media influences is important then to understanding the reasons why punitive and populist responses to crime may be embraced by this group.

Media Influences on Punishment Policy

Attitudes to punishment are obviously related to public perceptions of crime. The concern and focus on crime promoted by the media thus continually presents the issue of crime and punishment for debate. This capacity of the media to set the agenda for political debate was one of the first media influences to be discussed (McCoombs and Shaw, 1972) and remains one of the most important. Through both news and entertainment media, crime and punishment assume a much greater importance and presence for most citizens than could be achieved through direct experience. Crime policy thus assumes a special importance through its media status. It perhaps follows that the effectiveness of crime policy in this context will not judged by what might be considered normal benchmarks of success in crime control but through the symbolic and political results. Another consequence of the heavy media usage of crime themes then is that it restricts what is possible in the domain of public policy. In this environment politicians are seldom able (or willing) to provide various less punitive, alternative responses to crime for fear of how it will be depicted in the media.[22] This is despite a range of studies that demonstrate that the public would be receptive to carefully targeted and meaningful alternatives to the death penalty and imprisonment.[23]

Apart from their influence on public perceptions of crime, the media may have more direct influences on crime policy through the common assumption that they reflect the true nature of public opinion. One of the important ways the media are used by both politicians and the public is as a source of information about what "others" are thinking. The media gain a powerful role through this belief that they reflect the public agenda and portray the nature of public opinion.[24] The media then have the power to shape public opinion implicitly through the way crime is selected and depicted, as well as more explicitly by describing or suggesting what it is that the majority believe or support. The media can therefore "amplify" certain policies.

Media and political uses of "opinion polls" of often doubtful validity further confound attempts to discern "true" public opinion. The issue of public support and public opinion thus remains largely unknown and subject to a constant testing of claim and counterclaim. In a similar vein, a number of researchers have examined the way that victim advocacy groups have both used, and been used by, the media to further certain political objectives.[25] These groups are thus entwined not with the bulk of crime victims and their particular interests but with conservative groups pursuing an agenda of power and punishment.

Herbst (1998) argues that many policymakers gain their views of public opinion from the media. Judges also regularly cite public opinion as a factor in their sentencing decisions, particularly when these decisions involve dispositions likely to attract public criticism (see Roberts, Nuffield, and Hann, 1999). On closer examination, it is often the case that judges gain their impressions of public opinion in the same way that politicians do—from what they read in the newspaper.[26] Even more dangerous is the belief among some judges that they can "sense" the tenor of public opinion (see Fitzmaurice and Pease, 1986). However, it is media coverage, and in particular crime news, that is read uncritically by criminal justice agencies as reflecting public opinion.

For example, Dopplet (1992) conducted a survey in the United States which revealed that 30% of the government officials surveyed said that news coverage had led to recent changes in the operations of their agencies (p. 125). Dopplet found that about a third of judges, court administrators, corrections officials, and others in law enforcement believed that news coverage had led to substantive changes in the administration of justice. Chan (1995) reports a dramatic example of this phenomenon in one Australian jurisdiction. A minister in the government of New South Wales participated in a radio talk show to defend and promote the government's policy of cautioning juvenile car thieves. However, adverse reaction from callers led to the cancellation of the policy later the very same morning.

Beckett and Sasson (2000) also discuss the ways that key policy decision makers respond to media coverage as an indication of public opinion. For example, increased media coverage brings an issue on to the agenda, and it must be assumed that the media coverage reflects an increase in public concern. It would take a brave politician to dismiss increased media attention as not reflecting increased public concern. In short, it is better to be safe and assume that is the case than sorry after being labeled as aloof, out of touch, and uncaring. However, this places much power unwittingly into the hands of the media and risks setting up a closed loop, where media and political sources "talk up" a problem. A number of distinct instances of this phenomenon have been documented.

The best known is Fishman's (1981) account of how crime waves were developed out of a relatively small number of attacks against the elderly. The exigencies of news reporting quickly found a trend, political responses provided more fuel for the fire, and in a very short time the media were reporting on a crime "wave." Beckett (1997) and Beckett and Sasson (2000) provide a more detailed and recent example in relation to the way the war on drugs grew as its own political and media-driven crisis in the 1980s in the United States.

How are we to understand the nature of media and political interaction together with the influences on, and from, public opinion and key special interest groups? First and most important, we need to be aware of the way that the media, politicians, the public, and important interest groups are in dynamic interaction. The complex interweaving of influence and response emerges in the writing of many, who have examined the relationship between media crime and public policy. For example, Daly (1995, p. 6) noted that rather than linear, cause-and-effect relationships between the media and public policy, the relationships are reciprocal and interactive. Similarly, Dopplet and Manikas (1990, p. 134) talk about "a trisected chamber of reverberating effects among the media, the public and policy makers. Effects are multidirectional, prompted by the media and impacting on the media, by the public and on the public, and by manipulating policy makers as well as responsive policy makers."

A useful model that considers the operation of these reciprocal interactions was proposed by Kennamer (1992). This model may be useful as a device to

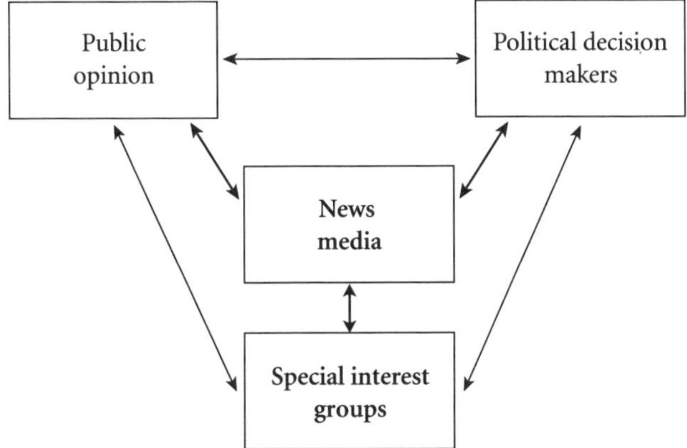

Figure 5.1.
A Model of the Interaction of News Media, Public Opinion, Special Interest Groups, and Political Decision Makers (adapted from Kennamer, 1992).

understand the position and dependent nature of the interaction between the four institutions (figure 5.1). In this model, the media are at the heart of the interaction of the three forces involved in the generation of public policy: policymakers, special interest groups, and public(s). Each of these parties may only express themselves to other parties in the process through its depiction in the media. The media are the conduit for expression, for conveying positions and expressing postures. The media, then, become a central pivot in the dynamic process of policy formulation, reaction, and adjustment. As long as there is a tacit understanding that the media are not pursuing their own policy agenda, the media reaction to policy is often read by all three groups as being akin to, or at least somewhat in sympathy with, public opinion. Thus, the media assume an importance to policymakers as both a source and an audience.

Media Influences on Policy Style

We have examined the influences of the media on public perceptions of crime and the politics of crime policy. However, there is one last aspect of media influences that is important to discuss and that concerns the influence of the media on the style of politics. Populism is a certain style of doing politics (Taggart, 2000), one that is very well suited to the dominance of the broadcast media and its focus on the emotional and dramatic story.

The key starting point in this nexus of media, public opinion, and populism is the central feature of the populist strategy to privilege and promote as unproblematic the concept of public opinion. It is fundamental to the claims of populists that public opinion does exist and is indeed concrete and unidimensional. The populist strategy is to claim not only to speak on behalf of the public but also to articulate public opinion that may appear to be hidden. Thus, there is an attempt to portray the articulation of public opinion as something profound, a revelation. By providing this sense of special insight, a populist may seem imbued with transcendent qualities. This may explain the purported sense of charisma often attached to populist leaders.[27]

The transformations of the media over the last two decades of the twentieth century have provided a perfect fit for the rise of the populist politician and accelerated the politicization of crime policy. Garland (2000) has identified some of the most relevant developments. First, television viewing emerged as a mass phenomenon at much the same time that high crime rates began to be regarded as a normal social fact. Crime itself was a boon to the TV journalist, offering unlimited action sequences complemented by the scenes of offenders being paraded into and out of court. Second, the dynamics of televised press coverage maximized the emotional force of popular opinion and victims' testimonies. This transformation of debate about crime policy to one of emotional montage has ensured that those attempting to speak more rationally about crime are seen as uncaring. Third, the depictions of crime on TV news naturally complement the heavy use of fictional crime shows and, together with the emergence of "reality TV," further exacerbate the merging of fact and fiction. Finally, the mass media shape and reinforce public concern about crime to the point that it provides firm ground for exploitation by populist politicians.

As noted, a central feature of the populist strategy is to accept public opinion as an unproblematic entity that has a distinct shape and direction. This view is contradicted by the findings of numerous studies on public opinion in relation to crime and punishment which find that it is malleable, is based on a series of false assumptions, and will readily respond to reasonable propositions or alternatives.[28] The populist strategy is to provide the allure of a single view, reflecting a singularity of will through a leader who is able to articulate this will.[29] It does not matter then how well informed the public is, or even whether the particular policy is effective or in the public's "best" interests. Populism works on an emotional rather than rational basis; evaluation and evidence matter less than feelings or opinions. Not everyone can have enough information to develop a crime policy designed to prevent crime, but everyone can have an opinion about what feels right to them. Populism works on the level of popularity but does not require or expect active and responsible citizen involvement. These qualities of populism therefore fit well with the demands of the media. Punishment in harder and more exotic forms has political appeal precisely because it has media appeal. Less "action-oriented" responses to criminals are likely to be depicted as soft and ineffectual.

Developing public policy on the basis of its media appeal exacerbates the existing tendency to dramatize uncertainty, crime, and the necessity for harder state control. Beckett (1997) has provided many examples of this in her discussion of the development of the "war on crime" and the "war on drugs" in the United States. Beckett argues that the "war on drugs" was a result of efforts by the federal government to feed and prime the media to change public opinion. The federal government had been expanding the budget and reach of the FBI and the Drug Enforcement Agency (DEA). Beckett and Sasson (2000, p. 67) cite the testimony of the DEA's New York director, Robert Stutman, explaining how he employed the media to promote his agency's interest:

> In order to convince Washington, I needed to make it [drugs] a national issue and quickly. I began a lobbying effort and I used the media. The media were only too willing to cooperate, because as far as the New York media was concerned, crack was the hottest combat reporting story to come along since the end of the Vietnam war.

Stutman's efforts paid off and the number of drug-related stories run in New York's leading paper, *The New York Times*, increased from 43 in the latter half of 1985 to 220 in the second half of 1986 (Beckett and Sasson [2000, p. 67]). Other media followed suit and drug use went on to become one of the most publicized issues in the nation. The 1980s drug scare in the United States provides a prime example of the way that political and media interests can operate in concert to exploit and enhance public concerns for their own benefit.[30]

New Frontiers of Fear: The Discovery of New Crimes and the Need for New Punishments

Naturally, the fear of dangerous offenders, especially the "new" crimes and "new" types of offenders evokes calls for protection. These fears are illustrated in archetypal media stories that have precipitated changes to sentencing laws in the 1990s. First, in the "released sex offender" stories, both fears converge and are amplified. Second, in "new crimes" the crime story serves to provide a graphic illustration of the ills of changing times. The mistrust of government is an underlying theme of both these types of story. This is particularly interesting to our investigation because this mistrust can be seen as reflecting the kind of anti-institutional sentiment that has been identified as one of the hallmarks of populism (Taggart, 2000).

Sex offenders released from prison who commit further offenses represent a double blow to public confidence in the criminal justice system. Not only has a heinous crime been committed—enough by itself to command considerable media attention and to generate public outrage—but also added to this is the spectre that the state had the offender in custody but then released him. Thus, a second powerful construct is attached to the story—that of an incompetent and lenient criminal justice system. The alleged incompetence of authorities is critical because it provides a conduit for the outrage evoked by the crime. Great emotion is evoked by the crime and a culpable target is found in lenient judges or parole boards. It is not surprising, therefore, that cases of released sex offenders committing further sex crimes have provoked some of the more extreme changes to sentencing law.

The case which contained all these elements and thus paved the way for a populist exploitation was the sexual assault and murder of a child (Polly Klaas) by a released sex offender in California. It was this case that precipitated the passage of the "three strikes" sentencing statute in California. This legislation served as a model for similar laws introduced around the world in the 1990s. In terms of the analysis of the media contribution to the public reaction to the crime, it is notable that out of all the threads in the crime that could have been the focus of attention (e.g., the failure of the police to quickly and correctly communicate information), the one detail that most stories highlighted was that the offender was a released sex offender.[31]

Other changes to the criminal justice system have drawn additional attention to released sex offenders. The most notable are the community notification laws developed after the furor surrounding the kidnapping, sexual assault, and murder of Megan Kanka from outside her home in New Jersey. This case and the reaction to it is described in more detail in chapter 8. The *News of the World* campaign in the United Kingdom involving the "naming and shaming" of pedophiles (see chapter 3) represents a significant development because the newspaper threatened to name pedophiles until a change in the law was introduced. Through these actions the editors openly displayed a posture of entitlement in terms of formulating public policy.

Newspaper "campaigns" on certain topics are hardly new. For example, Hogg and Brown (1998) give some examples of Australian newspaper campaigns on law and order. However, newspaper campaigns generally fall short of the aggressive stand-off precipitated by the *News of the World* campaign. These developments raise serious questions about the role and the power of the media in terms of public policy. Although much power already resides with the media, the *News of the World* campaign offers the prospect of cutting politicians out of the loop entirely.

Another type of media story feeds on the alienation and fear associated with the rapid pace of change and the breakdown of traditional social institutions. These amorphous fears can be captured in media depictions of "new" crimes. These are popular because they alert us to new frontiers often resonating with the uncertainty attached to new threats and demands in the changing society. These stories serve a useful purpose in allowing free-floating anxiety to be replaced by moral indignation: anger being a much more dignifying and reassuring emotional state than fear. Best (1999) has discussed the phenomenon of "discovering" new crimes. Some examples of "new crime" are child abduction (Straus, 1992), "home invasions" (aggravated burglaries) in Canada and high speed car chases in Australia, freeway shootings (U.S.), road rage (everywhere), "wilding" (U.S.), and stalking (everywhere).

By presenting these crimes as unprecedented, novel, and serious, it is implied that new levels of punishment are required. For example, throughout the

1980s and 1990s, the increasing awareness of sexual abuse offenses against children led people to overestimate both the prevalence in these offenses and the trends in these offenses (Scott, 1995). The alarm over the extent of the abuse led authorities to adopt extraordinary provisions in the interests of protecting victims or possible victims. The overreach of the law is probably best demonstrated by the sad development in a northern English city, where concern about child sexual abuse led to the false diagnosis by medical authorities of many cases of child sexual abuse using an experimental and highly contentious diagnostic tool. The tragic consequences of what might be thought of as a modern day witch hunt was so great that a full judicial inquiry was eventually instituted but not before much distress was caused.[32]

Crime provides everyday "combat" stories for the media. By constructing crime in militaristic terms, punishment can be seen as a form of retaliation. The populist-emotional "capture" of penal policy has led some (e.g., Freiberg, 2001) to counsel that those interested in advancing criminal justice reform must attune their message to the affective or symbolic wavelength. This resonates with earlier calls by criminologists such as Barak (1994) for a "newsmaking criminology" and Henry (1994) for efforts to provide the media with a "replacement discourse." These suggestions underlay some of the contemporary efforts to more robustly enter the fray and work with the dimensions we know of in the media and political processes. There are also a range of organizations working in different ways with the media to open up possibilities for social reform and other "pro-social" effects. These possibilities are discussed in the final chapter.

Conclusion

The discussion in this chapter reinforces the position stated in the previous chapter that crime policy is subject to a range of factors operating in the contemporary environment that favors populism. In this chapter we have discussed how the media treatment of crime promotes penal populism by focusing on certain types of crime, its framing of crime, and its discussion of the crime, the victim, and the offender. We have also examined the various channels or ways media treatment of crime impact on the key political actors. Finally, we have examined the way that the media shape the nature of crime policy by being receptive to the populist style.

The discussion in this chapter points to the importance and influence of the media on perceptions of crime and the politics of crime. This view is articulated well in Garland's (2000, p. 363) succinct account of the relevance of the media to crime policy: "It has surrounded us with images of crime, pursuit and punishment, and has provided us with regular, everyday occasions in which to play out the emotions of fear, anger, resentment, and fascination that crime provokes."

To summarize, the main ways that the media influence penal policy as discussed in this chapter are:

1. The systematic distortion of information about crime through crime "news";
2. The selective distortion of perceptions about crime through the entertainment media and the media that blur the line between news and entertainment;
3. The reinforcement of fears and simple views of the causes of crime;
4. The promotion of decisive, event- and action-oriented responses to crime;
5. The focus on crime, selection of crimes, and on enforcement action favor political styles such as populism that focus on emotionalism and the value of dramatic uncomplicated action.

6 Public Judgment in Real Criminal Cases

Throughout this volume we explore the relationship between public opinion and punitive penal policies and practices. In several domains we shall see how policies respond to (as well as create a desire for) a punitive response to offenders. In this chapter we pose a different question: When are populist penal initiatives founded on a false perception of the public's views? One answer is to point to surveys in which public sentencing preferences are compared to the practices of the courts (see Roberts and Stalans, 1997). These surveys generally find that in many instances the sentencing preferences of the public are not much harsher than sentences actually imposed and have been reviewed in chapter 2.

But this is only a partial answer to the question. A more complete response requires an examination of how laypersons respond to real cases, knowing that their judgments will actually have an impact on the life of another person. It is easy to be punitive in response to a hypothetical case, involving a vague (and brief) description of an offender and offense. In addition, sentencing studies involving the public take only a few minutes, hardly sufficient time to arrive at a thoughtful decision. Public responses to real cases are therefore more informative about people's conceptions of justice and tendency toward punitiveness.

This chapter provides an overview of the circumstances in which public preferences diverge from the punitive image that politicians and the media typically portray. We begin with a brief summary of the survey and experimental research that indicates the public is less punitive than opinion surveys suggest. This conclusion is further supported by the results from research which compares lay to professional magistrates' sentences in actual cases and the research on jury sentencing decisions. The most poignant example of the exercise of public thoughtfulness, leniency, and mercy—the exact opposite of the characteristics of populist punitiveness—is the phenomenon of jury nullification. Jury nullification refers to the decision of lay juries to acquit a defendant, despite the existence of overwhelming evidence to support a conviction. This chapter provides a conceptual overview of the areas where juries have acquitted defendants because a conviction would not fit the public's sense of justice or where the offender did not deserve the harsh sentence mandated by the law. The chapter concludes with a brief overview of public attitudes toward the death penalty, and the areas in which the law and the public disagree with respect to the imposition of a death sentence.

Sentencing by Lay versus Professional Judges

England, Canada, and Australia are of considerable interest in this context because in these countries, members of the public, serving as lay magistrates, sentence offenders. Sentences imposed by these lay magistrates provide a more adequate test of the hypothesis that the public are more punitive than the courts. How then, do the sentences imposed by lay magistrates compare to those imposed by professional, legally trained judges? One of the most comprehensive studies comparing lay and professional magistrates' sentences was conducted in England (Diamond, 1990). This study employed archival analysis, observations of sentencing hearings, and interviews with magistrates. A consistent finding emerged across the different methods of data collection: lay magistrates imposed *more* lenient sentences than did their legally trained, professional counterparts.[1] This study using sentences imposed in actual cases corroborates the findings from surveys using hypothetical survey data.[2]

Six states employ juries to sentence offenders convicted of felonies, thereby providing another opportunity to study lay responses to actual cases. One early study compared the severity of sentences imposed on offenders convicted of robbery in states that used jury sentencing with states that permitted sentencing only by judges. The findings suggest that on average, juries impose sentences of comparable severity (Smith & Stevens, 1984).

The final example we discuss pertains to the influence of popular will over the parole process. In Canada, juries have the power to change the parole eligibility dates of prisoners serving life sentences for murder. Prisoners serving life for first degree murder are eligible for parole only after having served 25 years in custody. However, a provision in the *Criminal Code* permits most such inmates to apply for a jury review of this restriction. The jury has the power to reduce the period without parole from 25 years all the way down to 15.

The results of surveys suggest that the public is opposed to people convicted of first degree murder (the most serious category) ever getting released on parole (Roberts, 1988). It might be anticipated therefore that applications under this provision would result in juries declining to make any change in the parole eligibility dates of such prisoners. In fact, the opposite is true; the vast majority of jury decisions have resulted in reductions to the number of years that these prisoners must serve before becoming eligible for parole (see Roberts, 2002c). This example provides additional evidence that popular justice does not always mean a more punitive response. [Jury Reviews of Parole Dates]

Findings from the Jury Nullification Literature

Further insight into public reaction to penal severity comes from the decisions of juries that can redress perceived injustices through their verdicts in criminal trials. Juries sometimes acquit a defendant, even though they know that the

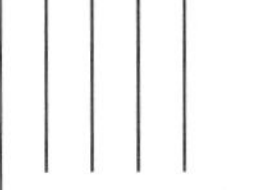

Jury Reviews of Parole Eligibility Dates for Inmates Serving Life for Murder

According to section 745.6 of the Canadian *Criminal Code*, almost all inmates convicted of first or second degree murder and who are sentenced to life imprisonment may apply for a jury review of their parole eligibility dates. Prisoners serving life for first degree murder must serve 25 years before becoming eligible for parole. However, at the 15-year point in the sentence, these prisoners can ask a jury to review their parole eligibility date.

The jury can reduce the number of years that the inmate has to serve prior to parole eligibility by up to 10 years. In almost all cases in which the jury has reduced the number of years that must be served before a parole application can be made, the parole board has subsequently granted the prisoner parole. Thus, the jury's decision is pivotal; it can mean the difference between the prisoner serving 15 years in prison instead of 25.

In fully four out of five applications to date, the applicant has received a positive response from the jury. That is, the juries have reduced the number of years that these prisoners must serve prior to becoming eligible for parole. In fact, the most common outcome of these reviews was a reduction of the full 10 years possible. However, according to the results from opinion polls, the Canadian public favor life without parole for cases of first degree murder! It is also important to bear in mind that these prisoners have been convicted of the most heinous crimes imaginable, and yet jurors are still willing to reduce by a substantial margin the amount of time that the inmate must serve in prison (see Roberts, 2002c).

prosecutor has proved, beyond a reasonable doubt, all the elements of the offense. Acquittals or convictions on lesser charges (based on conscience rather than hard evidence) are referred to as "jury nullifications." While the jury nullification literature pertains to verdicts, and not sentences, it is clearly relevant to sentencing: a frequent reason that jurors reach legally indefensible verdicts is that they perceive the punishment attendant upon a conviction to be either excessive or totally unwarranted.

Jury nullification may result when juries decide that statutes are inconsistent with higher laws of fairness derived from moral or religious principles or just plain common sense (see Finkel, 1995). Juries in all jurisdictions have the power to nullify the law, although such powers are rarely encouraged or publicly endorsed. All juries have the power to return a verdict of not guilty, even though the prosecutor has proven beyond a reasonable doubt that the accused intentionally committed the criminal act.[3] There is considerable public support for jury nullification. The vast majority of Americans (76%) in a recent national survey supported acquittals based on the jury's conscience, even though the defendant was guilty of a crime (Kopel, 1999). An earlier survey of Canadians found that over 75% of the public favored the use of instructions to the jury that decisions could be based on conscience in cases where a fairer outcome may be the result (Doob, 1979).

Whether citizens should be informed of their power to base judgments of guilt on conscience—and not evidence—is a question that has generated much controversy among legal practitioners. Those who defend jury nullification argue that citizens will not abuse this power. They argue that when jurors do acquit based on conscience, it is to improve the law—to bring justice and avoid an injustice in a particular case. Juries' acquittals based on conscience are considered rational because they are based on commonsense notions of fairness. Opponents of informing jurors of their power to nullify the law argue that jurors can and do misuse this power. They also argue that jury nullification is an act of flouting the law and creates situations where like cases are treated differently based on criteria that the law does not consider relevant. Those opposed to nullification believe that if juries know that they can follow their conscience, wrongful acquittals may arise out of mere prejudice. Acquittals based on gender, social class, or race would create unequal protection, discrimination, and unpredictability in the court system. Some extreme opponents are skeptical of the layperson's ability to apply the facts to a case; they argue that the role of the jury should be extremely curtailed in civil and criminal cases. From their perspective, experts with legal training can better serve the ends of justice. (For a more detailed discussion of jury nullification, see Scheflin, 1972; Scheflin & Dyke, 1980; Horowitz and Willging, 1991; St. John, 1997.)

After several high-profile defendants in the United States were acquitted, critics of the jury complained that the jury was using its nullification power too often. Data on conviction rates, however, do not support this complaint. Vidmar, Beale, Rose, & Donnelly (1997) found a conviction rate of over 80%. In the state of California, where many jury nullification acquittals allegedly occurred, the conviction rate was stable from 1981 to 1995, with an average conviction rate of 82%. It is clear then that jury nullification does not occur often enough to have much impact on the overall conviction rate statistics.

Jury nullifications are, in fact, rare events. Acquittals based on conscience constitute the rare exception and not the norm; most of the time juries faithfully discharge their responsibilities as fact-finders and come to the same decisions as legally trained experts. Evidence to support this conclusion comes from Kalven and Zeisel (1966), who compared verdicts from judges and juries in 3,576 trials in the United States. Jury verdicts and judges' verdicts were consistent in four cases out of five. In one-fifth of the cases, juries acquitted when the judge would have convicted. One-third of the disagreements occurred due to different interpretations of the evidence; two-thirds of the disagreements occurred because jurors relied on their values and conscience, whereas the judge focused on the evidence. Jury nullification therefore explained many of the disagreements. More recently, in New Zealand, a study of 48 jury trials found that there were only three verdicts which were "questionable" or "perverse" (Young, Cameron, & Tinsley, 1999).

Studies using mock juries have tested some additional hypotheses about jury nullification. Results show that juries are more likely to acquit sympathetic defendants if they are informed of their power to arrive at decisions based on their conscience. However, juries are unlikely to acquit defendants charged with very serious crimes (Horowitz, 1988). Also, if the prosecutor challenges the defense attorney's arguments to nullify, juries typically will continue to base their verdicts on the evidence adduced at trial (Horowitz, 1988). Furthermore, juries informed of their nullification power are no more inclined (than juries receiving standard instructions) to consider irrelevant factors such as race, gender, and social status (Niedermeier, Horowitz, & Kerr, 1999).[4]

Recent grass-roots efforts have emerged to counter the attempts of the United States Supreme Court to limit the jury to a fact-finding role. The "Fully Informed Jury Association" was founded in 1989 in the United States as a nonprofit organization, with a mandate to inform jurors of their historical right to return a verdict that reflects their conscience. Members send materials to interested citizens, distribute literature about the power to nullify the law, lobby for statutes supporting jury nullification, and monitor cases where jury nullification seems warranted. They also distribute leaflets at courthouses in an attempt to inform potential jurors of their power.[5]

Reasons for Nullification

There are several different reasons why jurors may follow their conscience rather than apply a strict interpretation of the law. Juries may acquit defendants because they believe that the behavior giving rise to a criminal charge should not, in fact, constitute a crime. In these instances, jury nullifications reflect public opposition to a law perceived to be unjust. Acquittals may also be based on a perception that the penalty is too harsh and disproportionately severe in light of the seriousness of the criminal act. Acquittals may occur when juries believe that the defendant has suffered enough, and that any further punishment would be cruel. Jurors informed about the power to base verdict decisions on conscience may also focus on the character of the victims and defendants. Defendants whose personal histories elicit sympathy from the jury may be acquitted, even though evidence clearly indicates that they were criminally responsible. We discuss support for these different reasons for jury nullification below.

Individual justice: Mercy as a Result of Extenuating Circumstances

Most jury nullifications involve a judgment that strict application of the law in a particular case will produce an injustice rather than general disagreement with the law in principle. Jurors may use their values and beliefs to evaluate the evidence and create a coherent story about the defendant's character and actions. If defendants are judged to have acted with good intentions, juries may see sentences as too harsh. For example, Leroy Reed, a mentally challenged offender on parole, was arrested for illegal possession of a weapon. Reed had wanted to be a private investigator and had been told that he would need a gun, which he subsequently acquired. Evidence adduced at trial indicated that Reed was only vaguely aware of what he was doing. His defense attorney made a nullification argument, and although it was clear that Reed had broken the law, he was nevertheless acquitted (Scheflin & Dyke, 1991).

There are many other examples of nullifications based on the motives of the defendants. In the United Kingdom and United States, defendants have been acquitted for growing and distributing cannabis to ill relatives or partners (Cowan, 1998; Conrad, 1999). In Idaho, two defendants were acquitted of aiding and abetting a kidnapping, when jurors heard the unusual circumstances of the case. The two defendants had kidnapped a young woman who belonged to a religious cult. The mother of the young woman hired the two defendants to kidnap and "deprogram" the woman from the cult beliefs of the religious group. The defendants had a laudable motive: they were trying to reunite a family and save a young woman from being brainwashed by the cult members (Threlkeld, 1993). Jury nullifications such as these provide further support of the public's endorsement of individualized rather than uniform justice.

Juries may also set aside the strict interpretation of the law and base their decisions on the extent to which the victim contributed to the offense. When a victim appears to have a bad character and a defendant has a good character, the latter may be acquitted of even serious crimes of violence. For example, a police officer in Australia shot and killed a man accused of molesting three girls who were relatives or family friends of the police officer. The officer argued that he had had no choice but to kill the man because the molester had threatened to kill the girls if they told anyone about the sexual abuse. The homicide was therefore justified as an act in defense of the children. The jury took mere minutes to acquit the officer of charges of murder and manslaughter (Balogh, 1999).

Kalven and Zeisel (1966) also found that juries were more likely to acquit the defendant of simple rape, in cases where the victim had been drinking or had violated social norms in some way. Jurors evaluate the extent of the victim's contribution to the offense in judging the moral blameworthiness of the defendant. Thus, contributory negligence resulted in the jury acquitting defendants (when judges would convict) in 60% of these rape cases (Kalven & Zeisel, 1966). Defenses such as battered woman syndrome and battered child syndrome are successful, in part, because jurors consider that the victim's past conduct justified the subsequent offense. These examples constitute departures from a strict interpretation of the law as a result of popular conceptions of moral blameworthiness.

Why is this the case? One explanation is that jurors may compare the defendant to their stereotypic image of offenders. Defendants with a history of good community involvement and who have a positive motive for the crime may not "fit" the stereotype and they are therefore accorded some leniency. Another possibility is that the public model of justice is broad and includes a number of mitigating factors that the law may consider to be irrelevant to the determination of guilt or innocence.

Nullifications as a Result of Perceptions That the Law Is Unjust

Only a very small percentage of jury nullifications occur because jurors believe that the law itself is unjust (Kavlen & Zeisel, 1966; Hans & Vidmar, 1986). If opposition continues, the law may be changed or it may fall into disuse. Many individuals in the United States in the 1800s were charged with violating the Fugitive Slave Law when they assisted runaway slaves; juries often acquitted these defendants (Barkan, 1983; Green, 1985).

Prohibition provides a good example of a law that proved to be unenforceable because it affronted public perceptions of fairness. The 1919 Volstead Act was clearly at odds with contemporary attitudes toward the regulation of alcohol, and juries routinely acquitted defendants charged with selling alcoholic beverages. The high acquittal rate in cases such as these rendered the prohibition laws largely unenforceable (see Scheflin & Dyke, 1980). Another example comes from the highly volatile political atmosphere in the United States at the time of the Vietnam War. Involuntary recruitment (the "draft") provoked considerable public resentment, principally among the young. In 1971, 28 war protesters went on trial in Camden, New Jersey, for destroying draft files at a local selective service agency. In the Camden trial, the defendants acknowledged that their conduct was unlawful but were allowed by the judge to raise a nullification defense.

Even though the FBI had caught the defendants red-handed (destroying draft files), they were all subsequently acquitted by the jury (Abramson, 1995). Other war protesters were found guilty of the charges because the court did not allow the jury to be instructed about their power to nullify the law (Barkan, 1983). More recently, in the 1990s, persons supporting a pro-life position on the abortion issue have been charged with unlawfully trespassing on the grounds of abortion clinics. Juries have acquitted some of these defendants, even though the evidence against them was overwhelming (Abramson, 1995).

An example from Australia also illustrates the public's unwillingness to enforce a law that offends its conception of justice. In Australia, a reverse onus provision operates for some defendants accused of drug violations. These defendants must prove their innocence, a requirement which is counter to conventional criminal procedure, where the defendant is innocent until proven guilty beyond a reasonable doubt. Juries have often been reluctant to accept the reverse onus of proof and have acquitted the defendants. One possible reason for these acquittals is the juries' unease with the reverse onus requirement (Sallmann & Willis, 1984). In criminal cases, it seems that the tried and tested criterion of "innocent until proven guilty" sits best with juries. Thus, juries can operate as a check on lawmakers who may want to reduce the evidentiary burden on the state and thereby facilitate the number of successful prosecutions.

Physician-Assisted Suicide

As noted, in the 1920s, the public were opposed to defining alcohol possession as a crime and blocked prosecutions arising from the application of the prohibition laws. Over the past few decades, another issue has arisen with similar consequences for the administration of justice. Considerable public debate has surrounded the question of whether a physician who has assisted a person to commit suicide is guilty of a crime. Some jurisdictions have legalized physician-assisted suicide, whereas other jurisdictions define assisting suicide as a crime comparable in seriousness to voluntary manslaughter. The state of Oregon and the Northern Territory of Australia have both passed laws permitting assisted suicide for terminally ill patients (Chochinov & Wilson, 1995).[6] In other jurisdictions (such as Washington and California), the majority of the public voted against enacting a referendum to legalize assisted suicide, even though public opinion polls showed that over 54% supported the referendum. An obvious conclusion to be drawn from these experiences is that supporting hypothetical situations is easier and requires less thought than making decisions about actual events.

The level of public support for permitting the acceleration of the death of a critically-ill patient depends on the method used and the nature of the individual's prognosis. A national sample of Canadians (85%) overwhelmingly supported foregoing life-sustaining treatment when a competent patient with a poor prognosis makes a request or has a living will, or the family makes the request on behalf of a comatose patient's prior wishes.[7] The public is less supportive of assisted suicide or active euthanasia in cases with a better prognosis, although over half of the Canadian and U.S. public endorsed these methods (Singer et al., 1995; Harris Poll, 1994; Maguire & Pastore, 1997). There is some evidence, however, that public support for legalizing assisted suicide is limited. When provided with the options of hospice care and information about potential abuses, only one-quarter of a national sample supported legalizing assisted suicides (Monmaney, 1997).

Jury decisions in actual cases of assisted suicide also reflect the divided and conflicting opinion of the public. The public considers the circumstance surrounding an incident of assisted suicide and supports assessments of morality on a case-by-case basis. For example, Dr. Kevorkian was tried and acquitted three times for assisting the suicide of terminally ill patients but was finally convicted for administering a lethal injection to a man suffering from Lou Gehrig's disease (Drell, 1999).

Throughout history, jury nullification has been used as a political tool to correct unjust laws or unjust practices. Recent proposals stretch the use of jury nullification to correct unfair racial discrimination by criminal justice professionals. Butler (1997) urges Black jurors to exercise jury nullification when Black defendants are on trial for nonviolent crimes in order to balance the inequality that has occurred due to discrimination. This discrimination covers education and employment opportunities, as well as discrimination in the criminal justice system.

In several recent cases, juries have been suspected of acquitting the defendant based on a principle that such acquittals of Black defendants will keep the system from sending any more Black men to prison. For example, in 1990, an all-Black jury in Washington, D.C. acquitted Darryl Smith of murder. After the acquittal, an anonymous letter from one of the jurors arrived at the superior court and stated that "while most jurors in the case believed Mr. Smith was guilty, the majority bowed to holdouts who didn't want to send any more Young Black Men to jail" (*Wall Street Journal*, Oct. 4, 1995, p. 1). Other Black and Hispanic defendants have been acquitted of drug possession and selling charges for similar reasons (Dodge, 1998). These nullifications show the potential misuse of nullification power and are similar to the jury acquittals of Klan members for killing Black people in the 1950s and 1960s in the southern states of the United States (Scheflin & Dyke, 1980). They also may be seen as similar to the acquittal of Los Angeles police officers in a state criminal trial by a primarily White jury for the assault on Rodney King.[8]

The public may also acquit defendants who are portrayed as scapegoats to cover up the misconduct of higher government officials. The split jury verdicts in the Iran-contra trial of Oliver North are an example of this principle at work. In that trial, the judge clearly instructed the jury that following the orders of higher government officials was not a legal defense that could excuse the criminal acts. The jury apparently rejected the judge's instruction. As Abramson (1995) notes:

> Of the three charges where the jury convicted, the evidence indicated that North acted alone, without authorization from superiors. On all charges where North credibly argued that his superiors knew of his false statements to Congress and his other steps to cover up the illegal contra-funding activity, the jury acquitted. After trial, one juror described North as "a scapegoat blamed unfairly for following the instructions of his superiors, and that is why we voted to acquit" him of charges of lying. (p. 66)

Nullifications Where the Punishment Is Perceived to Be Unjust

Some legal scholars assert that juries place a check and balance on the legislative and executive branches of government (Sauer, 1995). In a time of mandatory sentences, juries may base their verdicts, in part, on the severity of the punishment the defendant will receive if convicted. If the punishment is adjudged to be too severe or disproportionately harsh in light of the seriousness of the crime, jurors may acquit or convict on a lesser, included charge (partial jury nullification), which carries more appropriate punishment. In this section, we review the evidence of jury nullification based on the belief that the required punishment is unjust.

A good example of this phenomenon comes from Canada, where a murder conviction carries a mandatory penalty of life imprisonment, with no chance of parole until the individual has spent between 10 and 25 years in prison.[9] Robert Latimer took the life of his own daughter, who was severely disabled, but not critically ill. A jury found him guilty of second degree murder, and he received the mandatory sentence of life imprisonment without parole for 10 years. Upon hearing the sentence, several jurors expressed their shock at learning that the sentence was so severe for such a case. Notwithstanding the fact that it is illegal to discuss deliberations, some jurors interviewed on national television stated that they would not have convicted Latimer had they known beforehand about the severity of the sentence that would be imposed.[10] Thus, had the jury been aware of the mandatory sentencing provisions for murder, it seems likely that Latimer would have been acquitted as a result of jury nullification.

Traditionally, courts have not informed jurors of the punishment that defendants may receive if convicted and have discouraged jurors from considering the possible punishment in their deliberations (Sauer, 1995). Indeed, if this information comes to the attention of the jury during the course of a trial, it would likely result in the judge declaring a mistrial. Despite discouragement from the court, jurors often consider the likely sentence imposed, especially in cases involving extenuating or sympathetic circumstances. A pattern of acquittals of a specific charge may indicate that the mandatory sentence for that offense is perceived to be excessive. For example, jurors in Washington, D.C. have acquitted several defendants charged with possession of illicit drugs such as cocaine, crack, and marijuana. Interview data suggest that even without nullification arguments from the defense attorney or nullification instructions from the judge, jurors who are aware of the harsh federal sentencing laws for possession vote for acquittal because they believe that the mandatory sentences are too severe (Conrad, 1999).

Jurors may acquit defendants who have committed a serious offense which resulted in little actual harm; in these cases, the jurors know that the punishment imposed will be much harsher than is warranted in light of the harm inflicted. For example, a bank teller embezzled $20 but was caught immediately after leaving the bank. The jury acquitted the defendant of robbery because of the disproportionate punishment which would ensue from a conviction. In another case, a jury acquitted a defendant of robbery because the penalty for robbery was too severe in light of the fact that only two dollars were taken (Kalven & Zeisel, 1966).

In 1968, the owner of a gun store allowed prospective customers to try out his guns before buying them. He admitted on the stand that this practice was in violation of the Gun Control Act. The government had charged him with 88 felony counts, but the jury acquitted the defendant on every count, due in large part to the potentially severe term of incarceration associated with these offenses (Kopel, 1999). Mock jury research also supports the assertion that the severity of the penalty influences verdict decisions when jurors believe they are deciding an actual case and cannot alleviate the harsh penalty for particular kinds of cases. In cases that contain weak evidence or extenuating circumstances, experimental research shows that severe unjust penalties produce a higher percentage of acquittals (Kaplan and Krupa, 1986).[11]

Three strikes sentencing laws that count property offenses as strikes also conflict with popular conceptions of doing justice. Research using mock juries demonstrates that the public perceives a life sentence as disproportionate and unfair when applied to defendants convicted of nonviolent crimes (see Finkel, 1995). Several juries have acquitted offenders facing life imprisonment when the third "strike" involved a minor property or drug offense. In the United States, a defendant who had two prior felony convictions was charged with possession of a small amount of crack cocaine. If convicted, the defendant would have been sentenced to at least 25 years in prison under the Three Strikes legislation. The defense made a plea to the jury, and the jury acquitted, even though the state's evidence was overwhelming (NPR, 1995).

Jurors in California took nullification a step further and refused to continue deliberations, once they learned that a defendant charged with a property crime would be subjected to the three strikes law (cited in King, 1998). There have been many other acquittals of offenders eligible to be sentenced under the three strikes rule when their third strike is a minor property or drug offense. This pattern of acquittals for property and drug offenders suggests that legislators have exceeded the public's conception of just sentences. Penal populism thus is refuted by the decisions of people in cases where the severity of the penalty seems excessive. In Australia, considerable public outcry to change mandatory sentencing laws in the Northern Territory of Australia arose after the suicide death of a boy convicted of a minor property crime. [Australia Reconsiders Mandatory Sentencing]

The Death Penalty

The United States remains the only Western nation to execute offenders and the only nation in the world to execute juvenile offenders convicted of murder.[12] Why do legislators continue to support the death penalty and why do the public serving as jurors continue to impose it? Ironically, legislators may persist with the death penalty as a legal punishment as a result of misinformation about what the public actually wants. Studies have shown that legislators overestimate the level of support for the death penalty among their constituents. For example, half of the Indiana legislators indicated that most of their constituents preferred the death penalty to alternatives such as life without parole, work, and restitution to the victim's family. However, when actually given the choice of these alternatives, only 26% of the public still preferred the death penalty (McGarrell & Sandys, 1996). Other data examining death sentences in actual cases indicate

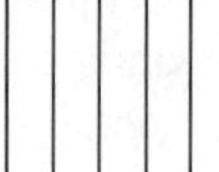

Australia Reconsiders Mandatory Sentencing in the Face of Tragedy

John, a 15-year-old aboriginal boy, committed suicide on February 9, 2000, after being sentenced to a mandatory 28 days in jail under Australia's Northern Territory mandatory sentencing laws. He had stolen 90 Australian dollars worth of office and school supplies. According to Northern Territory Law, juveniles 16 years old and younger must be sentenced to a minimum of 28 days in jail after a third conviction for property, violent, or sexual crimes. His death sparked a public outcry against the mandatory sentencing laws and provoked demands for the Australian federal government to intervene. Coupled with a report by the United Nations Committee on the Elimination of Racial Discrimination, this case increased pressure on the government to recognize discrimination against Aborigines.

The United Nations report urged Australia to consider overturning mandatory sentencing laws in the Northern Territory and Western Australia because "mandatory sentencing leads to Indigenous children being imprisoned at the rate of up to 9:1 relative to Non-Indigenous children" (Facts.com, March 29, 2000). Prime Minister Howard and Northern Territory Chief Minister Denis Burke agreed on a deal, where the mandatory sentencing laws for juvenile property offenders would be amended to allow judges more discretion in sentencing juveniles, but the mandatory sentencing laws for adults would remain intact. The prime minister also agreed to provide 5 million Australian dollars for diversion programs for juveniles (Facts.com, April 19, 2000). This example of politics illustrates how an atypical tragic case and media coverage can stir public sentiment and create pressure for politicians to change unjust laws.

that the public is more lenient than legal professionals. Kalven and Zeisel (1966) compared sentencing decisions from both judges and juries in over 100 capital cases and found that juries were less likely than judges to impose the death penalty.

Politicians are not alone in being misinformed about this issue. Important research on jurors in the United States has demonstrated that jury-decision making in death penalty cases can reflect ignorance of the alternative punishment that would be imposed if the offender is not executed. When deciding to sentence a defendant to death, jurors' beliefs about parole eligibility dates for life sentences affect their eventual sentencing decision. Jurors that estimate that the defendant will be released after a few years are more likely to support the imposition of the death penalty. In fact, the majority of the public tend to underestimate the length of time that a defendant convicted of murder will spend in prison if he is not executed. The end result is that some defendants have been sentenced to death because jurors deliberating on their penalty held erroneous perceptions of the period of imprisonment mandated by state law (Steiner, Bowers & Sarat, 1999).

The response of the public in England sent a clearer message to Parliament. In the 1950s, English law allowed the death penalty only for offenders convicted of murders involving police officers as victims, involving repeated murders, or occurring during the commission of a theft. Juries in England often acquitted defendants of such murders because they believed that the death penalty was an unjust punishment (Kalven & Zeisel, 1966). This form of jury nullification created the impetus for the total abolition of the death penalty in England.

Although over three-quarters of the public support the death penalty in principle, the public believes that it is an unjust punishment for certain forms of murder and some categories of offenders. For example, 34 states allow accessories to a murder that occurred during the commission of a felony to be sentenced to death, even though the accessory may not have actively participated in the murder. Several experimental studies have examined whether the public supports treating principals and accessories alike in a felony murder (Finkel, 1990; Finkel and Duff, 1991; Liss, Finkel, and Moran, 1994; Finkel and Smith, 1993; Robinson and Darley, 1995). These studies show that over half of the respondents acquitted the accessories of first degree murder, thus nullifying the assumption of the felony-murder rule. Aggregate jury data also demonstrate the reluctance of both jurors and prosecutors to support the execution of accessories and principals in felony murder cases.

The Canadian public opposes the death penalty for killings that occur during the commission of a felony; over 90% of Canadians supported the death penalty for premeditated murder compared to only 60% for unplanned killings that occurred during the course of burglary (Focus Canada, 1987). Another source of injustice in the administration of the death penalty is allowing states to execute mentally challenged offenders convicted of murder. Although this practice is legal and constitutional in the United States, the majority of the public believes that it is unethical and unjust. When asked in public opinion polls, 75% of the public opposes the death penalty for mentally challenged offenders (Roberts and Stalans, 1997, p. 237).

Conclusion

A closer examination of how juries and lay magistrates make decisions in actual cases contradicts the image of a universally punitive public that is often projected by populist politicians. Juries and lay magistrates are often more lenient than professional magistrates. The review of the jury nullification literature highlights another important theme. The public endorses individual justice and wants to be merciful when offenders act from good motives. Thus, the trend toward placing the sentencing decisions in the hands of the legislators (rather than judges) is inconsistent with the public's support for individualized justice.

Penal populists have created inflexible penalty structures that are based on extreme crimes involving extreme physical harm which simply do not reflect the average case before the courts. A penal structure built on a foundation of political rhetoric, media stories, and public demands about extremely violent and chronic offenders cannot do justice in typical cases. The public's punitiveness dissipates when the public must decide average cases that face disproportionate punishment.

In a time of harsher sentencing measures and punitive approaches to crime control, the results of jury decisions in real life cases demonstrate more clearly than perhaps any other measure that arbitrary rules cannot serve justice. These rules attempt to ensure that serious crimes result in severe penalties. However, the findings presented in this chapter reveal that the public are just as interested in ensuring that the sentence is fair and in proportion to the circumstances of the case. In a time of harsher sentencing measures and punitive approaches to crime control, the public are still able to show mercy to offenders of victimless crimes or violent offenders acting from good motives.

7 Juvenile Crime and Juvenile Justice

Throughout the 1990s, juvenile crime and juvenile justice generated more public concern than any other criminal justice issue. Most juvenile justice scholars believe that this public anxiety about escalating juvenile crime rates and a lenient juvenile justice system has resulted in significant legislative change in most countries. Zimring (1998), for example, notes that "the climate of concern in the early 1990s has produced a bumper crop of legislative responses" (p. 111).[1] There are, however, some notable examples of resistance to penal populism in New Zealand and Canada. The issue of juvenile crime has largely been synonymous with concern for crime, in general, and many populist penal policies have been directed at juveniles. For example, Australia's first mandatory sentencing law was originally drafted in response to alarm about levels of juvenile crime. [Mandatory Sentencing of Juveniles]

All five jurisdictions have witnessed a rapid escalation in public concern over crime by juveniles, particularly when it involves serious crimes of violence. The perception held by most people is that crime by juveniles has been increasing in volume and seriousness in recent years. As we shall show, while there was an increase in juvenile crime rates in the 1980s, recent statistics show stable or declining rates of juvenile crime in all five countries. Still, the perception persists that there has been a significant transformation in the seriousness of crimes committed by juveniles.

It is widely believed that children today are capable of criminal acts that would have been inconceivable for their counterparts decades or centuries ago. The Bulger case in England, in which two 10-year-old boys killed a five-year-old, springs readily to mind as an example. More recently, the tragic killing of a 10-year-old by two other children, barely teenagers, has aroused further public concern about youth crime. However, as anyone who has read historical accounts of crimes involving juveniles can attest, these tragedies have many precedents in history (see examples in Radzinowicz, 1948). The killing of James Bulger was interpreted by many people as clear evidence that today's children were capable of the worst forms of criminal violence, and that a new level of criminality had been reached. These specific cases tend to color perceptions of an entire generation. Few would deny that the premeditated (even rehearsed) homicide of young James Bulger was an act of inexplicable depravity, but did it really "say" something about the moral turpitude of the generation to which his killers belonged?[2]

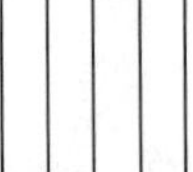

Mandatory Sentencing of Juveniles in Australia

The mandatory sentencing of juvenile offenders in Australia has been a political issue that has developed as a populist punitive response to juvenile offending in the two remote "frontier" states—Western Australia and the Northern Territory. Western Australia developed Australia's first mandatory sentencing laws in 1992, aimed specifically at repeat juvenile offenders. The laws were very much developed "on the run" following a "rally for justice," partly organized by a talk-back radio host which attracted 20,000 angry protestors to the steps of the legislative assembly complaining about the leniency of the juvenile justice system. The laws that developed in this way were eventually repealed. However, they were subsequently replaced by a new government inspired by the American "three strikes" statutes. In 1996, this government introduced its own form of "three strikes," law aimed specifically at the offense of home burglary.

Meanwhile, in the Northern Territory, a region with a significant proportion of Australia's indigenous population and intractable social and crime problems, the government sought to emulate America's experience with "zero tolerance" policing and "silver bullet" solutions that featured swift sudden punishment (including mandatory imprisonment). It was the mandatory sentencing laws introduced by the Northern Territory government in 1997 that eventually led to Australia's mandatory sentencing crisis of 2000. Although the new laws specify that juvenile offenders must have at least one prior conviction, there was no shortage of eligible juveniles convicted of trivial earlier offenses.

The number of young juveniles sent to detention under the new mandatory laws for trivial property offenses started to rise. When one of these young people committed suicide in prison, the issue of mandatory sentencing assumed a new national importance and attracted growing international attention. The issue became a cause celebre and even threatened to split the right-wing government of John Howard, as many parliamentarians considered crossing the floor to vote with the opposition on various proposals. Eventually, the prime minister managed to broker a deal to defuse the crisis. (For information on these events and a copy of a report on mandatory sentencing by a parliamentary committee, visit: http://ms.dcls.org.au/.)

As with other issues examined in this volume, public concern with youth crime has crystallized into a desire for harsher juvenile justice. There have been calls for the creation of a single criminal justice system that would encompass adults and juveniles, with the result that the severity of punishments would not vary if the offender happened to be under 18 years of age. However, since the beginning of the nineteenth century, Western societies have recognized that juveniles should not be held fully accountable for their criminal actions and should be treated differently from adult offenders.[3]

For many years now, a vocal minority has advocated the imposition of "adult" sentences on juvenile offenders. In light of widespread public concern over rising rates of juvenile crime—particularly when it involves violence—this message has struck a chord with penal populists. The result is that over the last two decades of the "War on Crime" we have witnessed an erosion of the principle that juvenile offenders should be treated more leniently than adults. The "get tough" movement has tried to include these juvenile offenders within the ambit of the adult criminal justice system. An example of this "get tough" movement is legislation from California. [Proposition 21]

The populist response to crime by juveniles has consisted of an attempt to dismantle the separate system of justice that has been created for juvenile offenders. Populist politicians have used the fact that juveniles receive mitigated punishments (compared to adults) to argue that juvenile sentences are too lenient, as though the adult disposition were the norm and the youth court sentence a lenient aberration. The imposition of milder punishments on juvenile offenders has also been cited as a *cause* of juvenile offending, the same way that leniency throughout the criminal justice system has been described, by politicians and members of the public, as a cause of crime.

The syllogism that links the severity of punishments to crime rates emerges more clearly at the level of juvenile justice, where it is often argued that tougher penalties will put a stop to rising levels of juvenile violence and prevent juveniles from turning into adult offenders. The source of the frustration may be the widespread perception that young people will not behave unless the punishment for wrongdoing is severe. But as Jackson Toby noted as far back as 1957, the main factors distinguishing delinquents from nondelinquents is whether a young person has a "stake in conformity" (Toby, 1957). Giving a young person a reason not to offend is, therefore, likely to be a much more effective strategy than threatening punishment.

The claim that "a crime is a crime" and should result in the same punishment for adults and juveniles has also developed popular appeal, spurred on by

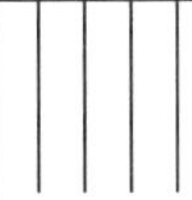

Proposition 21 in California

A recent, punitive reform of the criminal justice response to juvenile crime in the United States emerged in California in 2000. Proposition 21 was ratified by 62% of voters in that state in March of that year. This legislation introduces a number of changes to the juvenile justice system. For example, it requires adult trials for juveniles as young as 14 years of age, if they have been charged with one of a list of enumerated offenses. In addition, the statute transfers from judges to prosecutors the unfettered discretion to decide whether a juvenile accused should be tried as an adult. The legislation also restricts the authority of judges to refer juveniles for treatment or probation (rather than incarcerate such offenders). Opponents of the restrictive and harsh legislation have pointed to the fact that it was passed at a time when the state's juvenile crime rate had declined significantly: the number of felonies declined by 30% and the number of homicides by fully 50% during the period from 1990 to 1998.

Proponents of tough, populist legislation appear to ignore the declining crime rates and continue to justify their policies by reference to the incidence of crime. Thus, although as noted, California's crime rate dropped 30% between 1990 and 1998, the former governor who sponsored Proposition 21 was still able to talk about "high rates of juvenile and gang-related violence" (Governor Pete Wilson quoted in AP interview with Martha Mendoza, March 3, 2000).

populist politicians who claim simplicity as a virtue in itself. In addition to calls for the abolition of the separation between youth and adult courts, proponents of the "get tough" movement have promoted a number of specific changes to the system of juvenile justice, including facilitating the transfer of juvenile accused to adult court; lowering the minimum age of criminal responsibility; lowering the maximum age limit of the juvenile justice system; relaxing the constraints on the publication of the names of juvenile accused, and imposing adult sentences on juvenile offenders. In all these areas, the impetus to amend legislation has been greatest in the context of serious crimes of violence.

In this chapter, we review some of the principal policy changes that have been implemented or proposed, especially those pertaining to young persons charged with violent offenses. Wherever possible, we evaluate the degree of concordance between these proposals and the views of the public. At the conclusion, we describe some developments that are inconsistent with penal populism.

In considering the extent of public support for punitive juvenile justice policies, several themes emerge. First, public support for punitive measures reflects misperceptions of the kinds of crimes committed by juveniles and the severity of the criminal justice response. Second, part of the widespread support for punitive responses to young offenders is a result of the polling methodology employed; respondents are asked if they support a particular policy (tougher sentences) without being asked to consider alternate options. Third, concern about violence underlies public dissatisfaction with reformative efforts and explains the support for harsher punishment. Fourth, despite all the media attention to violent crimes committed by juveniles, the majority of the public nevertheless still believe in the value of attempting to reform young persons who come into conflict with the law. For example, a significant proportion of the public believes that violent juvenile offenders who suffered an abusive childhood should be treated with leniency (Stalans and Henry, 1994). Finally, we shall discuss the experience in jurisdictions such as New Zealand, Canada, and the United Kingdom, where despite the heated rhetoric about youth crime, legislative reform has not necessarily been populist.

Before reviewing public reaction to specific reform proposals, however, it is important to understand (a) the nature of news media coverage of juvenile crime and juvenile justice, (b) public perception and reality of juvenile crime trends, and (c) public knowledge of trends with respect to juvenile justice.

Media Coverage of Juvenile Crime

The media are responsible for distorting the public's view of juvenile offenders and the juvenile justice system (see Schwartz, 1989 for a discussion of media-based myths about juvenile crime). One study of newspaper stories in California found that two-thirds of stories about violent crime portrayed juveniles as offenders, and over half of all stories about youth involved some form of violence (Shepherd, 1998). Research in Canada has shown that newspapers rarely contain information about the background or circumstances of juvenile offenders or provide information about the justification for the sentence imposed. Instead, newspapers emphasize the seriousness of the offense and the impact of the crime on the victim (Sprott, 1996). Also, this same study found that the coverage of youth crime was heavily skewed toward violence: only one-quarter of court cases—but 94% of news stories—involved violence.

Television coverage of juveniles is just as biased, with about half of its stories about youth focusing on crime and violence (Shepherd, 1998). Dorfman and Schiraldi (2001) reviewed media coverage of youth issues and concluded that "relatively few youth are arrested each year for violent crimes, yet the message from the news is that this is a common occurrence" (p. 13). From this skewed portrayal of youth, members of the public have developed a distorted view of the true nature and extent of crime by the young.

To the Public, Juvenile Crime Is Violent Crime

To the public, juvenile delinquency has become synonymous with violence (e.g., Sprott, 1996). In Australia, juveniles regularly feature in the media as members of gangs, car thieves, as a menace to the public on trains, and for street parties which escalate out of control. When most Americans think about juvenile crime, images of the shootings in Columbine come to mind or, more recently (in March 2000), the killing of a six-year-old Michigan girl by a schoolmate of the same age. In a similar way, Britons' image of juvenile offenders was influenced by the killing of James Bulger, and Canadians were shocked to learn of the murder of Reena Virk, a teenage girl, by a gang of her acquaintances, many of whom were girls.

These tragedies are highly memorable, even without the repetition which comes from continuous media coverage during the course of the subsequent trial. Research has demonstrated that people generalize from single incidents and infer that a general trend is emerging with respect to youth crime. These high-profile offenders become symbolic of all teenagers, and their parents' generation tends to attribute criminality to most young persons. This has consequences for public opinion with respect to juvenile justice.

The media seldom give sufficient context about crimes, and this omission encourages a punitive response from the public. Covell and Howe (1996) demonstrated this phenomenon with respect to public attitudes toward juvenile offenders. Half the respondents in their study were asked to read a very brief, newspaper-length account of a teenager charged with rape. The other group read the same summary of the facts but were also provided with some background information about the offender's family life that would not typically emerge in a newspaper story. When asked to sentence the offender, people who read this additional information were far less punitive.[4] One lesson from this study is that when thinking about crime by juveniles, the public tend to focus on the seriousness of the offense and do not naturally consider the offender's background. When this information is made salient (as it would be in court, in the course of a sentencing hearing), public perceptions shift significantly.

Juvenile Crime Trends: Public Perception and Reality

In chapter 2 we documented the discrepancy between public perception and reality with respect to adult crime trends. Public views of juvenile crime trends are little more accurate than perceptions of adult rates. Polls in the United States of America and Canada reveal that the majority of the public sees juvenile crime as increasing in frequency: four out of five Canadians surveyed in 1999 thought that youth crime rates had increased over the previous five years (Roberts 2001; see also Belden, Russonello & Stewart, 1997; Baron & Hartnagel, 1996; Lee & Wellford, 1997). This perception of rising juvenile crime rates existed in periods where such rates were decreasing or stable from year to year, as well as in periods of increasing crime rates.

Although the juvenile crime rate climbed in the late 1980s, as with the adult crime statistics in Canada (and elsewhere), rates began to fall in the 1990s. In fact, apart from a brief period in the 1980s, the level of police-reported crime in Canada changed very little during the period from 1977 to 1996 (Carrington, 1999). Sprott and Snyder (1999) reviewed juvenile crime trends in the United States and Canada and concluded that there was no evidence to suggest that rates of serious violent juvenile crime (the form of criminality of greatest concern to the public) had changed significantly during the period from 1991 to 1996.

The most recent statistics in Canada reveal a decline in the youth crime rate for the eighth consecutive year (Tremblay, 2000). Rates of violent crime involving juveniles have been stable or declining for almost as many years (Savoie, 1999).[5] Despite these trends, Canadians continue to believe that matters are getting worse with respect to crime by juveniles. In addition, although there is considerable emphasis on juvenile violence in the media, the percentage of juvenile crime involving violence is actually lower than the percentage of adult crime involving violence (Tremblay, 2000).[6] Similar results emerge from Britain. Two-thirds of respondents to the 1998 British Crime Survey believed that juvenile crime had increased within the previous two years, while in reality it had declined by 12% (Mattinson & Mirrlees-Black, 2000).[7]

The Public Overestimate the Proportion of Crime for Which Juveniles Are Responsible

Consistent with the perception that things are worse than they are, the public overestimate the amount of violent crime for which juvenile offenders are responsible. For example, 60% of California respondents believed that young people commit most of the violent crime recorded by the police (Belden et al., 1997). In reality, juveniles are responsible for approximately 12% of crimes reported to the police (see Snyder and Sickmund, 1999; Sickmund, Snyder & Poe-Yamagata, 1997).

Widespread media coverage of a few incidents has clearly changed public perceptions of the magnitude of the problem of school violence. Dorfman and Schiraldi note that "in the 1998/99 year there was less than a one in two million chance of being killed in a school in America, yet 71% of respondents to an NBC/*Wall Street Journal* poll felt that a school shooting was likely in their community" (2001, p. 2).

In the United Kingdom, approximately one recorded crime in 10 is committed by a juvenile, but this is not the way that the British public see things. The British Crime Survey asked respondents whether young persons (between 10 and 17 in the UK) or people older than 17 were mainly responsible for crime; over one-quarter responded that juveniles were mainly responsible for crime (Mattinson & Mirrlees-Black, 2000). Less than one-fifth of all recorded crimes in Canada in 1999 involved a juvenile suspect (Savoie, 1999). However, public estimates of this statistic are much higher: most people estimate over 50%. It is also interesting to note that teenagers—who might be expected to have a more accurate perception of the amount of crime committed by the young—share the same misperception held by adults (Angus Reid, 1997).

Juvenile Crime Becoming More Serious as well as More Common

Finally, a common perception held by the public is that in addition to changes to the *volume* of youth crime in recent years, there has been a marked change in the *seriousness* of crimes committed by juveniles. There is scant statistical evidence for this public perception either. Doob and Sprott (1998) examined crime statistics in Canada and found no evidence to support the conclusion that violent acts by juveniles had become more serious throughout the 1990s.

Public Knowledge of Trends in Juvenile Justice

Public Knowledge of Juvenile Justice Is Poor

If people know little about trends in juvenile crime, they probably know even less about the criminal justice response. For example, one survey found that most Canadians knew little or nothing about the sentences available in youth court. Over half of the sample believed (erroneously) that the maximum penalty for a minor assault was six months imprisonment (in fact, it is much higher). The vast majority (over 80%) of respondents did not know that 17-year-olds could be tried in adult court, regardless of the seriousness of the offense of conviction, and that offenders as young as 14 years of age could be tried in adult court if they had been charged with a serious offense (Sprott, 1996).

A similar lack of public knowledge about the juvenile justice system in the United States has been demonstrated. For example, one survey found that although most respondents knew that juveniles under the age of 18 could be tried in adult court for violent crimes, they could not identify the minimum age at which this takes place (Survey Research Laboratory, 1995). Most people believed that a 15-year-old juvenile tried and convicted in juvenile court for murder had to be released by age 18, when in fact the maximum age of release is higher (Stalans & Henry, 1994).

Public Underestimate Severity of Sentencing in Youth Courts

Public estimates of sentencing trends for young offenders tend to be inaccurate. Canadian respondents underestimated by a considerable margin the percentage of young offenders who receive a custodial sentence (Sprott, 1996). Data from Statistics Canada further undermine the view that sentencing patterns in youth courts are much more lenient than adult courts. This study compared the use of custody for adults and young offenders and found that for a number of high-volume offenses, *sentence lengths were actually longer for juveniles*. For example, 65% of youth court custodial terms for assault were longer than one month, compared to only 43% of adult court sentences (see Sanders, 2000). Sentence lengths were longer for youth than for adults for theft, failure to appear (in court); burglary; property damage, mischief; possession of restricted drugs, assault causing bodily harm; possession of stolen property (see Sanders, 2000).[8] These offenses account for a significant percentage of caseloads in youth courts. Simply put, the juvenile justice system in Canada is harsher than many Canadians realize.

Public Critical of Sentencing Trends Involving Juvenile Offenders

In light of the public misperceptions about juvenile crime trends and the absence of familiarity with the juvenile justice system, it is not surprising that the public around the world tend to think that sentencing in youth court is too lenient. Recent data from the United Kingdom illustrate the point. Respondents participating in the 1998 British Crime Survey were asked the standard question posed about adult sentencing: "*Would you say that the way the courts deal with young offenders is too tough, too lenient, or about right?*" Six out of 10 respondents were of the opinion that youth courts were too lenient; fully one-quarter believed that they were *much* too lenient (Mattinson and Mirrlees-Black, 2000). The public tend to see leniency in sentencing as a greater problem in youth courts. These findings explain why the public express less confidence in juvenile courts than any other component of the criminal justice system. A recent survey of Canadians found that although the public supported a number of strategies to reduce youth crime rates, "making sentences harsher" topped the list in terms of public support. Almost all respondents (93%) believed that sentences imposed on juveniles were too lenient (see Sprott, 1998).[9]

Punitive Juvenile Justice Policies

Changing the Purpose of the Juvenile Justice System

Perhaps the most fundamental change advocated involves the purpose of the juvenile justice system. Policymakers in several jurisdictions have tried to shift the purpose of the juvenile justice system from rehabilitation to accountability and punishment, goals traditionally ascribed to sentencing at the adult level. The juvenile court's jurisdiction has been extended several years past the age of majority to allow for the imposition of longer sentences of incarceration. Other statutory changes have further undermined the purposes of reform and rehabilitation.

The Public Remain Supportive of Rehabilitating Young Offenders

Although government policies in most countries have shifted toward a more punishment-oriented approach to juvenile offenders, few of these punitive policies attract strong support from the public. The vast majority of the American public (82%) agreed that it is important to try to rehabilitate juvenile offenders who are in the correctional system (Applegate, Cullen & Fisher, 1997).[10] In a Tennessee poll, respondents were asked to identify the purpose behind juvenile prisons. Support was much greater for rehabilitation (63%) than for punishment (18%; see Moon, Sundt, Cullen, and Wright, 2000).

Similarly, a strong majority of Canadians (70%) believe that for juveniles, rehabilitation is more important than punishment, particularly the use of prison (Baron and Hartnagel, 1996).[11] The most recent survey conducted on this issue in Canada found that the public continued to subscribe to a different sentencing "model" for juveniles. More support emerged for rehabilitation when considering juveniles; incapacitation on the other hand attracted more support from the public when considering adult offenders (Doob, 2000).

Indermaur (1990) conducted a study of public views of youth justice in Australia and found that when asked to identify the main purpose of sentencing juveniles, 13% chose rehabilitation with respect to "a serious violent offender," but the proportion endorsing rehabilitation doubled if the question pertained to a "young property offender." Support for retribution was also much lower if the "target" offender was a young property offender rather than a violent offender. Also, public support for proposals to shift the purpose of sentencing away from reform to punishment is limited to repeat offenders and certain violent offenders. In this respect, punitive proposals in the field of juvenile justice may be out of step with community views.

When respondents are asked to choose between rehabilitation and prevention programs or punishment and enforcement programs, several U.S. surveys during the period from 1994 to 1996 show that most respondents (between 51% and 71%) believe that rehabilitation and prevention programs are more important (see Belden et al., 1997; Survey Research Laboratory, 1995). Moreover, the public cited increasing investment in children's programs as the most effective strategy to reduce crime and believed that sending more juveniles to adult prisons was the least effective strategy (Lee & Wellford, 1997). Over 60% of respondents to a survey in California believed that youth correctional facilities make juveniles become hardened criminals (California Poll, 1988). Clearly, public support for prevention and rehabilitation programs for youthful offenders has not diminished, despite the media's portrayal of juvenile offenders as hardened criminals.

Public Also Support Rehabilitation even for Juveniles Convicted of Crimes of Violence

There also appears to be support for rehabilitating even violent juveniles. A poll of Chicago residents found that 60% believed that "violent youths are still children who can learn to turn away from crime" (Lawrence, 1999, p. 14). An earlier poll in California found that 75% of respondents believed that youth who commit serious crimes could be rehabilitated and should not be sent to secure facilities for as long as the law allows. Similarly, over two-thirds of a sample of Californians believed that youth of all ages charged with violent offenses could be reformed (Belden et al., 1997).

Support for reforming juveniles is also seen in the public's disapproval of some punitive policies that can create future difficulties for juveniles when, as adults, they seek employment. Americans also opposed allowing colleges to have access to juvenile arrest records and expelling teenagers from schools for possession of marijuana (Schiraldi & Soler, 1998). Most respondents in a Virginia poll also wanted judges (rather than prosecutors) to decide whether a juvenile accused should be tried as an adult. These respondents also opposed detaining juveniles and adult offenders together in the same jail while they were awaiting trial (Survey Research Laboratory, 1995).

The public is willing to provide even violent juveniles with a chance to turn their lives around. Most people oppose many of the provisions in the Violent and Repeat Juvenile Offender Act that may hinder efforts to rehabilitate the young person. For example, respondents to a survey on the act strongly rejected provisions such as granting prosecutors exclusive discretion over the decision to transfer a juvenile accused to criminal court (see Schiraldi and Soler, 1998). An earlier nationwide survey found that just over half (53%) of the respondents supported community-based programs such as regular or intensive supervision probation or a community residence for a first-time juvenile offender convicted of a violent crime, but the vast majority (83%) favored secure residence for juveniles convicted of a second violent crime (Schwartz, 1992). The public are willing to provide a chance to first-time violent juvenile offenders, but juveniles who repeat violent crimes may be seen as posing a clear threat to public safety.

Facilitating Transfer of Juvenile Accused to Adult Court

Policymakers across a number of jurisdictions have proposed or passed legislation to permit juveniles convicted of serious crimes to receive sentences as severe as those imposed on adult offenders. One trend has been to amend laws so that certain juvenile offenders (usually repeat or serious offenders) can be more easily tried as adult offenders. The most common minimum age that a juvenile can be tried as an adult is 14 across the United States. Forty-one states have now passed laws that increase the number of juveniles that can be tried as adults and that lower the age at which juveniles can be transferred to adult court.

An additional incentive for the states to move in this direction came from the federal government in 1998, when Congress made some federal grants contingent on the recipient state allowing the prosecution of teenaged accused as adults (Young & Gainsborough, 2000). The result has been that significant numbers of juvenile accused have been transferred for trial to adult court; there were 10,000 such cases in 1996 (Young & Gainsborough, 2000) of which racial minorities accounted for a disproportionately large number. Moreover, over half these transfers were for nonviolent or drug offenses.[12] This illustrates yet again one of the adverse effects of penal populism: punitive measures arise in response to the most serious cases of violence, yet affect the much larger numbers of people convicted of less serious crimes.

The decision to try juveniles as adults is often based on the goals of providing adequate punishment and protecting public safety. Most jurisdictions consider an accused's age as an important criterion for determining whether juveniles should be tried and punished as adults. A national survey in the United States found that a little over half the sample (53%) indicated that 17 is the age at which juveniles should be tried as adults (Schwartz, 1992). Similarly, a majority of Canadians (70%) also favored trying all 16- and 17-year-old juveniles as adults (Gallup Canada, 1994). There appears to be a public consensus that 16- and 17-year-old juveniles who commit serious crimes should be tried as adults.

Members of the public appear divided in their views as to whether 14- and 15-year-old juvenile offenders should be tried and punished as adult offenders, though many jurisdictions employ 14 as the minimum age at which juveniles who commit serious crimes can be tried in adult courts. Close to two-thirds of respondents in U.S. polls indicated that juveniles aged 15 or older who committed violent crimes should receive the same punishment as an adult offender (Lee & Wellford, 1997). Support for the "same crime, same punishment" principle diminishes for the younger offenders: 14-year-olds are seen to be too young to warrant adult-level punishments; less than half the sample in one survey supported prosecuting 14-year-olds as adults (Belden et al., 1997). A sample of Canadians also assigned less severe sentences to the younger juvenile offenders, but the difference between younger and older offenders decreased for very serious crimes (Zamble & Kalm, 1990).[13]

In a study using brief descriptions of a juvenile who had no prior convictions and was charged with murder, respondents were twice as likely to recommend a trial in adult court for a 16-year-old than a 14-year-old juvenile.

Age of the accused also affected recommendations to try in adult court a juvenile who had two prior convictions and was charged with homicide: 16-year-old juveniles were more likely (than 14-year-olds) to receive a transfer to adult court (Stalans & Henry, 1994). Across surveys, the age of the youth had an important impact on public views. There was a consensus that 16-year-old youths who commit violent crimes should be tried in adult court, but opinion was divided about transferring 14-year-old juveniles, even when charged with serious violent crimes.

Public support for trying juveniles as adults is much greater for juveniles who have prior criminal records. If the juvenile had no prior convictions, only one-quarter of the respondents supported an adult trial (Stalans & Henry, 1994).[14] However, if the juvenile charged with the murder of his father has two prior convictions, half of the respondents wanted the juvenile tried as an adult. Thus, the public's relative tolerance for the offender diminishes when the juvenile has had numerous opportunities to reform him or herself. Moreover, the public considers both the prior record and the seriousness of the offense in their decisions to try juveniles as adults and to recommend placement in a secure facility. The public are sensitive also to background information about the juvenile and do not support policies that automatically require all juveniles to be tried as adults, even those who are charged with serious violent crimes.

The type of crime also has an important influence on the public's sentencing recommendations for juvenile offenders. Surveys show that about two-thirds of the public oppose the imposition of similar penalties on juveniles and adults for crimes in general, drug possession, or serious property crime. Although two-thirds of the respondents want juveniles facing their first charge to be tried as adults and to be placed in secure or residential facilities if the charge is a serious violent crime or drug dealing, the public is divided over whether these juveniles should be sent to adult prisons: 44% support the imposition of adult prison sentences for serious violent crimes and 30% support adult prison sentences for juveniles convicted of drug trafficking (Schwartz, 1992).

Finally, it is important to point out that although there is considerable populist pressure to transfer juvenile accused to adult court, research evidence suggests that in terms of crime prevention, such transfers may actually be counterproductive. A study by Bishop and Frazier (1997) compared the recidivism rate of juveniles transferred to the adult system with that of juveniles who remained in the youth court system. These researchers were able to match the samples on important background variables such as age, gender, and the seriousness of the current and previous charges. The findings indicated that a higher percentage of the transferred group reoffended within two years. In addition, the transferred juveniles were more likely to be subsequently rearrested for more serious offenses. It appears then that penal populism may result in more, not less, crime.

Changing the Age Limits of the Juvenile Justice System

Lowering the age of criminal responsibility and thereby increasing the number of children entering the criminal justice system has been a popular proposal in many jurisdictions. It is worth noting that although there has been considerable popular clamour to lower the age of criminal responsibility in Canada and the United States, the minimum age of criminal responsibility is already lower than many other countries. In Italy, for example, criminal responsibility begins at the age of 14. In Canada, there have been numerous calls to lower the age of criminal responsibility from 12 to 10 (or even lower). In 1998, a Parliamentary Committee advocated lowering the age limit, and this proposal was endorsed by most political parties at the federal level. Moreover, in every recent federal election, both principal opposition parties have proposed lowering the age of criminal responsibility. Despite this pressure, the federal government has retained the current age limit of criminal responsibility. The minimum age of criminal responsibility in Australia is already lower than in Canada; it is 10 years of age in most states and even lower in two jurisdictions.

In addition to lowering the minimum age of criminal responsibility, some states have lowered the maximum age at which juvenile courts have jurisdiction. Thus, several states automatically try all 16- and 17-year-old offenders as adult offenders. Sentencing laws pertaining to juveniles have evolved in the same direction as sentencing laws for adult offenders. Juveniles tried in adult court for serious felony crimes are subject to mandatory minimum periods of incarceration. Juvenile court judges can now impose both juvenile and adult sanctions on juveniles found guilty of serious felonies in the juvenile court. As of 1995, 15 states in the United States had laws that permit judges to combine juvenile and adult sanctions.[15]

Although Canada has not lowered the maximum age of young offenders, such a reform has been proposed repeatedly in recent years. It appears to have some degree of public support: two national surveys (conducted in 1994 and 1998) found that 70% of respondents favored lowering the maximum age from 17 to 15 years of age. It is important to note, however, that the question was posed in the context of violent crimes (Stein, 1999). Responses to this issue are highly influenced by the manner in which the question is posed. Researchers in Canada gave the public a choice between either a child welfare or a criminal justice response to "under age" offending; under these conditions, support for criminalizing youth fell from over three-quarters to under one-quarter of the respondents (Sprott and Doob, 1997).

Increasing Accessibility to Information Relating to Juvenile Accused and Offenders

One of the differences between adult and juvenile court is the degree of public access to information. In order to protect the young accused and his or her family, juvenile justice systems impose significant restrictions on the freedom of the news media to publish the names of juvenile offenders. This practice has been changing, in part, as a result of pressure from news organizations, for whom restriction on publication is seen as a threat to freedom of the press. Media organizations have launched legal challenges to judicially imposed restrictions on the publication of the names of juveniles accused of crimes. Some newspapers in Canada have argued that they need to publish the names of young offenders not so much to exercise freedom of the press but rather to ensure public safety. In this way, the media have represented themselves as an extension of the criminal justice system rather than simply a source of information.

As a result of this pressure, several jurisdictions now permit the limited publication of juveniles charged with certain violent crimes. Even in Canada, a country which has resisted most of the more punitive changes to the juvenile justice system, new legislation permits the publication of names of certain young offenders.[16] The public appear to support the relaxing of rules regarding publication, but only for those sentenced for violent crimes: 80% endorsed such a position. Finally, many jurisdictions have made changes to make it easier for certain agencies, especially criminal justice agencies, to have longer-term access to juvenile court records.[17]

Establishment of Boot Camps for Juvenile Offenders

A popular proposal in many Western countries has been the creation of military style "boot camps" for juvenile offenders. As with other populist justice innovations, this concept originated in the United States, where marine-style discipline was believed to be the antidote to offending by crime-prone teenagers. Boot camps emerged in the early 1980s, and by 1990, approximately 50 such camps existed in state prison systems (MacKenzie, 1994). By the time that boot camps were introduced in Canada and Australia (in the late 1990s), research evidence had already demonstrated that this idea had little merit in terms of crime control or rehabilitation (e.g., Mackenzie, 1994).[18]

The introduction of boot camps in Western Australia had all the hallmarks of penal populism. The camp was announced just before a state election; little thought had been devoted to the kinds of offenders who would be sent there, or what might be done with them at the camp (established hundreds of miles into the wilderness). Courts were reluctant to send young offenders to such an institution, and after several years and several million wasted dollars, the government put the boots to the camp itself. The experience in Ontario, Canada was little different.

Making Parents Responsible for Crimes Committed by Their Children

Should parents suffer for the crimes of their children? Concern over rising violent crimes committed by juveniles has led to proposals to hold parents accountable for the crimes committed by their children. Some jurisdictions in the United States have enacted laws to allow the government to impose fines or jail time up to one year for knowingly failing to control or supervise a child who is suspected or convicted of crimes (see Chapin, 1997; Geis & Binder, 1991). For example, one Detroit suburb passed such legislation in 1996; the ordinance holds parents responsible for the crimes of their children and subjects parents to fines and the possibility of further punishment if these are not paid (Barak, 1994). Similarly, two provinces in Canada have passed legislation making parents financially responsible for wrongful acts committed by their children. In Ontario, parents are held financially responsible even for non-criminal acts of their children. An individual simply has to convince a small claims judge that money is owed as a result of some action by the "defendant's" children.[19] Limited parental responsibility legislation also exists in the United Kingdom.

The theory behind parental responsibility laws is that such legislation will motivate parents to educate and control their children. The public clearly believes that lack of parental guidance is a major cause of juvenile delinquency. An American poll in 1998 found that almost all respondents (90%) indicated that lack of adult supervision of children contributed "a lot" to violence in our society (Sourcebook of Criminal Justice Statistics, 1999). Polls conducted between 1994 and 1997 found that the majority of respondents believed the most important causes of crime were lack of morals and values, illegal drug use, and the breakdown of the family (Lee & Wellford, 1997).

What do the public think about this kind of parental accountability legislation? Generally speaking, Americans seem to be in favor of such legislation, while Canadians are less enthusiastic. An American poll found that the majority believed that parents of juvenile offenders should be held accountable in some way (Belden et al., 1997). Surveys in the United States revealed that almost two-thirds of the respondents supported making parents financially responsible for loss and damage caused by their children. Not surprisingly, perhaps, people with children were less supportive of this policy, although even half of the parents still supported the policy. In Canada, a survey conducted in 1994 found that less than half the sample supported making parents financially responsible for crimes committed by their children (Insight Canada, 1994).

Neither Americans nor Canadians, however, support the use of criminal sanctions as a way to hold parents accountable for the crimes of their children. In Canada, such a provision is opposed by over two-thirds of the respondents to a 1999 nationwide survey (Gallup Canada, 1999, see also Roberts & Stalans, 1997; Belden et al., 1997). As an alternative to criminal sanctions, some jurisdictions require parenting classes for parents of children adjudicated as juvenile delinquents (see Chapin, 1997); surveys have yet to be conducted to assess the degree of public support for this approach.

British Juvenile Justice

The evolution of the juvenile justice system in England and Wales over the past two decades clearly exemplifies the tensions between populist and rational policy making. Juvenile offending and the juvenile justice system have been the focal points for popular concern about crime. The 1998 British Crime Survey found that of all parts of the criminal process, the public had least confidence in the juvenile justice system (Mattinson and Mirlees-Black, 2000).

As is the case with other jurisdictions, this lack of confidence can be traced in part to the representation of youth crime and youth justice in the national media. Various themes have been consistently sounded in the tabloid press. One is an image of feral juveniles totally beyond the reach of any form of parental or official control. Over the past decade, the press has reported on a number of highly persistent young offenders, the most notorious of whom was dubbed "Rat boy," as he lived roughly in the underground drainage system of a northern city.

Another media theme involves naive and incompetent social workers and probation officers, grappling with offending that is beyond their comprehension. This paradigm is best illustrated by "Safari boy," a persistent young offender whose "punishment" involved a trip abroad designed to increase his self-esteem. This sentence was widely covered and condemned by the popular press. A final theme is that of total moral collapse, evidenced by increasingly heinous crimes committed by younger and younger offenders; here the crimes of very serious violence committed by children are offered as evidence of a growing trend, rather than as the rare and unique tragedies that they really represent.

The political response to public concern has at times been unequivocally populist. Faced with an intense "moral panic" over persistent juvenile offenders in the early 1990s, the Conservative administration introduced Secure Training Orders (STO) for persistent offenders aged 12, 13, or 14, for whom only very limited custodial options existed. This initiative ignored the fact that social services already had statutory provisions for placing such offenders in secure accommodation; the problem lay less in lack of powers than in a lack of resources.[20] The Criminal Justice and Public Order Act of 1994 doubled the maximum custodial sentence for offenders aged 15 to 17.[21] The population of sentenced young offenders in custody, which had fallen by half between 1980 and 1993, rose by over two-thirds during the period from 1993 to 1998.

However, following the election of the Labour government in 1997, the youth justice system has been substantially reformed. Some commentators have regarded these reforms as further examples of populist authoritarianism. In particular, criticism has focused on parenting orders, anti-social behavior orders, curfew orders, and much more inflexible arrangements for police cautioning. Some of these orders are based in the civil rather than criminal law and require a lesser evidentiary standard. A consistent criticism is that their net effect will be to draw more people into the ambit of formal social control.

On the other hand, this legislation makes it clear that priority is attached to rehabilitation. Considerable store is set on integrating the efforts of probation officers, social workers, and the police. A new custodial order, the Detention and Training Order, replacing Secure Training Orders and Detention in young offender institutions, is intended to provide the framework for rehabilitation within custodial settings. There is also a great deal of emphasis on reducing delays in the administration of juvenile justice. In short, many of the reforms fall firmly within the long-established tradition of liberal reform, which has characterized penal thinking since the Second World War. The climate of opinion within which the reforms are implemented will probably determine the balance that is eventually struck between punishment and rehabilitation. [Reforming Youth Justice in the U.K.]

Reforming Juvenile Justice in Canada

Canada seems to have resisted the slide into penal populism witnessed in other jurisdictions, and it is worth exploring the reasons why this is the case. There have been some punitive changes to the juvenile justice system of course. As noted in this chapter, the Young Offenders Act (YOA) was amended on several occasions, with each amendment making the system somewhat tougher. Still, during the period from 1992 to 2001, the pressure on the ruling Liberal Party to replace the YOA with a new, more punitive juvenile justice act has been intense. According to a 1999 poll, responding to crime by young persons was identified as the most important criminal justice issue for Canadians (Stein, 1999). Moreover, comparisons with surveys across our five countries reveals that if anything, Canadians are less informed about juvenile crime trends than the public in other countries.

In 1999, the government did finally introduce a new statute to replace the old YOA. The Youth Criminal Justice Act (YCJA) constitutes a complete overhaul of the juvenile justice system. Since the act had been anticipated for many years, and all opposition parties (with the exception of the left-leaning New Democratic Party) have been clamoring for harsher sentencing arrangements for young offenders, many people anticipated a highly punitive new bill.

As it turns out, the YCJA is not the punitive legislation many critics of youth justice demanded. Indeed, this is borne out by the fact that opposition politicians in the federal parliament and provincial politicians continued to berate the government for being "soft on youth crime." It was the sentencing provisions that most critics wished to see toughened. This change did not occur; while a number of changes were made which seemed to make the system more punitive, with respect to the use of custody, the new legislation actually heads in the other direction. Although it talks tough, in reality, the bill is not an example of populist legislation. For example, the bill contains strict criteria that must be met before a judge in youth court can sentence a young person to

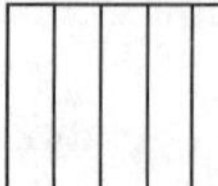

Reforming Youth Justice in the United Kingdom

Not all radical reform is radically punitive. The changes to the youth justice system in England and Wales provide a good example of continuity with rehabilitative traditions. Reform was clearly needed. The system was subject to very considerable delays and inefficiencies; public confidence in youth justice was low; and it was strongly suspected that young offenders had little respect for the system. The Crime and Disorder Act 1998 established Youth Offending Teams (YOTs) in England and Wales effective April 2000. A new Youth Justice Board for England and Wales oversees the work of the YOTs. It was significant that responsibility for establishing YOTs was not placed with a criminal justice agency. Rather, local authorities (municipalities) were required to set up partnerships that included the police, probation service, and health authorities. Smaller authorities were encouraged to set up joint arrangements with neighboring areas. These YOTs are multidisciplinary teams staffed by probation officers, social workers, police, and education and health staff.

The Crime and Disorder Act 1998 articulated a clear—and largely rehabilitative—philosophy for youth justice. It gave the whole system an overarching aim of preventing offending and reoffending, though the main task of YOTs is to respond to young offenders who have come to official notice. Key elements of youth justice now include

- the final warning scheme, which limits the scope for repeat cautioning (or warning) of offenders;
- rapid response by youth courts where young offenders reoffend;
- more open and accessible court procedures;
- early intervention to stop their offending;
- a range of new orders, such as Parenting Orders, Referral Orders, and Reparation Orders;
- secure Training Centres, overseen by the Youth Justice Board.

Some of these developments could be portrayed as examples of populist authoritarianism. For example, Parenting Orders place new responsibilities on parents to control their children's offending, and extra Secure Training Centres have been purchased from the private sector. However, the overall tenor of the system remains rehabilitative and restorative rather than punitive. Whether public confidence in youth justice recovers over the next few years remains to be seen, of course. It is unlikely that many people in England have the slightest idea of the considerable reforms that have occurred since 1998. If the public sense of a failing system remains unchanged, the philosophy of the youth justice system will remain vulnerable to attack from penal populists.

custody. Also, the government rejected a number of radical changes to the juvenile justice system (such as lowering the age of criminal responsibility). So far the public seems divided about the new act. A poll, conducted several months after it was introduced, found approximately half the sample thought that the proposals were "about right" (Stein, 1999). While this is far from a strong majority, it is much higher than the percentage of people who supported the previous Young Offenders Act.

What general lessons can be learned from this example? Or, more bluntly, how did the government succeed in introducing moderate legislation with respect to an issue so frequently the target of penal populism? There appear to be three explanations. First, the ruling Liberal government had a comfortable parliamentary majority when the legislation was introduced, and the polls indicated little reason to believe that this would change as a result of a general election. Policymakers may have felt more secure, knowing that another majority mandate was likely. Punitive responses to crime are clearly more likely to emerge when a government feels threatened by the prospect of being bundled out of office following an election.

Second, the government packaged the proposed act in such a way that it seemed to be tougher than it actually was. This explains why two youth justice experts described the new legislation as "A Sheep in Wolf's Clothing" (Doob and Sprott, 1999). Just prior to the official release of the proposed legislation, parts of the act appear to have been selectively leaked to the press. The media reported that the act would introduce a number of punitive provisions, which were highlighted in newspaper headlines. (For example, the bill expands the list of offenses for which a young offender would be presumptively liable, upon conviction, to an adult sentence). By the time the draft legislation was available, the perception of a relatively tough act had been absorbed by the media and transmitted to the public. Third, the government was aided by the rapid creation of a "consortium" of academics and practitioners who opposed passage of the bill, on the ground that it was *too* tough. This gave the government much-needed ammunition with which to respond to opposition politicians, provincial government critics, police organizations, and victims' advocacy groups, all of whom declared the new act to be insufficiently punitive. Whether the act will be accepted by the public is another matter; media coverage has contributed to widespread disenchantment with youth justice in Canada. [News Media]

Although the focus has been on Canada, the experience may be reflective of something of a "countercurrent" movement that is evident also in other countries. [Against the Punitive Tide]

Conclusion

As Zimring (1999) observes, "The 1990s have witnessed the broadest and most sustained legislative crackdown ever on serious offences committed by youth within the jurisdictional ages of American Juvenile Courts" (p. 260). This flurry of punitive responses to youth crime has not emerged because of any real increase in juvenile crime rates. If this "crackdown" was linked to an increase in juvenile crime, it should have occurred earlier, in the mid-1980s, when juvenile crime rates in America, particularly homicide rates, were increasing dramatically.

Over the course of this chapter, we have seen that most of the public concern about juvenile crime (and also criticism of the juvenile justice system's response) pertains to juveniles convicted of a serious crime of violence. Yet such offenders represent a very small proportion of all juveniles who come in contact with the law. Canadian statistics illustrate the point well. In 1999, there were approximately 2.5 million young persons within the age limits of juvenile crim-

News Media and Public Attitudes toward Juvenile Justice in Canada

Evidence of the power of the media to shape public perceptions comes from the Canadian experience with respect to juvenile justice. In 1984, the Juvenile Delinquents Act (JDA) was replaced by the Young Offenders Act (YOA). The new act stressed the concept of accountability, and while holding juveniles more accountable, also provided young persons in conflict with the law with more procedural protections. Members of the public were slow to learn about the new act: a survey conducted in 1992 found that half the sample admitted that they were "not at all" or "not very" familiar with the YOA (Decima Research, 1993). A poll conducted the next year found the public equally divided in terms of their evaluation of the act, half opposed and half the sample expressed support (Roberts, 1994). Thereafter, public opinion with respect to the act shifted dramatically. By the late 1990s, the public rated the youth justice system more negatively than any other component of criminal justice. By 1997, fully three-quarters of the population expressed "little or no" confidence in the YOA (Angus Reid, 1997). A year later, more than four out of five respondents (90%) identified reforming the YOA as an "important issue" for the government (Angus Reid, 1998). In fact, reforming the YOA was more important than balancing the budget or fixing the health care system, two traditional sources of anxiety for Canadians in the 1990s. So what changed the public's views?

The change in public attitudes to juvenile justice was not a reaction to escalating youth crime rates. The crime rate by young persons declined by a fully 40% during the period from 1991 to 1999, exactly when public attitudes toward the juvenile justice system were hardening. Nor was it a response to any changes to the statutory framework of youth justice that would result in more lenient treatment; as noted elsewhere in this volume, the YOA was amended three times during the period from 1984 to 1996, and each amendment made the system tougher. Finally, the change in public mood cannot be described as a response to more lenient dispositions being imposed. In fact, quite the opposite occurred. In 1987, less than one-quarter of cases in youth court resulted in a custodial term (Leesti, 1992). A decade later, the custody rate was over one-third (Carriere, 2000). So while crime rates declined, and the youth justice system became tougher, the Canadian public moved from a position of ambivalence toward the YOA, to one of heavy criticism.

The change in the public mood can plausibly be attributed to media coverage of the problem of youth crime. In particular, although there had been no change in the number of young persons accused of murder, there was extensive media coverage of several murders involving young people in the mid-1990s.

inal responsibility (12 to 17 years of age). In that year, 45 teenagers were charged with murder or manslaughter (Tremblay, 2000), and less than half of these were eventually convicted. Regrettably, the public are unaware of this statistical reality. Part of the public's punitiveness springs from ignorance of the volume (and seriousness) of juvenile offending and the actual severity of the criminal justice response.

Public views of justice for juvenile offenders are clearly more complex and tolerant than the policymakers have represented in their rush to pass punitive legislation. The best illustration of this comes from responses to a question on the British Crime Survey which asked people about ways of dealing with young

Against the Punitive Tide: Restorative Justice in Australia and New Zealand

Restorative justice is a broad movement that means different things to different people. At the core, however, is a concern for healing the damage caused by crime in a more productive way than is offered through formal, adversarial, and, above all, punitive methods of justice. Although still in its infancy—and not without its critics—restorative justice offers an alternative to punitive sentencing. In an era of punitive, mandatory sentencing, two developments in Australia and New Zealand involve reforms which feature the possibilities of using a restorative justice (RJ) approach for dealing with young offenders.

At the core of these initiatives has been the notion of conferencing and involves a meeting between the offender and the victim along with various families and supporters. The conference is generally mediated by a representative of one of the leading agencies such as police or justice. Most jurisdictions in Australia and New Zealand now have some form of conferencing, however, the method used and the types of offenders it applies to varies considerably (see Daly, 2000 for an overview). The first major piece of legislation introducing family group conferencing in New Zealand was the Children, Young Persons and Families Act of 1989. At the same time, John Braithwaite was writing his seminal work *Crime, Shame and Reintegration*. It is likely that the book combined with the implementation of the restorative scheme in New Zealand fostered the widespread interest in a positive approach to juvenile justice that appeared to offer a way out of many of the dilemmas in the field—the most important of which were victim dissatisfaction and ineffective sentencing. It is ironic that these efforts in Australia should be largely overshadowed by populist sentencing and the mandatory sentencing crisis of 2000. More details on restorative justice in Australia, including the article by Daly (2000), can be found at the Australian Institute of Criminology website: www.aic.gov.au.

Although most countries have witnessed an increasing punitiveness toward juvenile offenders through the 1990s, New Zealand in this period has been experimenting with an altogether new form of justice for juveniles. Restorative justice in New Zealand draws much of its inspiration from that country's Maori culture. Restorative principles permeate the Children, Young Persons and Families Act, introduced in New Zealand in 1989. This piece of legislation transformed new Zealand's approach to dealing with juveniles, most (estimated to be 80%) of whom are now diverted away from formal court proceedings. The intention was to allow most cases of juvenile offending to be mediated by appropriate parties, using a restorative approach. The most important part of the system is the family group conference. However, about one-quarter of cases are dealt with by police giving a warning (cautioning). About three-quarters of juvenile cases are dealt with by the Youth Aid section of the Police Department who approach the matter from a social casework perspective and consult with all the relevant parties and determine what informal sanctions are needed—usually this also amounts to a warning, but it can involve the making of an apology, providing reparation, or doing community work. In about 10% of cases, the family group conference procedure is used (see Brown and Young, 2000).

offenders. No single response attracted the support of even a quarter of the respondents. This finding is itself interesting because it undermines the position that the public feel that there is a single effective way of responding to youth crime, and that this way involves harsher punishment. Parental responsibility attracted the most support (one respondent in five). Harsher punishment was supported by only one out of 10 respondents (see Mattinson and Mirrlees-Black, 2000, table 4.4). In an era in which punitive measures are advanced as solutions to juvenile offending, the public have not lost their ability to express understanding and compassion for juvenile offenders.

8 Sex Offenders and Sexual Predators

No form of offending provokes greater public condemnation and desire to punish than crimes of sexual aggression, especially when the victims are children. These tragic crimes attract intense news media attention, and punitive legislation often emerges in the wake of this coverage. Also, it is with respect to sexual offenders that the most extreme outbursts of "street" punitiveness occur, as witnessed by the attacks in England against innocent people suspected of being pedophiles (see chapter 3). Surveys suggest that many people believe that sex offending is on the rise, and that there has been an increase in the number of sexual predators. Unfortunately, such crimes have always occurred, although they were less likely to come to official attention in previous decades. We begin this chapter by discussing penal policy responses to sex offending in several countries and then examine the research that has accumulated on public attitudes toward this form of offending. Our thesis is that populist politicians have exploited the widespread public concern about sexual offending to pass punitive legislation that only poorly addresses the true nature of the problem of sexual aggression. This chapter discusses how politicians and the media have shifted public focus toward sexual predators, which diverts public attention away from the more prevalent and equally serious forms of sexual offending such as child molestation and rape by family members and acquaintances.

Although many people believe that the frequency of sex offending is increasing, there is little convincing evidence that this is, in fact, the case. There is also nothing particularly new about public demands for the harsh punishment of sex offenders. In the 1990s, in an era dominated by technologies of control and risk assessment, many people have called for greater surveillance of these offenders, including electronic monitoring and other such devices. The latest proposal is to employ the Global Positioning System (GPS) to monitor the location of offenders with convictions for crimes of sexual aggression involving children, and is being used in some jursdictions in the United States and is being considered in the United Kingdom. Another change in the 1990s is the degree to which politicians are willing to place themselves at the forefront of those advocating harsher punishments for this category of offender. It is as if politicians fear being usurped by more alert political opportunists also claiming the prize of media attention and public popularity.

For example, after media coverage of a child who was raped and murdered in New Zealand, legislators quickly came in line with media and public calls to enact more punitive sentencing laws for sex offenders (Thorp, 1997). Similarly, media reports appear regularly in the United States, Great Britain, Australia, and Canada about paroled sex offenders committing sexual assault and murder involving young children. Politicians debated (and subsequently enacted) legislation creating more stringent prison sentences for sex offenders and passed other laws to tighten controls on sex offenders serving sentences in the community.

These laws, which allow very long prison sentences in cases of a violent or sexual offender, were promoted on the promise that the community would thereby be better protected (Ashworth, 1997; Freiberg, 1997a, b; La Fond, 1998; Pratt, 1998b; Thorp, 1997). Several states have also created indefinite detention for sexual predators through a civil procedure that confined sexual predators until they were rehabilitated.[1] California became the first state to create a law requiring sex offenders convicted twice of molesting a child under 13 years old to undergo chemical castration, and Florida, Georgia, and Louisiana have passed similar laws (Miller, 1998). A law in the United Kingdom enacted in 1996 created a mandatory life sentence for offenders convicted of a second serious violent or sexual offense (see Hough & Roberts, 1998). In 1995, the Louisiana state legislature enacted a law allowing courts to impose the death penalty for aggravated rape, where the victim is a child under the age of 12 (Schaaf, 2000).[2]

Such legislation is often accepted more because of the moral indignation it satisfies than its ability to make the community safer from sexual offenders. While there may be some marginal gains in safety, the cost (both in financial and humanitarian terms) of such policies is great. If the ultimate goal is community safety, then these laws would need to be subjected to much more scrutiny. A more appropriate cost-benefit analysis would include a comparison of how the money spent on punishment might otherwise be spent on preventing these incidents from occurring. In addition to these populist measures, both the United States and Canada have created specialized intensive supervision probation and parole programs for sex offenders that provide intensive supervision and treatment.[3] These programs are far more cost-effective than the lengthy incarceration sentences. For example, Arizona has an intensive supervision parole program that imposes life-time probation, weekly counseling sessions, routine polygraph tests, and random home searches on released sex offenders (Gordon, 1998).

These programs were designed in response to the perception that the level of supervision associated with standard probation and parole, which typically requires only one office visit per month, is insufficient for many sex offenders. Many sex offenders are now sentenced to these intensive supervision probation programs (see English, Pullen & Jones, 1996), and preliminary evaluations suggest that they have a more positive effect of keeping offenders under control in the community than do standard probation programs (Stalans, Seng & Yarnold,

2001; Berliner, Schram, Miller & Milloy, 1995). Moreover, the programs are more cost effective than sexual predator laws (La Fond, 1998). The annual cost of the lifetime probation program in Arizona is $1,400 per offender compared to an annual cost of between $60,300 to $127,750 per offender to incarcerate or civily commit sexual predators under the sexual predator laws (La Fond, 1998). The fact that few people are willing to question the efficacy of spending money on incarcerating sex offenders indefinitely relieves politicians of both responsibility and accountability. It also reveals the ascendancy of neoconservative influences over neoliberal influences on New Right penal policies (O'Malley, 1999).

Evolving Public Views of Sex Offenders

In the 1990s, a great deal of attention focused on child sexual abuse and sexual violence against adults. The public has come to perceive child sexual abuse as a serious or major problem that causes great emotional and physical harm to victims (Alabama Poll, 1995; Tabachnick, Haydenville & Denny, 1997). The public also believe that it is quite prevalent among children; for example, half of the respondents to a Kentucky poll estimated that 35% or more of children have been victimized (Kentucky Poll, 1992). Moreover, among women, fear of sexual assault is a common experience. For example, a national opinion poll conducted in the United States in 1995 found that almost half the female respondents (47%) and almost a third of the male (29%) were frequently worried that they or someone in their family will be sexually assaulted. Respondents indicated that they more often worried about sexual assault and burglary than becoming a victim of any other crime (Haghigh & Sorensen, 1996).

The evolving societal image of sex offenders is, in part, responsible for this widespread public apprehension. When people think about sex offenders, predatory stranger rapists and child molesters most readily come to mind. As discussed earlier, Surette (1994) has demonstrated the importance of the image of the sexual predator to the media. The public is, it seems, highly influenced by media coverage of this problem. The public is far less likely to define sex offending in terms of the less serious offenses, such as flashing or voyeurism, which in reality account for significant proportions of offenders.

Public knowledge of the nature of sex offenses involving children has undergone a transformation over the last decade. In 1985, the child-protection movement in the United States focused on incest cases and attributed sexual abuse primarily to fathers, stepfathers, or grandfathers of victims, and these offenders were perceived as treatable (Jenkins, 1998). Thus, the child-protection movement in the mid-1980s provided reliable information about the individuals who most often sexually abused children. However, due in part to the changing rape shield laws and a number of high profile child molester cases involving strangers, the public focus shifted away from incest to repeat child molesters in the mid-1990s.

Media stories began to emphasize the predatory nature of child molesters by using the term "sexual predator." While the term sexual predator was never used in the 1980s, by 1995, 924 media stories had employed the phrase (Jenkins, 1998). These stories have used the label sexual predators to represent sexual offenders as an unmanageable threat to the community (Simon, 1998). The image of the sexual predator is consistent with the extensive media exploitation of this archetype in a number of Hollywood films. The public's attention is drawn once again to the most extreme forms of sexual assault: where strangers commit sexual assault and physical violence against young children or where strangers commit serial rapes at random against adult women. In reality, sexual predators and serial sex killers are very rare. However, their appeal to the media is undeniable. The consequence is that public apprehension about this rare form of sexual violence is inflamed, and public interest is diverted away from the far more prevalent forms of offending.

The image of a sex offender has been shifted from someone in the immediate family to strangers and possibly friends, and from an immoral (but treatable) behavior to an incurable and dangerous perversion that is often promoted by organized groups ("rings") of pedophiles. Along with this evolution in the public's views about sex offenders, penal policy has evolved from a need to treat sex offenders to a philosophy of simply warehousing offenders who are perceived to be incurable (Simon, 1998). This populist punitiveness is hostile to treatment and focuses on managing high-risk offenders by means of the imposition and threat of severe punishment (Simon, 1998). The most widely accepted treatment for sex offenders, cognitive behavioral group therapy (which focuses on relapse prevention), recognizes that sex offenders will remain at risk of committing new offenses throughout their lives. However, this therapy focuses on teaching offenders to manage their risk and stop the cycle of sexual assault before actually committing another sex crime.

Survey research has demonstrated the societal shift away from the perception of familial, curable incest offender and toward the incurable dangerous repeat pedophile. A 1995 survey in Alabama revealed that strangers, adult friends, and familiars other than parents were believed to be the three types of people who are the most frequent sexual abusers against children (Alabama Poll, 1995). The majority of respondents in a representative survey believed that child molesters were incurable and could not stop their offending, even if motivated to do so (Tabachnick, Haydenville & Denny, 1997).

Many people can neither forgive nor forget the acts of child sexual abuse. Evidence of the intransigence of public views of sex offenders comes from research that has explored reactions to ex-offenders. A recent survey of North American Roman Catholics concerning their views of priests who have been convicted of child sexual abuse found that respondents were divided on whether a priest who sexually abuses children should be allowed to return to the ministry (Rossetti, 1995). The biggest proportion (42%) supported expelling the priest from further ministry, 31% were unsure, and 27% believed the priest should be allowed to return to the priesthood. Only half (51%) would accept a former priest who had undergone treatment back into their parish, whereas 27% were unsure, and 22% would not accept the priest back.

These results demonstrate that even religious persons (for whom forgiveness constitutes a critical element of their faith) are reluctant to forgive and allow a child molester to return to a position of moral authority. Furthermore, over two-thirds of the polled adults in England opposed the placement of a treatment center for sex offenders in their community and indicated that they would take action to prevent creation of such a center. Similarly, 75% stated that they would be unwilling to rent a flat to a sex offender who has undergone treatment, and 37% would never hire a convicted sex offender (Brown, 1999). Unlike other offenders, for whom the public can countenance reintegration, sex offenders are clearly seen as a category apart.

Movements in Great Britain, Canada, and Australia also have shifted the emphasis from incest to sexual attacks by strangers with an incurable condition. These countries have relied on American authorities and turned their focus to less prevalent and organized forms of child sexual abuse such as organized pedophiles, satanic and ritualistic sexual abuse, on-line pedophiles, and serial pedophiles or molesters. The mass media in these countries were receptive to the feminist criticism that the media focused too much attention on stranger-to stranger rapes, organized pedophile rings, and repeat offenders. This receptiveness, however, was short-lived after the passage of rape reform laws in the mid-1980s which did not fully support the ideology underlying feminist views of sexual assault. A study of the content of sexual assault stories in Canada's newspapers before and after the rape reform laws found that the passage of the laws appeared to have affected the content of news stories on rape (Los & Chamard, 1997). Newspaper coverage after the reform law was passed included many articles on acquaintance and date rapes. Articles on date rape, however, portrayed women victims as often contributing to the attack or lying about the assault. The media reports did little to buttress feminists' views of sexual assault, and actually reinforced the public view that real rapes involve strangers, random attacks, and the infliction of physical injuries.

Media stories on child sexual abuse also failed to support feminists' attempts to highlight the reality that a great deal of sexual abuse occurs in families. In New Zealand, media accounts began to promote the view of child sexual abuse as extremely pathological behavior that could not occur in normal families (Atmore, 1996). Most interestingly, when incest cases were covered in the media, the emphasis was on the ways in which feminists had pressured government officials to accuse innocent fathers and how therapists had fostered the misdiagnosis of sexual abuse (Atmore, 1996). Media stories have reinforced and created misconceptions about sexual assaults and have not supported the transformation in public conceptions of sexual assault that law reforms attempted to accomplish.

Consistent with media accounts, individuals from a variety of backgrounds perceive an allegation of sexual assault to be most credible when a stranger accosts a woman on a street with a weapon and inflicts injuries during the rape (Williams & Holmes, 1981). Earlier research by Kalven and Zeisel (1966) found that juries acquitted defendants of rape in only 12% of cases involving strangers or injuries, but 60% of the cases in which none of these aggravating factors were present but where the judge would convict. The public appears to regard sexual assault victims with more skepticism if the perpetrator is a spouse, dating partner, or acquaintance. In these situations, the public defines an event as a sexual assault if the perpetrator used force, inflicted visible injuries, or if the victim had resisted the assault. Members of the public attribute less responsibility to the victim and more responsibility to the perpetrator, as the force of the perpetrator and resistance of the victim increases.

The public in all of these countries endorses misconceptions about sexual assault that condone and support violence and force under some circumstances. Moreover, these misconceptions about sexual assault are formed before adulthood. For example, a survey of Australian adolescents found that their stereotypical view of sexual assault was very similar to the stereotypes found in research with adults (Davis & Lee, 1996). Most adolescents believed that rape generally involved a perpetrator using violence and carrying a weapon, and one-third of the boys believed that the rapist would be a stranger. At least 40% of the adolescents subscribed to a number of myths about rape, for example, that women often lie about being victims of sexual assault, and that men cannot control themselves when they are sexually aroused (for a review of the rape myth research, see Roberts & Stalans, 1997). Furthermore, Wells and Motley (2001) argue that the sexual predator laws have reinforced rape myths such as the "crazed rapist," especially in light of the fact that sexual predator laws are limited to offenders who victimize strangers in some states (e.g., Missouri and Washington) or refer to "mental abnormalities."

Public Knowledge of Sentencing Practices in Crimes of Sexual Aggression

Members of the public in all jurisdictions surveyed tend to be ill-informed about sentencing practices involving offenders convicted of sexual assault. Before demonstrating the public's lack of knowledge about sentencing of sex offenders, some statistics on sentencing patterns will illustrate the severity of penalties imposed on sex offenders. Approximately 82% of convicted rapists in the United States and 95% of convicted rapists in England are imprisoned (Langan & Farrington, 1998). Sentences for rape were significantly longer in the United States than the United Kingdom. For those sentenced to prison, judges in the United States imposed an average sentence of 10 years, which remained stable from 1985 to 1993. However, the actual time served increased from 1985 to 1993 from three and a half years to five years (Greenfeld, 1997).

In England, the average term of imprisonment imposed was 6.4 years in 1994, an increase of three years from the previous decade (Langan & Farrington, 1998). Convicted sex offenders imprisoned for sex offenses other than rape experienced the second highest growth in prison population with an annual average increase of 15%, while the number of rapists grew an annual average of 7% from 1980 to 1994 (Greenfeld, 1997).[4] Canadian sentencing statistics show a similar pattern. In the mid-1990s, while the number of crimes recorded by the police declined, and with no apparent increase in the seriousness of offenses appearing before the courts, the length of sentences imposed on sex offenders increased by 50% (Roberts & Grimes, 2000). These statistics suggest that sentencing practices have become more punitive in recent years, and that populism may, in part, be responsible.

The public rarely has statistical information about sentencing patterns for sex offenders. Instead, atypical cases portraying lenient sentences are highlighted in the media, and the public assumes that such cases are representative of standard practice in the courts (Hough and Roberts, 1998). Fewer than one person in five in England could correctly estimate (within 10% of the right figure) the proportion of convicted rapists actually sent to prison; the remainder of the sample gave estimates that were too low, and more than half of these provided estimates that were large underestimates of the correct figure (Hough & Roberts, 1998, pp. 13–15).

Similarly, in the United States, many respondents underestimated the amount of time that sex offenders serve in prison (Illinois Policy Survey, 1997). Canadian data, too, show that the public underestimated the severity of sentences imposed on offenders convicted of sexual assault (Doob and Roberts, 1988). In this punitive climate, the public endorses longer prison sentences for child sexual abusers in the absence of knowledge about sentencing practices (Skibinski & Esser-Stuart, 1993). The belief that sex offenders are getting off lightly is an important influence on the way in which public views of sentencing are shaped. First, the perception itself reflects and expresses moral indignation regarding this type of offender. Second, the spectre of sex offenders evading adequate punishment also captures the news media's attention, thereby reinforcing the public perception of excessive leniency.

Public Preferences for Sentencing Sex Offenders

A common perception in all countries is that offenders convicted of sex crimes are not punished severely enough. A member of the public reading a brief description of a sex offender will tend to imagine a repeat offender who has molested a great number of children. This image will then influence public sentencing preferences. As with drug trafficking offenses, violence is a defining characteristic that generates a punitive response from the public. For example, one study found that over half of the sample selected the death penalty or life without parole as the preferred sentence for a first-time child molester, and 86% selected these harsh punishments for a repeat child molester when provided with a description of child sexual abuse (Alabama Poll, 1994).[5] In response to general questions, Canadian female students wanted sex offenders to serve at least two years in prison and receive treatment (Vallient, Furac and Antonowicz, 1994).

In the case of stranger assaults on adult women, the public overwhelming endorses the use of long prison sentences. Almost all respondents in England (94%) endorsed the imposition of a prison term for rapists, which is, in fact, quite congruent with actual sentencing practices (Hough, Moxon & Lewis, 1987). The majority of respondents in two American surveys supported prison for a first-time offender who raped a woman in a park (Doble, 1997). (The average sentence for a stranger who uses force to rape is 13.4 prison years [Robinson & Darley, 1995]). Similarly, when given a choice between a community-based sanction with mandatory counseling or a prison sentence, 94% of North Carolina respondents endorsed prison for a man who stalked and viciously raped a college student (Doble, 1995). A sample of adults in England supported treatment for sex offenders in prison, but were opposed to sentencing sex offenders to treatment alone, without any element of punishment (Brown, 1999).

The public, however, is less certain about how to sentence offenders who do not fit the image of the perpetrator as a violent stranger or predator against children. Some offenses such as statutory rape and date rape elicit an ambivalent response from the public. Respondents in research by John Doble recommended the use of alternatives to imprisonment for a first-time offender convicted of statutory rape of a 15-year-old girl (Doble, 1995; Farkas, 1997). Although all respondents recommended that the perpetrator of stranger assault receive some form of punishment, fewer (71%) respondents recommended that the perpetrator of a sexual assault against a date companion be punished (Robinson & Darley, 1995).

Public debates about high-profile "date rape" cases (such as the William Kennedy Smith case) also illustrate the ambivalence and controversy that surround the labeling of forced sexual assault on a date as a criminal offense equivalent to a sexual assault against a stranger. Moreover, if two people are living together and are in the process of a separation, a substantial proportion of respondents oppose the imposition of any punishment for forced intercourse if the victim was in a common-law living arrangement (31%), if the act was against a spouse (66%), or if the act was against a homosexual partner (66%) (Robinson & Darley, 1995). Other research supports this pattern of less severe punishment for forced intercourse as the intimacy of the prior relationship increases (Sigler, 1995).

The Case of Incest Offenses

Politicians and the media in the last decade have been silent about the harm caused to incest victims and have failed to provide adequate laws that would protect victims from further sexual abuse by family members. Victimization by family members represents a significant proportion of child sexual abuse. Family members committed just over one-third of all sex crimes against children, and abused 49% of the victims under age 6, 42% of children between the ages of 6 and 11, and 24% of adolescents (Snyder, 2000). Furthermore, many of the young victims may remain silent and not report the abuse, which will create a false sense that incest offenders have lower recidivism. Incest offenders that prey on young vulnerable children commit considerable harm relative to other types of sex offenders. There is considerable evidence that incest victims, because of the trust and dependence on the parental relationship, suffer more psychological and social harm both in the short-term and long-term than do victims from stranger or acquaintance molestation or rape (for a review of this research, see Lurigio, Jones & Smith, 1995). Research also suggests that incest offenders can be very tenacious, repeat offenders. In an anonymous survey, 159 of the 561 incest offenders that violated girls reported 12,927 sexual abuse acts against 286 victims, which also included victims that were acquaintances (Abel et al., 1987). These findings suggest that many incest offenders prey on children as much as the stranger sexual predator that politicians and the media have constructed.

Given this evidence, it is puzzling that politicians divert public attention to the infrequent stranger sexual predators. Researchers also have not focused much attention on public views of the appropriate punishment for incest. Moreover, when research has assessed public views, the questions often present inaccurate or inappropriate descriptions of incest. For example, in one study respondents were asked how they would sentence an incest case involving a 45-year-old man who fondled his stepdaughter without her consent after "she initially encouraged him" (Doble, 1995, p. 49). In this case, respondents were almost evenly divided between choosing prison or an alternative sanction. As formulated, however, this question provides a distorted view of incest, one which implies the complicity of the victim.[6]

Moreover, research has demonstrated that the lay public, mental health professionals, child protective professionals, and criminal justice professionals attribute more blame to adolescent victims of incest than to prepubescent victims (Maynard & Wiederman, 1997; Eisenberg, Owens & Dewey, 1987; Reidy & Hochstadt, 1993; Waterman & Foss-Goodman, 1984), though the majority of the blame is attributed to the perpetrator. A small percentage of professionals (3% to 5%) in several studies indicated that the father initiated the incest as a result of the child's seductive behavior (Eisenberg et al., 1987; Johnson, Owens, Dewey & Eisenberg, 1990), and one-third of a sample of law enforcement officers and 69% of child protective service workers in a rural county in the United

States indicated that 15-year-old and 13-year-old daughters were just as guilty as the father when sexual penetration occurred (Wilk and McCarthy, 1986).

Do incest offenders receive more lenient treatment from the U.S. criminal justice system? A few studies have found that incest offenders are less likely to be arrested and formally charged in the criminal justice system than nonfamilial sex offenders (see Stroud, Martens & Barker, 2000), but if convicted and sentenced to prison, they serve a comparable length of prison time as child molesters who victimize children outside their family (Simon, 1996; Levesque, 2000). These studies, however, have not determined whether incest offenders are more likely to be sentenced to probation. Clearly, more research is needed to determine whether in actual practice prosecutors and judges treat incest offenders more leniently than child molesters who victimize children outside the family.

If mitigated punishments are imposed for incest crimes, they have not arisen as a result of their popularity with the public. One survey has assessed public support for this discount. The vast majority of Alabama respondents (87%) disagreed with the statement that the court should treat first-time child sexual abusers who abuse their own children more leniently than other sex abusers (Skibinski & Esser-Stuart, 1993). Other jurisdictions such as England and Canada have legislation that makes incest an aggravating factor in child molestation, which should result in a harsher punishment.[7]

Juvenile Sex Offenders

Politicians and the media have also ignored another important feature of sex offenses: children often sexually abuse other children. Studies show that children between the ages of six and 12 are responsible for up to 18% of all substantiated child sexual abuse crimes in the United States (Pithers and Gray, 1998). Compared to adults, child offenders are twice as likely to be a victim of a sexual assault, and these victims may develop sexual behavior problems that lead to abusing other children. Children and adolescents were the perpetrators of sexual crimes in one-third of the children referred to treatment for sexual behavioral problems (Pithers and Gray, 1998). When children abuse children, a double tragedy occurs, and one that is difficult to respond to effectively and fairly. With the increasing punitiveness toward juvenile offenders, many of these offenders will not receive any treatment and will be incarcerated beyond the age of majority. It is likely that they will commit additional sexual crimes when they are eventually released from prison.

Some jursidictions are experimenting with alternatives. New Zealand and South Australia have a unique early intervention that may be an effective way of handling juvenile crimes that involve sexual abuse. The government of New Zealand, from the Maori culture, has adopted the use of family group conferences to control juvenile sexual offenders; these conferences were later developed in jurisdictions in Australia with some variations. Braithwaite and Daly (1998) describe the family group conferences as "citizenship ceremonies of reintegrative shaming." The family group conferences are used for a wide range of juvenile offenses, and sexual offense accounts for about 1% of all conferences (Daly, 2000). From 1994 through 1998, there were 92 conferences for juvenile sex offenders in South Australia.

The offender's family or other community members who care about the offender, the victim's supporters, the offender, the victim, and the police are invited to attend a conference. All parties discuss the impact of the offense and are encouraged to suggest a plan of action. Victims and their supporters must agree on the plan of action before it is accepted by government representatives. A number of benefits can emerge. The offender's family and supporters are better able to understand and appreciate the harm. The conference coordinator and the dialogue may confront stereotypical beliefs of the offender and his supporters, which may reduce the likelihood of further offending. And finally, the conference typically ends with the offender making an apology to the victim.

The plan of action adopted may include extended family and parents watching and keeping track of the offender more closely, the offender entering a formal treatment program, the offender making an active effort to clear rumors that placed the blame on the victim, and other productive strategies. New Zealand is so committed to these conferences that it often pays the travel costs of offenders' relatives, when there are no immediate family or friends in the local area. Family conferences are obviously in the experimental stage, but there are encouraging signs documented in Daly's work for this method to offer better outcomes for the victim, the offender, and the community, particularly in regard to juvenile sex offenders on less serious charges.[8]

Other Criminal Justice Responses to Sexual Offending

Not all the legislation that has been introduced to respond to sex offenders involves the sentencing process. Extraordinary measures with respect to sex offenders have been proposed and enacted that test the boundaries of the criminal law, sometimes involving the imposition of sanctions in the absence of a conviction. Although these laws have been justified on the grounds of community safety, very little research has evaluated their effectiveness.

Community Notification

Most states in the United States have enacted laws requiring sex offenders to register with law enforcement or a central registry. By the mid-1990s, 32 states had enacted community notification statutes that made information about sex offenders available to the public through dissemination by law enforcement authorities to the relevant community or through the request of specific individuals (Finn, 1997). Over half the states have developed a website that allows the public to obtain information about where sex offenders live in their community and provides a picture of the sex offender along with information about his convicted sex offense (see Adams, 1999). A judge in Texas recently took community notification even further when he ordered sex offenders to erect signs in their yards saying "Danger: Convicted Sex Offender Resides Here" and to drive with bumper stickers stating "Danger! Registered Sex Offender." The limited evidence, from newspaper letters to the editor, with respect to public reaction suggests that most people oppose such "disintegrative shaming" sentences (Corpus Christi, May 20, 2001).

The most well-known sex offender registration and notification statute was named Megan's Law, in memory of a 7-year-old girl, Megan Kanka, who was raped and murdered by her neighbor, a convicted sex offender. Megan's mother argued that if she had known that a sex offender was living next door she would have taken greater precautions with Megan. In response to public demand, within a month of Megan's death, New Jersey legislators passed a sex offender registration and notification law (Jenkins, 1998). These notification laws typically require convicted felony sex offenders to register for a 10-year period, and offenders convicted as sexual predators to register for the remainder of their lives, and allow the release of this information to the public.

England and Wales have also enacted a registration requirement in the Sex Offender Act of 1997 that requires offenders to register with police departments and keep police informed of their home address (Plotnikoff & Wolfson, 2000). The British parliament also was under pressure from the media and public in 1997 to enact a community notification law similar to "Megan's Law" so that the public would be informed of the whereabouts of convicted sex offenders. Parliament created the registry requirement but rejected the idea of enacting a community notification law after receiving advice from police and probation authorities (Dean, 2000). This is an interesting example of political restraint in the face of public pressure. Ontario created a sex offender registry in the spring of 2000, although the federal government has yet to indicate whether it will follow suit. In contrast to the United States providing the public with open access to information about where sex offenders reside through a simple click on a website or requesting the information from the police department, England and Canada created registries for police use but do not allow public access; these registries are a more benign response to controlling sex offenders.

Preventive Sentencing

Some jurisdictions have created preventive sentencing provisions that limit the freedom of individuals alleged to pose a risk of committing sexual offenses. A good example can be found in section 810.1 (1) of the Canadian *Criminal Code*. This provision permits anyone who fears on reasonable grounds that another person will commit a crime of sexual aggression against a juvenile to lay such information before a judge. The court will then cause the parties to appear, and if the judge is satisfied that the informant has reasonable grounds for his or her apprehension, the defendant will be ordered to sign a recognizance and to comply with a number of conditions. If the defendant (who is not, it is important to note, even suspected of having committed a crime) refuses to enter into the recognizance, or if he violates the conditions of the recognizance, he may be sentenced to up to a year in prison. The recognizance is renewable year after year. The potential offender can therefore be subject to considerable restrictions on his freedom for a sustained period of time. The provision has proven popular with Crown counsel and the police, but has been criticized by civil libertarians and by academics in the area of sentencing. Critics have argued that it involves the imposition of a punishment in the absence of any evidence of wrongdoing.

Allowing Propensity Evidence in Sex Offense Trials

In the United States, evidence about the character of the defendant or his/her prior arrests or convictions is not admissible at trial. Congress, however, has changed the evidentiary laws for sex offender cases, with the result that propensity evidence regarding prior arrests or convictions of sex offenses can now be introduced at trial. The purpose of the new federal rule of evidence (413–415) is to increase the likelihood of conviction; however, courts have great discretion to interpret the rule and can deny propensity evidence if it is more prejudicial than probative. It appears that courts are more willing to allow propensity evidence in stranger rape cases and child molestation cases than in acquaintance rape cases (Wells & Motley, 2001).

Public Support for Strategies to Prevent Sexual Assaults

How much public support do these measures attract? Consistent with their response to reducing crime in general, the public endorses a wide range of strategies to respond to sexual offenders. The majority of respondents indicated that it is very important for parents to teach children to report all cases of sexual abuse by relatives, teachers, or other adults (California Poll, 1986). The public, in general, also believes that several agencies should intervene to prevent child sexual abuse, including social service agencies, law enforcement, churches, mental health professionals, and courts.

Most respondents endorsed the use of a wide range of sanctions for all sex offenders, including mandatory treatment, incarceration, and compensation in the form of reimbursement for treatment for the victim and his or her family (Alabama Poll, 1995). Moreover, respondents want the criminal justice system to prosecute a higher percentage of sex offenders and impose longer prison sentences, but at the same time to restrict the need for the child's testimony (Skibinski & Esser-Stuart, 1993). Most respondents also oppose diversion programs, in which the offender agrees to participate in a treatment program, and as a result, no conviction is registered (Skibinski & Esser-Stuart, 1993). This suggests that the public sees the purpose of the sanction as consisting of more than just curing the offender; they want the criminal law to make a statement about the criminal conduct. Public responses to sexual offending thus go beyond the utilitarian goal of reducing the risk of reoffending.

Conclusion

Conservative politicians have enacted simplistic punitive sentencing measures in response to public outrage over high profile, extremely violent cases of child sexual abuse. It is clear that the public demands more severe punishment for crimes that involve violence. Consistent with this theme, public preferences for long prison sentences for sex offenders also depend on whether there was violence, physical harm, or the threat of physical harm with a weapon. Additionally, the public defines sexual assaults as more serious and deserving of punitive measures if children are involved, even if they are family members.

However, as we have seen, public views do not (and cannot) exist in isolation. There is a synergistic relationship between public reaction, the media, and political initiative. The lead, and therefore the control, almost entirely lies with the latter two components. In this context, then, politicians have a weighty responsibility to sift through fact, fiction, and justifiable indignation. If everyone agrees that the goal is community safety, it is incumbent on politicians to offer more than just punitive responses. They have an important role in providing information and leadership to communities alarmed by media coverage of the problem. Once the media hyperbole subsides and emotions cool, the public is left with ineffective laws that address only a small minority of cases.

By defining crimes of sexual aggression in terms of sexual predators, penal populists have helped to keep the vast majority of sexual assault and abuse cases in the shadows. Sexual crimes are disproportionately committed against children who are family members or acquaintances. This form of offending that causes serious harm to its victims has not been brought to the attention of members of the public, whose eyes remain fixed on the image of predators. The result is an inappropriate response to sexual aggression. Disproportionately long and indeterminate sentences for "sexual predators" are costly and create strain on overcrowded correctional and mental health systems. The greater cost, however, may well be the indirect result: public attention is directed away from the majority of sexual assaults committed against family members and intimate partners. An additional effect of this emphasis on the sexual predator may well be a depreciation of the seriousness of familial sexual assault when seen against a background of sexual predators.

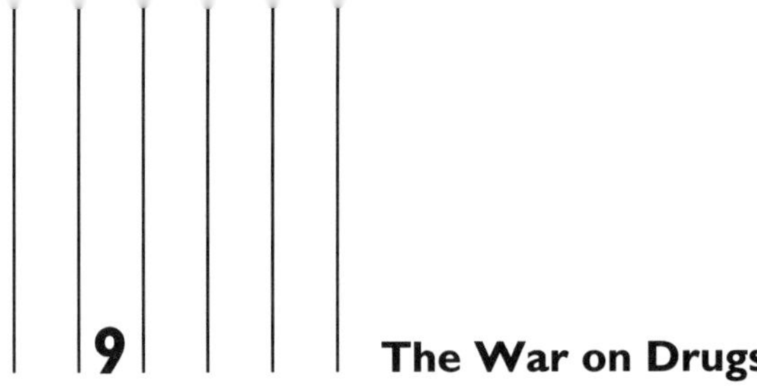

9 The War on Drugs

Politicians around the world have campaigned long and hard against drug offenders, who are often held up as the most visible (and harmful) evidence of declining moral standards. As such, they have been frequent targets of "get tough" campaigns in several countries, particularly in the United States. The "War on Crime" conducted around the world over the last two decades has focused considerable attention on protecting public safety through the imposition of harsher sentences on offenders convicted of drug crimes. Evidence of this can be found in the fact that the United States, Canada, the United Kingdom, and one Australian State (Queensland)[1] have all instituted mandatory minimum prison sentences for some drug offenses.

Although these laws are usually promoted as a means of stopping the drug trade, in reality, the people usually affected are the easy targets—the casual user. For example, in 1994, approximately two-thirds of all drug-related arrests in Canada were for simple possession (Fischer, 1998, p. 163, 171); in Australia, simple use of cannabis accounts for approximately three-quarters of all drug charges.[2] In England in 1999, 90% of drug offenders were cautioned or found guilty of unlawful possession, with the majority of charges involving possession of marijuana (Ramsay and Partridge, 1999). Of the more than 1.5 million arrests in the United States in 1994 for drug-law violations, 80% were for simple possession (Drugs and Crime Facts, 2001), and drug offenders accounted for 21% of the state prison population and 59% of the federal prison population in 1998 (ONDCP, 2001). Indeed, it is America's "War on Drugs" that is often seen as the major cause of its steeply rising incarceration rate (see Blumstein and Beck, 1999). Although political trends, issues, and public attitudes move on, the legislation left on the statute books lingers. The consequences of this legislation are economic and will continue to consume valuable government resources well into the future.

Penal populism is evident in the U.S. politicians' creation of a War on Drugs, and this chapter explores Americans' growing intolerance with that War. The American politicians' War on Drugs is placed in an international context as trends and drug policies in European countries, Canada, Australia, and New Zealand are explored. Within each country there are jurisdictions that take a different approach to drug crimes. This chapter focuses on salient aspects of the relationship between public opinion and drug policies. Politicians have enacted several harsh mandatory prison terms for drug crimes in anticipation that the public would support such laws. Scientific surveys that have compared public opinion to the current penal laws provide evidence that politicians did not accurately perceive public views' about drug users and traffickers. This chapter highlights the areas of drug policy that do not attract public support. For example, the public believes that current mandatory prison terms for drug traffickers who use violence are too lenient, whereas current laws requiring mandatory prison terms for marijuana possession are too harsh.

We first describe how the U.S. War on Drugs began and then highlight the public's growing intolerance with this war. We question whether the United States started such a war because of more serious drug abuse problems compared to other countries, and discuss the war's ineffectiveness at reducing drug abuse. We then turn to public support for penal policies associated with this war. We start with the "harder" illicit drugs such as heroin and cocaine and then turn to public support in all five countries for decriminalizing marijuana and for allowing the use of medicinal marijuana, where doctors can prescribe marijuana to alleviate symptoms affecting terminally ill or seriously ill individuals. In this discussion, we highlight active measures that the public has taken to oppose some of the tough penalties and how politicians have responded to this public opposition. The political responses have ranged from discrediting public views to active interference with the public will.

The American "War on Drugs"

The "War on Drugs" began with some states adopting harsh mandatory sentencing laws for possession of illicit drugs. In 1973, New York legislators passed the first mandatory sentencing laws (the Rockefeller Drug Laws), which mandated a sentence between 15 years to life in prison for possession of four ounces of narcotics. Many other states as well as the federal government soon enacted similarly harsh, mandatory sentences for drug possession and trafficking. Beckett (1997) shows that rather than riding a wave of public concern about drugs, policymakers and politicians initiated and maintained this concern about drugs. She argues that the war on drugs allowed the conservative forces in power in the United States through the 1980s to shift attention away from the underlying causes of crime, such as unemployment and inequality, toward drug use.

Evidence that politicians created, rather than responded to, public concern can be found in several public opinion polls (Beckett, 1997). In early 1986, polls revealed that only 3% of the public was "most concerned" about drugs. Even after all the publicity and the anti-drug initiatives of the government, only one-third of the public in 1989 identified drugs as the most important social problem. When politicians and the media stimulate public concern, it is often short-lived, and this is the case with drug abuse. When asked to describe the single most important problem facing our country, only 5% polled in 2000 identified drug abuse (Drugs and Crime Facts, 2000). Moreover, when asked to identify the two most important issues for the government to address, during the period from 1993 to 1999, less than 10% of Americans cited drugs (Sourcebook of Criminal Justice Statistics Online, 1999).[3] In response to the media blitz, politicians have introduced initiatives, claiming they were legitimated by the "growing public concern about drugs," sometimes even claiming specifically that polls demonstrated this growing public concern. However, when pressed, it seemed that politicians took, as their evidence of public concern, the amount of media attention given to the issue.

Although conservatives such as President Reagan were elected to office promising to deal with street *crime*, they eventually shifted the focus to street *drugs*. The War on Drugs escalated under Reagan with Nancy Reagan leading the "Just Say No" campaign that advocated abstinence from all drug use. Media campaigns warned of the harmful effects of drugs and how consuming marijuana could lead to the use of hard-core illicit drugs such as heroin and cocaine. The media focused particular attention on crack cocaine. The number of drug stories appearing in the *New York Times* increased 400% between the latter half of 1985 and the corresponding period a year later (Beckett, 1997). Similar increases were observed in other print and electronic media. This degree of media attention provided the federal government with justification to treat possession of crack cocaine as an offense carrying a much more severe prison sentence than possession of cocaine or heroin. The story of how government agencies, but particularly an uncritical media, drove the drug panic of the mid-1980s is by now well documented (e.g., see Orcutt and Turner, 1993).[4]

This political and legislative activity has both reflected and stimulated the way that the news media represent drug offenders. The media often portray drug-users as immoral, deviant, and potentially violent individuals. Drug use and drug users are often the subject of "threat to youth" stories aimed at middle-class, middle-aged parents. This image both promotes and justifies punitive sentencing policies (see Pratt, 1998b).[5] Politicians have adopted a strategy of linking drug use and violence to support their "War on Drugs"(e.g., National Drug Control Strategy, 1999).[6] These efforts appear to have influenced public opinion; in a 1998 national survey, 90% agreed that drug use often leads to crimes of violence (Gallup, 1999).[7]

Thus, politicians and media outlets feed off themselves and can create a crisis, to which a response is needed. Although the media have not changed the public's priorities, media publicity has made a difference. In a Gallup Poll conducted in November 1998, over half of the national sample indicated that their concern about drugs has increased over the last five years. Most people stated that they were more concerned because they had become more knowledgeable about drugs, that drugs were becoming more widespread, and that they were worried about their children and grandchildren. Consistent with the media blitz around crack cocaine, over half considered crack cocaine to be the biggest drug problem (Gallup, 1999).

Prevalence of Drug Use

One justification often advanced for the rigorous law enforcement approach taken in America is that rate of drug use among offenders is higher in the United States than elsewhere. The results of systematic research, however, do not support this assertion. Taylor and Bennet (1999) compared the United Kingdom and the United States, using both self-report data and urinalysis data from detained arrestees. Based on the urinalysis data, a larger percentage of detained arrestees in England than in the United States had recently consumed marijuana, benzodiazepines, opiates, and methadone. The use of cocaine proves the exception to this pattern: 40% of detained arrestees in the United States tested positive for cocaine, compared to only 9% of arrestees in England. Thus, while the overall percentage of offenders who use any drug was significantly higher in the United States than England, this differential is explained by the incidence of cocaine use. Similarly, rates of drug usage in Australia and the United States are very similar, with the exception of cocaine use which is much higher in the United States (Makkai, 1994).

Makkai compared National Household Survey results in the United States and Australia in 1991 and found that although rates of cocaine usage are three times higher in the United States, Australians have slightly higher rates of exposure to heroin and amphetamines. With regard to more regular usage (within the past year), the rates are considerably higher in Australia than the United States. Based on a 1998 New Zealand National Survey, the rates of marijuana use in New Zealand are also similar to the United States. However, compared to Americans, New Zealanders reported a higher percentage of people who used LSD in the last year, whereas Americans had a higher use of cocaine and heroin (Field & Casswell, 1998).

Comparative data on the annual prevalence of marijuana use also illustrate that the United States is not the world leader in illegal drug usage. The percentage of people five years of age and older who used marijuana in 1998 was 17.9% in Australia, 15% in New Zealand, 12.3% in the United States, 9% in the United Kingdom, and 7.4% in Canada (World Drug Report, 2000). The United States, however, does lead in the percentage of people using cocaine, with its estimate of 3.2% at least double the estimate of the other four countries (World Drug Report, 2000). Whereas cocaine is the second most illicit drug used in the United States, residents of the United Kingdom have a much higher rate of consuming amphetamine-type stimulants (Global Illicit Drug Trends, 2000). The five countries have similar percentages of the population using opiates (World Drug Report, 2000). The use of illicit drugs is clearly prevalent throughout the world; the United Nations estimates that 4.2% of all persons 15 years and above were consuming illicit drugs in the 1990s (UN Information Service, 2001).

American Public Reaction to the "War on Drugs"

Even in the 1980s, the public was divided on how to deal with drug users. In a national survey conducted in 1983: half supported the imposition of a mandatory prison sentence for possession of a small amount of cocaine and 45% opposed such sentences (Yankelovich, Skelly, & White, 1983). Moreover, whatever public enthusiasm there might have been in the United States in the 1980s for the War on Drugs, it seems to have waned. Politicians and law enforcement officers may have retained their enthusiasm for a "War on Drugs," but there is evidence that the public have adopted a far less aggressive posture. Americans are particularly skeptical that the government's "War" on Drugs has in fact reduced drug use. Although 85% of Tennessee residents approved of former President Bush's War on Drugs, over half expressed no confidence in the federal or state government's ability to fight drug abuse (Tennessee Poll, 1990). When asked if imposing mandatory prison sentences for drug users would affect the incidence of drug-related crime, 53% of respondents in a national survey in 1994 indicated that such sentences would have only a minor impact or no impact at all (Drug Strategies Survey, 1994). In two national surveys conducted in 1995, over half of the respondents believed that the War on Drugs had had no effect on drug use (Attitudes on Substance Abuse and Addiction Survey, 1995; Cintron & Johnson, 1996). In March 2001, a national survey revealed that 74% of the respondents agreed that we are losing the drug war (Associated Press, 2001).[8]

Self-report data from adolescents support this pessimistic perception. Although illegal drug use in all five countries decreased in the 1980s, it subsequently increased in the 1990s. Comparisons with respect to any illicit drug use among high school seniors in the United States show an increase from 16.4% in 1991 to 24.9% in 2000 (National Drug Control Strategy, 1999). Similar trends are seen with grade school children in the United States. Use of any illicit drugs has been rising since 1994 for adults between the ages of 18 and 25 with almost one in five reporting using drugs in 2000. In 1999, an estimated 208,000 Americans were using heroin—triple the number in 1993 (DEA, 2001). And although cocaine use declined from 1985 to 1992 and then remained stable, the number of new adult cocaine users has significantly increased since 1990. Since the 1990s, deaths related to heroin use have been rising in the United States (DEA, 2001) and Australia (Makkai, 2000). Similar trends toward increasing drug use in the 1990s have been observed in other countries. Canadian student surveys also show a significant increase in the use of marijuana since the late 1980s (Fischer, 1998). In Australia, the use of illicit drugs (either on a casual or more substantial basis) also increased from the mid-1980s (AIHW, 1999; Makkai and McAllister, 1998b). In England, use of illicit drugs increased until the mid-1990s and then stabilized (World Drug Report, 2000).

American Public's Strategies and Active Resistance

The American public's skepticism has turned to intolerance and demands for a different approach in some jurisdictions. The public's response, however, varies widely from jurisdiction to jurisdiction, and there is little public consensus regarding the overall strategy to reduce the harms associated with illicit drug use. The public tends to endorse a balanced approach to deal with drugs. The preferred strategies to reduce the drug problem selected in a Maryland poll were education/prevention and reducing the supply of drugs (Maryland Poll, 1997). Similarly, a national poll of Americans found that about half of the sample believed that treatment and education were the most effective ways of dealing with the drug problem. Half believed that border patrol and law enforcement were the most effective approaches (Cintron & Johnson, 1996). The public strongly endorses a balanced approach to drugs, with over 82% favoring anti-drug education in school, anti-drug education in the community, increased job training for at risk youth, increased funding for the police, as well as more severe penalties (Blendon & Young, 1998).

There is a similar lack of consensus regarding the most effective approach for dealing with the drug problem in public schools: 52% of Americans support an educational approach, 42% support the imposition of severe penalties (6% responded "don't know") (Maguire & Pastore, 1998, p. 103). By comparison, the Australian public shows more consensus and prefers education and treatment to deal with marijuana, allocating 70% of the resources to these strategies and only 30% to enforcement strategies. Similarly, the Australian public would assign 60% of resources to education and treatment to address cocaine and heroin use and only 40% to law enforcement (Makkai, 2000).

Politicians often rely on unscientific opinion polls to assess public sentiment and as a result have overestimated the public's support for punishment through prison terms compared to treatment. Many surveys contradict the image of a punitive public and reflect a public that is merciful and supportive of treatment. In a 1991 Georgia Poll, 87% agreed that drug addicts should be viewed and treated as persons who are ill, and a similar percentage believed that they could be successfully treated (Georgia Poll, 1991). A national survey conducted in 1998 found that 80% believed that drug treatment programs should be more widely available (Gallup, 1999). The majority of Oregon residents who participated in focus group research endorsed court-ordered treatment for drug addicts. Participants believed that treatment provides a second chance for offenders, even though they estimated that only about one-third of offenders who complete treatment will subsequently refrain from further offending (Begasse, 1997). The vast majority of North Carolina respondents (84%) favored sentencing offenders addicted to drugs to mandatory treatment, even if this sentencing option was more expensive (Doble, 1995). In 1998, 58% of respondents to a national survey agreed that the country was spending too little to deal with drug addiction (Gallup, 1999).

The American public, at least in some states, have actually taken action to stop the "War on Drugs" policies that place offenders convicted of unlawful possession in prison. Seven states have held referenda concerning lowering the penalties for drug possession, and five of these have passed. California's Proposition 36 in 2000 passed with a 61% approval and requires treatment rather than jail for offenders convicted of drug possession, and allocates $180 million for start-up costs and then $120 million a year to pay for the additional treatment. Arizona passed a similar bill in 1996. Oregon and Utah also passed laws that require the police to have probable cause before seizing and selling property belonging to suspected drug offenders. These states also passed legislation requiring the proceeds of the forfeitures to be directed toward drug treatment and education (Jacobs, 2000). Finally, as noted in chapter 6, the literature on jury nullification also sheds light on the nature of public attitudes toward the sentencing of drug offenders. When juries in the United States are aware of the harsh, mandatory minimum sentences for drug offenses, the defendants were often acquitted—even though substantial evidence pointed toward a conviction (Conrad, 1999).

Politicians have heard the public's growing intolerance of America's War on Drugs. US politician's, however, have dealt with the public's growing intolerance by changing their rhetoric rather than their budget or the laws. The rhetoric may have changed to fall more in line with public sentiment, but the approach still places more emphasis on law enforcement than on prevention and treatment. [U.S. Politicians Change War]

Evidence for the continual emphasis on law enforcement comes from the 2001 fiscal year National Drug Control budget. The budget of $19.2 billion allocates 68.9% to law enforcement, including breaking sources of supply,

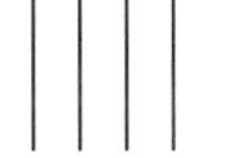

U.S. Politicians Change War on Drugs Metaphor

One strategy that politicians often use is to change rhetoric to suggest a change in their practice but to keep the same policies and strategies. Politicians have used this strategy to deal with the public's intolerance of the War on Drugs and demands for a more treatment-oriented approach. In the 1999 U.S. National Drug Control Strategy, the "war on drugs" metaphor has been replaced with a "cancer" metaphor. Political leaders have asserted that "the metaphor of a 'war on drugs' is misleading. Although wars are expected to end, drug education . . . is a continuous process. . . . Cancer is a more appropriate metaphor for the nation's drug problem. Dealing with cancer . . . requires the mobilization of support mechanisms—medical, educational, social, and financial—to check the spread of the disease and improve the patient's prognosis" (p. 7). This medical metaphor suggests a more balanced and treatment-oriented approach, but one which still has abstinence as its foundation and clearly regards drug use as an intrinsic evil that must be eradicated through restricting both supply and demand.

shielding America's frontiers, and reducing drug-related crime and violence, and 19.5% to reduce the consequences of drug use through drug treatment and diversion in drug courts and 11.6% to reducing drug use among youth. Clearly, law enforcement continues to receive the bulk of the resources, and this appears to be inconsistent with the public's preference for a more balanced approach. This distribution of resources, however, is not unique to the United States. In 2000, the New Zealand government reserved 62% of the total $224 million allocated for drug control to law enforcement strategies, 24% to treatment services, and 14% to primary prevention (New Zealand Country Report, 2001). Unlike the United States, however, the New Zealand government funds programs that address and attempt to reduce the harms associated with drug use. [International Trends in Harm Reduction]

As the discussion on needle exchange programs in the box on "International Trends in Harm Reduction" shows, the American public is unwilling to support programs that do not send a clear message of abstinence from hard illicit drugs such as heroin. Politicians in the United States, however, often generalize the public's support of abstinence to include marijuana, and as a result are overzealous in their punishment of marijuana users, as a later section of this chapter demonstrates.

Overzealous punishment in the form of prison sentences for drug users is also inconsistent with global trends. For example, America's overuse of prison sentences can be contrasted with the approach in England and Canada. In 1999, only 5% of persons charged with unlawful possession in England were imprisoned (22% were placed on probation or given a conditional discharge, 26% were given a fine, and 45% were cautioned). Moreover, the rate of imprisonment has not changed over the past decade. In 1999, 14% of persons convicted of unlawful production (primarily of cannabis plants) were sentenced to prison, and approximately half of those charged with unlawful supply or possession with intent to supply were sentenced to prison (Ramsay & Partridge, 1999). At the present, possession of less than 30 grams of marijuana in Canada carries a maximum penalty of $1,000 and six months in jail (Erickson, 2000). However, the typical sentence is a discharge or a small fine.[9]

Public Attitudes toward Narcotic Use and Drug Trafficking

The public appears not only to support deterring users of hard illicit drugs such as cocaine, crack, and heroin through a prison term but also favors treatment for certain hard-core users. Although most respondents favored incarceration for offenders convicted of cocaine, crack, or heroin possession for personal use, the average prison sentence was under three years. The public concurs with the U.S. federal sentencing guidelines on sentences for crack, cocaine, and heroin possession, with the exception that the public does not make a distinction for crack cocaine (Rossi & Berk, 1997).

International Trends in Harm Reduction

While the U.S. government continues to emphasize abstinence and a law enforcement approach to the drug problem, Americans are clearly growing weary of this approach. Many other countries are focusing on reducing the harms associated with drug use rather than placing abstinence of illicit drug use as the number one priority. Several innovative programs have developed to address the negative collateral consequences of taking illicit drugs. Injecting drug users (IDU) taking heroin and other illicit substances had high rates of hepatitis, AIDS, jaundice, and other diseases communicated by sharing needles.

In 23 countries including England, Canada, Australia, and New Zealand, government initiatives started needle exchange programs that allowed drug users to exchange used needles for clean ones, and such programs were not politically controversial (Lane, Lurie, Bowser, Kahn, & Chen, 2000). Instead, these programs were construed as one way to reduce AIDS, and many of these programs continue to receive federal government funds. Currently, New Zealand has 13 needle exchange programs that supply more than one million needles and syringes a year to illicit drug users through pharmacies that are subsidized by state funds. By contrast, the American public appears unwilling to accept the benefits of needle exchange programs, and such programs are highly controversial. In 1997, 90% of respondents in a national survey believed that needle exchange programs would increase crime and create public health hazards from discarded needles. In addition, about 60% of voters believed government-funded needle exchange programs could encourage illegal drug use among teenagers and could send the message that the federal government condones illegal drugs, and they wanted members of Congress to terminate needle exchange programs and focus on abstinence and drug rehabilitation (Bowdy, 1999). Other polls suggest that the American public opinion is divided in its position on needle exchange programs (Blendon & Young, 1998; Southern Focus Poll, 1997). Currently, a U.S. federal law bans the federal government from funding needle exchange programs and allows the government to withdraw funds from agencies that exchange needles. City and state legislators, however, can enact needle exchange programs and 33 programs in the United States have received positive evaluation (Lane et al., 2000).

Other efforts to reduce the number of deaths from overdose of hard illicit drugs and to eliminate the prevalence of dirty needles are being tried. In May 2001, Australia implemented the first injecting room for heroin-injecting drug users to inject drugs in a safe environment (Associated Press, 2001). A total of 42 injecting facilities are open in Germany, the Netherlands, Switzerland, and Austria (Drug Policy Expert Committee, 2001). Other legalized heroin-injecting rooms are being considered in Victoria and New South Wales in Australia. However, a recent national poll found that the Australian public was divided concerning legalized heroin-injecting rooms with 52% disapproving, 37% approving, and 11% neutral (Morgan Poll, Oct. 17, 2000). Time will tell whether the Australian public changes its support or whether Australian politicians heed public disapproval.

There is substantial disagreement between public preferences and the U.S. federal sentencing guidelines with respect to drug trafficking offenses. The two major differences are whether trafficking of certain drugs (e.g., crack cocaine) requires a more punitive response and whether different forms of violence require different sentence lengths. First, the public makes no distinction between crack cocaine, powder cocaine, and heroin, whereas the U.S. sentencing guidelines impose an additional nine years if the offender was trafficking in crack cocaine.

Judges also agree with the public that U.S. sentencing guidelines for drug offenses are too harsh. A 1996 survey administered to U.S. district judges and chief probation officers found that these professionals rated sentences for drug possession and drug trafficking as "too harsh" compared to other federal crimes (Johnson & Gilbert, 1997). Federal judges also believe that the sentencing guidelines for drug trafficking are often too harsh. In 1997, 17,622 offenders convicted of drug trafficking were sentenced in U.S. federal courts, and judges often departed from the guidelines and imposed a more lenient sentence (U.S. Sentencing Commission, 1998).

Some research supports the view that public opinion is more in line with federal judges' opinion than with the severe mandatory federal sentences for drug trafficking. The majority of the public believes that a mandatory prison sentence for drug dealing would not make a major difference in reducing drug-related crime (Drug Strategies Survey, 1994). Research has demonstrated that the American public favors alternative community-based sentences (with mandatory counseling) over a prison sentence for different types of offenders selling drugs. Before they were made aware of community-based sanctions, over half of the respondents preferred such alternatives for a first-time offender who was convicted of a small amount of cocaine and was a probable drug dealer. If a first-time offender who is addicted to drugs sells a small amount of cocaine to undercover police officers, over two-thirds of respondents favor a community-based sentence involving mandatory treatment. Half of the respondents favor a community-based sentence, even if a first-time offender sells a small amount of cocaine to high school students. Over two-thirds of the public, however, support prison for a repeat offender trafficking small amounts of cocaine or for a first-time offender selling large amounts of illicit drugs (Doble, 1995).

Finally, research has demonstrated that the public is also treatment-oriented when sentencing detailed, realistic cases. In a study using videotapes of simulated sentencing hearings, the public endorsed rehabilitation and recommended treatment for a drug addict convicted of selling cocaine, whereas judges usually emphasized general deterrence and recommended a prison sentence (Diamond and Stalans, 1989). The public appears willing to give a second chance to small-time drug dealers addicted to drugs but is unwilling to extend the same leniency to major drug dealers.

This area of drug policy also illustrates how conservative politicians continue to support punitive policies, even in the face of evidence that the public does not support such laws. Tonry (1995) and others, moreover, have shown that crack cocaine penalties were imposed disproportionately on lower-income minorities. The federal U.S. Sentencing Commission has also recommended the removal of differences in the penalties for crack and powder cocaine. Although Congress did lower the penalties for crack (in 1999), the difference still remains;

crack cocaine penalties are still 10 times higher than for powder cocaine (they were 100 times higher previously) (National Drug Control Strategy, 1999). Thus, there is little public or professional support for the legal distinction and the differences in penalties for powder or crack cocaine. In the face of this opposition, Congress has upheld these laws which can be seen as systemically discriminatory (see Tonry, 1995).

When Linked to Violence, Drugs Trigger a Punitive Public Response

Respondents recommended on average much longer prison sentences for drug trafficking offenses when violence was involved than the sentencing guidelines required. For example, respondents recommended an average increment of five years imprisonment if "the drug dealing organization was known to use weapons and violence as a way of doing business," whereas the guidelines require only an increment of two years in these circumstances. Moreover, respondents make fine distinctions about how weapons are used in their sentence recommendations, whereas the guidelines merely require an increment of two years for all types of weapon use and violence. Punitive penal policies appear to be supported by the public only when there is a direct link between drug trafficking and violence (Rossi & Berk, 1997). Rossi and Berk concluded: "Clearly the public makes fewer distinctions among drugs and is far less punitive. . . . What may matter most about drug trafficking to the respondents is the violence that may be associated with it" (1997, p. 113). This could well reflect the general fear and concern associated with violence rather than a concern with drugs.

Moreover, in Australia, politicians have sacrificed the movement toward a more liberal policy in order to capitalize on an association with punitiveness that elements of the media are seeking (Christie, 1998). Australians are largely supportive of the use of strong penalties for drug trafficking. Close to 90% of Australians support or strongly support increased penalties for the sale or supply of heroin or cocaine, and the proportion strongly supporting harsher penalties has increased in recent years (Makkai and McAllister, 1998).

Decriminalization of Marijuana

The public clearly sees marijuana use as less serious than the use of cocaine, crack, heroin or other illicit drugs, even though drug policies in the five countries have only recently recognized the difference. We have alluded to the fact that U.S. politicians have enacted penalties for marijuana possession that exceed public support. In this section we examine public support for lowering the penalties for marijuana possession to a fine or community-based sentence, a kind of "decriminalization." Much evidence indicates that the public opposes the complete legalization of marijuana.[10] Policies to reduce the penalties associated with possession of a small amount of marijuana, however, attract considerable support from the public in all five countries. Moreover, legislators have been successful in enacting laws to reduce the penalties associated with possession of small amounts of marijuana. Three jurisdictions in Australia have enacted laws that make possession of a small amount of marijuana punishable by a small on-the-spot fine, and if the fine is paid, the individual avoids acquiring a criminal conviction (Makkai, 2000). All other Australian jurisdictions have provisions for the cautioning (rather than charging) of those found using or possessing small amounts of cannabis (Lenton, McDonald, Ali & Moore, 1999). These laws seem to have the backing of the Australian public. At least half of Australians who are opposed to legalizing personal use also believe that violation of this law should not carry a criminal conviction (Bowman & Sanson-Fisher, 1994). Moreover, several polls indicate that almost half of the Australian respondents oppose the incarceration of individuals who merely smoke marijuana (Makkai & McAllister, 1993).

In New Zealand, a Parliamentary Select Committee held an inquiry into marijuana laws in 1998 and reported that the cost of the existing prohibition could not be justified. Although no changes to the law have yet been introduced, new inquiries have been established to further investigate the consequences of marijuana prohibition. In July 2000, the New Zealand Parliament enacted legislation prohibiting the importation and sale of drug-related paraphernalia, such as marijuana pipes (New Zealand Country Report, 2001). It is unclear which direction the New Zealand Parliament will now take. The new drug policy released in 1998 emphasizes the reduction of collateral harms to health, social, and economic costs from drug use as the number one priority, but at the same time attempts to reduce the prevalence of cannabis use. Government agencies have examined proposals for early court intervention with young offenders who have a drug problem (similar to the specialized drug courts; New Zealand Country Report, 2001). In New Zealand, sentences for possessing drugs are generally fairly small; however, the severity of sentences for "dealers" has significantly increased.

In July 2001, British police began a six-month experiment in an area of London where police will caution users, and seize drugs, but will not arrest the offenders. This approach keeps drug users out of jail and saves police an average of five hours for each individual who otherwise would have been arrested. On October 23, 2001, the Home Secretary announced plans to significantly reduce the penalties for marijuana offenses. Under the proposals, marijuana would be reclassified as a class C substance, and this reclassification would reduce penalties for possession, use, and dealing of marijuana. This announcement was in response to widespread calls by users, doctors, and police to relax the penalties against marijuana consumption and is justified as allowing the police to spend more time on enforcing laws against harder illicit drugs such as crack cocaine. The proposal if passed would begin in the spring of 2002. A study in England found that public sentencing preferences concur with actual sentencing practices: the public favored a community-based sentence for a young cannabis user (Hough, Lewis & Walker, 1988).

In the United States, support for decriminalization varies widely across jurisdictions, though many nonprofit groups are now actively trying to generate public support for decriminalization. For example, a nonprofit organization in the United States recently started an advertising campaign on the Boston subway system to suggest that marijuana use should be decriminalized. In a national survey, 54% of American adults believed that smoking marijuana in a private residence should be permitted but regulated or should be permitted and not regulated, whereas 46% believed it should be totally prohibited (Harris and Associates, 1990). By contrast, the majority of the voting public in Mendocino County California in the United States voted to support a countywide initiative to decriminalize backyard marijuana gardens (Jacobs, 2000).

When given more alternatives and information about the cases, the public, however, overwhelmingly supports a much more treatment-oriented response involving less severe punishment than the U.S. federal laws currently allow. For example, about 80% of residents in Maryland chose a treatment program for an adult convicted of possessing illegal drugs for the first time (Maryland Poll, 1992). Before they were made aware of alternative sanctions, over half of the respondents preferred community-based sanctions for a first-time offender convicted of possession but who was a probable drug dealer. After learning about the availability of community-based sanctions, 83% preferred this option (Farkas, 1997). Most respondents (80%) selected a treatment program as the appropriate sanction for a first-time offender convicted of possessing illegal drugs for personal use (Maryland Poll, 1992). Similarly, almost 60% of a sample of Americans recommended probation for offenders convicted of marijuana possession for personal use, and thus it appears that Americans are more lenient in their sentencing preferences for marijuana possession than the U.S. sentencing guidelines (Rossi & Berk, 1997).[11]

In Canada, government policies with respect to marijuana users also tend to be more punitive than public opinion. The proposed revisions to Canada's drug law in 1995 did not change the repressive punitive policies toward users, but instead merely adjusted the statutes in line with current sentencing practice. A Health Canada survey during this time period found that a significant majority of the Canadian population favored either the imposition of relatively lenient penalties or total decriminalization of cannabis possession (see Fischer, 1998, pp. 172–173). In a recent poll, 69% of residents in Vancouver, Canada, favored decriminalizing marijuana possession (Cohen, 2001).

The trend toward decriminalization of marijuana also is occurring in other European countries, though enforcement of their drug laws have been relaxed to an even greater extent. In Portugal, the legislature voted in July 2001 to decriminalize the use of a range of recreational, illicit drugs. Individuals caught in possession of small quantities will receive no sanctions; those caught with more than 10 days' supply will be required to appear before a tribunal composed of social workers, psychologists, and medical specialists. In Belgium, people are permitted to grow marijuana for personal consumption. Spain permits personal use of any illicit drug, as long as it is consumed in a private residence. In Norway, the typical penalty for possession of hashish is a fine.

Politics Surrounding the Use of Marijuana for Medicinal Purposes

Although the public oppose the total legalization of marijuana, they do support the limited legalization for medical purposes. Legalizing the therapeutic use of marijuana attracts greater support among the public than politicians. The majority of respondents in statewide polls and national polls believe that doctors should be allowed to prescribe marijuana for patients suffering from serious illnesses (Arizona Poll, 1998; Illinois Policy Survey, 1997; Wyoming Election Year Survey, 1998; Blendon & Young, 1998; Gallup Poll, 1999). When given choices of legalization, making it a minor violation, a crime, or requiring a medical prescription, half of the respondents in a national sample of U.S. adults chose the method of prescription as the way to regulate marijuana use. However, overwhelming support for the use of marijuana under a doctor's supervision appears to be only for patients suffering from serious illnesses (see Maryland Poll, 1990; Blendon & Young, 1998).

In addition to public opinion poll data, referenda indicate that the majority wants terminally ill and chronically ill medical patients to be able to access marijuana to control their pain. Seven states (Alaska, California, Colorado, Maine, Nevada, Oregon, and Washington) have passed laws through public referenda, allowing terminally ill patients to use marijuana to alleviate their symptoms. Hawaii is the first state where legislators passed a law allowing the medicinal use of marijuana. Conservative politicians are, however, opposed to providing the public with a voice in the creation of such laws. Congress initially withheld money from the District of Columbia to count the ballots from its referendum on whether terminally ill patients should be legally allowed to use marijuana to alleviate symptoms, but a federal court allowed the votes to be counted and the referendum passed with 69% approval (Facts.com, Sept, 23, 1999).

The U.S. federal government has interfered with the implementation of medicinal medical programs in states that have passed such laws in several ways.[12] First, federal agents have arrested numerous patients for violation of federal laws prohibiting possession of marijuana, even though these patients have valid legal state cards permitting the possession of marijuana. Second, the federal government has attempted to stop California from distributing marijuana to patients who have qualified for its use. On August 14, 2000, the Ninth Circuit U.S. Court of Appeals ruled against the federal government to stop the distribution, but the federal government sought a stay of the decision to stop the distribution of marijuana (Cowan, 2000). The U.S. Supreme Court ruled in May 2001 that California cannabis clubs could not distribute marijuana to seriously ill patients because the U.S. Congress has determined that marijuana carries no medical benefit (AAP, 2001). Finally, the U.S. federal government has threatened doctors that they may lose their right to participate in federal programs such as Medicaid and Medicare if they talk to patients about the use of marijuana to alleviate their symptoms. This has led a group of California doctors, patients, and nonprofit organizations to sue the government, alleging violation of freedom of speech (Weikopf, 2000).

The topic of medicinal use of marijuana represents an example of the selective use of public opinion by politicians to support their own conservative views. Although both public opinion polls and referenda show that the public perceives no negative effects arising from the use of marijuana for medical reasons, U.S. politicians refuse to listen. Conservative politicians in the United States and elsewhere have been unwilling to loosen the prohibition against marijuana and continue to harass and arrest individuals who use marijuana with their doctors' consent. The federal government in December 2001, however, has relaxed its tough stance by approving three medicinal marijuana trials that will test the efficacy of marijuana for medical use. The trials with take place at a university in California (NORML, 2001).

There are also struggles between the public and politicians in other countries. New Zealand's public appears divided, with educators, district councils, and the National Party demanding that the decriminalization of marijuana should be taken off the government's agenda. Members of Parliament, including the founder of NORML, want to allow the use of marijuana for medical purposes. In South Australia, persons are allowed to cultivate up to 10 marijuana plants for this purpose. In New South Wales, the premier announced that the government would continue with its medicinal marijuana trial and allow seriously ill patients to grow up to five marijuana plants without fear of prosecution (Doherty, 2001).

In Canada, the Ontario Court of Appeal ruled in 2000 that Ottawa had one year to amend the blanket prohibition on marijuana possession in the Controlled Drugs and Substances Act. Justice Marc Rosenberg wrote in the unanimous decision that "it has been known for centuries that in addition to its intoxicating or psychoactive effect, marijuana has medicinal value" (McNulty, Aug. 9, 2000). A survey conducted in Vancouver found strong public support for legalizing marijuana for medicinal purposes (Cohen, 2001). The health minister announced in April 2001 that the government would enact regulations by July 31, 2001, allowing people suffering from AIDS, multiple sclerosis, spinal injuries, epilepsy, severe arthritis, and other conditions to possess and use marijuana (Evening Post, April 7, 2001). On July 30, 2001, Canada enacted legislation to permit patients suffering from a chronic or terminal disease to grow, buy, possess, and consume marijuana to alleviate their symptoms.

England also is considering decriminalizing marijuana possession for medicinal purposes. In 1999, British physicians supported legalizing marijuana, arguing that it posed no serious threat to health and was safer than tobacco or alcohol. The United Kingdom began clinical trials on the use of marijuana for medicinal purposes in October 1999 (Venters, 1999), and in October 2001, the home secretary of Britain announced a proposal to allow doctors to prescribe marijuana to terminally or chronically ill patients (Facts.com, Nov. 1, 2001).

Conclusion

In the political arena, particularly in America, drugs constitute a highly volatile electoral issue. The lengths to which President Clinton went to disavow inhaling marijuana and George W. Bush's prevaricating responses with respect to his past behavior are clear evidence of this phenomenon. Based on much evidence from scientific surveys of public opinion, the "War on Drugs" in America has lost its popular appeal and is seen as a costly waste of resources. The policies from the War on Drugs also fail to reflect public preferences. The U.S. public prefers much longer prison terms for drug traffickers that use violence than the sentencing guidelines allow and prefers less severe punishment for marijuana possession. In all five countries, the public is in support of decriminalizing marijuana and also supports allowing doctors to prescribe marijuana to alleviate the symptoms of terminally ill or chronically ill individuals. Despite the public's willingness to consider alternative sanctions and treatment programs, sentences for offenders convicted of drug possession in the U.S. federal court have dramatically increased in severity over time.

Indeed, the public's intolerance with the drug war has changed to action in some states through enacting state laws to divert offenders charged with possession to treatment programs. Similarly, at least the rhetoric in Canada of harsher law enforcement toward drug users is out of line with Canadian public sentiment. Another clear example of the political punitiveness which underlies drug policy in the United States is the highly punitive sentence applied to crack cocaine. The U.S. Congress ignored public opposition, expressed both in polls and the media, and the Sentencing Commission in its creation and continuation of the harsher law for crack cocaine.

Why have U.S. politicians used strategies such as changes in rhetoric and active resistance to respond to public opposition? Politicians have not abandoned the tough-minded punitive approach toward drug users and traffickers, in part, because the public views about drug abuse are complex. The public supports the "War on Drugs" message of abstinence from hard illicit drugs such as crack and heroin and are suspicious of programs such as needle exchange programs that do not promote abstinence. However, even for users of crack, cocaine, or heroin, the public is willing to support community-based treatment for a first arrest. The public, however, disagrees with the "War on Drugs" message that marijuana is as dangerous as the harder illicit drugs and can lead to the use of harder illicit drugs. Evidence of the public's distinction between marijuana and the harder illicit drugs can be seen in their support for the decriminalization of marijuana. The War on Drugs has failed to represent public views, in part, because it failed to appreciate the nuances and contextual nature of public opinion about drug offenders.

In addition, politicians may be resistant to moving their policies in line with public views for several reasons. Some politicians may sincerely believe that marijuana is as harmful as other harder illicit drugs and that abstinence is the best policy and are pursuing a policy in line with their own ideology. Other politicians may be focusing on a particular segment of the public and believe that their core constituents support mandatory minimum prison terms for marijuana. Both of these explanations may have merit. Conservative politicians generally are opposed to drug use. Moreover, evidence from public opinion polls show that at least in America, the consensus of public opinion varies by jurisdiction.

The topic of using marijuana to alleviate medical symptoms illustrates the role of conservative ideology in the government's creation of mandates to outlaw medicinal marijuana. In the debate about medicinal marijuana, conservative politicians in the United States cannot point to public support for their ban; instead, politicians are in a battle with their constituents, who have voted to create laws allowing the use of marijuana when a doctor prescribes the drug to alleviate medical symptoms. Moreover, governments in England, Canada, and Australia have been more open to legalizing marijuana for medicinal purposes after medical research showed no serious adverse health effects. Thus, American politicians are also out of step with the global trend toward acceptance of medicinal marijuana and the decriminalization of marijuana.

An alternative explanation is that politicians support punitive drug laws because they serve to mainly punish that group which is viewed by the "aspirational middle class" as a threat—the poor and marginalized groups of the inner city; this view may be particularly true for sentencing laws regarding crack cocaine. If this is true, it reveals another way that populists can use crime policy as a wedge issue attracting voters while sacrificing the group that are seen more and more as an object of punishment and derision rather than compassion and assistance.

The volatile politics of drug crimes means that it is an area where clear and decisive leadership is needed. However, this is precisely the kind of action which is shunned by populist politicians. The public subscribe to a mixture of views, but there is every indication that they are receptive to more treatment and less punishment as a way of handling the problem. This requires a cogent and well thought-out policy that recognizes the existence of public anxiety about drugs. Such a policy is possible only in an environment in which the media and politicians avoid the creation of crises.

10 Responding to Penal Populism

This book has been concerned with the emergence, over the 1990s, of increasingly punitive sentencing policies and practices in the English-speaking world. These punitive policies have been applied to juvenile, as well as adult offenders, and to a wide range of offenses. This final chapter proposes some strategies with which to halt, or at least impede, the seemingly inexorable drift toward more punitive sentencing; only if this occurs, we believe, will it be possible to ensure more rational sentencing policy development.

Understanding the Drift to More Punitive Criminal Justice

Our point of departure was that harsh sentencing and, in particular, mandatory sentencing achieves little by way of crime reduction, imposes large financial and social costs on the community, and often violates consensual sentencing principles such as *proportionality* with respect to the imposition of punishments, in general, and *restraint* with regard to the use of imprisonment. Most populist penal policies create disproportionate punishments and are profligate with respect to the use of incarceration. Although we support the application of deterrent theories, which advocate maximizing the *certainty* and *celerity* of criminal punishments, there is little evidence to support the assumption that animates penal populism—namely, that increasing the severity of punishment will reduce crime rates. In other words, we think that this trend in penal policy is irrational since it is inconsistent with the results of criminological research.

The emphasis on imprisonment as the *primary* criminal justice response to offending is also, in our view, inappropriate and outmoded. We have not argued this case over the course of this book; others have done so persuasively enough for us (e.g., Currie, 1998; Rubin, 1999). Instead, our aim has been to examine the factors that underlie the move toward more punitive policies. The attempt has been to explain why politicians promote costly penal policies that are demonstrably ineffective, socially divisive, and frequently unfair in their application.

We have not given much credence to the view that in advocating harsher sentencing, populist politicians are simply being appropriately responsive to the democratic will. In the first place, public opinion is much more complex and nuanced than is generally supposed. While the public have strong views about the treatment of offenders—and their sentencing preferences can sometimes be harsh—a wealth of research questions the conclusion that members of the public invariably favor the imposition of harsher sentences. Public attitudes toward punishment have evolved considerably over past decades, and we now know far more about the most effective strategies to inform the public about crime and justice issues (see Roberts & Hough, 2002).

Unfortunately, the research qualifying the general conclusion that the public are punitive is seldom referred to in debates about the future of sentencing. Second, a careful analysis of penal politics shows that politicians *lead*, as much as follow, public opinion. It would be a simplistic form of democracy that delivered flawed criminal justice policies simply because there was an apparent public demand for them. This would amount to democracy by uninformed plebiscite, quite different from the form of government by elected representatives that our five nations purport to uphold.

In large measure, of course, our argument has been precisely that politicians *have* been populist in their promotion of tough penal policies. Although populism can be employed to distract attention from other areas of social policy, it often leads to a chain reaction or penal "arms race." It is the fear of being seen as "soft on crime"—or at least as being softer than one's political opponents—rather than a commitment to "out-tough" them that tends to drive politicians to the extremes of penal excess. However, there are other factors at work which give the current forms of penal populism their precise shape and texture. We have argued that penal politics in developed democracies are characterized by misinformation on the part of both politicians and the people whom they were elected to represent. In addition, politicians are likely to have a distorted view of the true mood of the public, with negative consequences for criminal justice policy development, in general, and sentencing reform, in particular.

It might be argued that this perspective is intrinsically conservative, implying that whatever the nature of public perception, the penal systems in our five countries were in good shape prior to the advent of penal populism. In suggesting that penal policy is being distorted by populist politics and public misinformation, we do not mean to advocate a return to some Golden Age of sentencing. For decades the justice systems in all our countries have been riven with problems, and these have contributed to widespread public cynicism toward the courts. However, these problems have less to do with leniency per se than with reductions in the probability that offenders will be apprehended and punished, delays in imposing punishment, sentencing disparity, and a lack of responsiveness to the needs of victims.

Explaining the Success of Penal Populism

Throughout our research we have sought to identify—and explain—areas of criminal justice that seem particularly susceptible to the influence of penal populism. It is no easy task, for while no area of criminal justice policy development has been completely compromised by populism, no topic has been completely untouched either. Nevertheless, our tentative conclusion is that there are certain conditions that facilitate the promotion and adoption of populist punitive initiatives. In terms of the legislative environment, penal populism seems most likely to emerge in the run-up to elections and in the course of the electoral campaign itself. Another period of heightened susceptibility arises when a government rules by minority or enjoys only a narrow majority in the legislature. This is particularly true when the government is confronted by a vigorous and populist parliamentary opposition.

Some of the features that are likely to facilitate the adoption of populist criminal justice legislation are when

- the issue is one with which the public have limited *direct* contact but which attracts widespread media coverage;
- the crime problem is one which, in its most extreme form, carries catastrophic consequences for the individual victim and his or her family and community;
- the crime problem threatens or harms particularly vulnerable victims such as young children or the elderly;
- the crime problem is represented by a tragic crime with features which attract widespread media attention;
- the crime problem is one which provokes the greatest degree of public abhorrence;
- the issue is one for which the media have constructed a paradigm example.

Sex offending fits many of these criteria. Most members of the public have limited direct contact with sex offenders; this means that the stereotype of a sex offender is likely to be as divergent from reality as is possible. The range of conduct included within the category "sex offending" is very broad and encompasses a wide range of seriousness. Despite this, the public image of a sex offender is drawn from the most serious pole of the spectrum of seriousness. The extreme forms of sex offending include the most serious offenses, and the media have clearly constructed a stereotype of the sexual predator to which many people can resonate. The numerous examples of high profile sex offenders in recent years have done more than simply focus public attention on certain individuals; they have colored our perceptions of large groups of people. In addition, they can spawn legislation that affects large numbers of other offenders who may share few characteristics with the cases covered by the media. Finally, by virtue of its inherent seriousness and violation of deeply held values, the media image of sex offenders provokes (not unreasonably) widespread public anxiety and outrage. When inappropriately channeled, these emotions give rise to the kind of mob mentality seen in England as a result of the tabloid campaign to "weed out the pedophiles" in British society (see chapter 3).

The evolution of populist legislation with respect to drug offenders may be explained in the same way. Although a significant proportion of the population (particularly the generations under 40) may use soft drugs such as marijuana, few middle-class members of the public in our countries ever encounter someone who *sells* hard drugs for a living: a drug *dealer*. An image of drug dealers can therefore be promoted by the media, and casual consumers of illegal drugs are drawn into the same frame. Even in the United Kingdom, where principles of harm reduction and demand reduction have guided drug policy, the rhetoric surrounding initiatives to curb the supply of drugs is nevertheless fairly bellicose.

Burglary is another form of crime that causes widespread public alarm; and at the same time very few people will have direct contact with people who end up being convicted for this crime: few people have ever encountered a *burglar*. The image of such people that most of us carry in our heads bears little relation to reality, as has been demonstrated by systematic research (e.g., Stalans & Diamond, 1990). In jurisdictions where burglary is a serious problem (such as Britain), it is therefore not surprising to find "three strikes" legislation, resulting in mandatory prison terms for this kind of offender.

Juvenile justice would seem to fit the criteria of populism less well, and this may explain why there has been less populist legislation in this domain. There is no doubt that the news media representations of crime by juveniles, and the high-profile tragedies to which we have referred, have certainly rocked public sensibilities and influenced public support for juvenile justice policies. But the public obviously have far more direct contact with young people and are less inclined to adopt a "throw away the key" attitude with this group. The stereotype of a "juvenile offender" does not have the clarity that characterizes the sexual predator, the drug dealer, or the professional burglar. People who are worried about increasing youth crime rates are concerned about a *range* of criminal activity which includes, in its most extreme form, homicide, but also many lesser examples of deviance such as groups of young people who seem threatening but whose conduct borders on being merely disrespectful.

When someone suggests that the answer to juvenile crime lies in the greater use of incarceration, people may think of their own offspring, and in the spirit of "there but for the grace of God, go they," this makes them rather uneasy with punitive sentencing policies for young offenders. The mandatory minimum term of imprisonment for juvenile offenders in Australia is a good example of a tough juvenile justice policy that struck many Australians as exceeding the limits of reasonable policy making, in part, because of its mandatory nature and, in part, because of the severe impact that imprisonment may have on young people.[1]

Having documented some of the major examples of penal populism and considered its causes, it now becomes important to convert this understanding into some form of action. We attempt, therefore, in the remainder of the book to consider what steps can be taken to respond to penal populism and to outline areas for possible action.

Responding to Penal Populism

The Importance of Action, Rather than Reaction

What hope is there for more research-based and rational crime policy development in light of the existence of populist pressures? It is now clear that against the emotional and dramatic appeal of populist crime policy, "rational" information-based and "criminological" perspectives are often considered irrelevant. People are not satisfied by what appears to be cold rationalism. This is partly because deliberation is often seen as something that prevents rapid action. It is hard to "hold fire" in the face of distress, let alone the panic that can follow in the wake of a very serious crime. Therefore, the benefits of rational crime policy must be "sold" and the costs of our actions clearly highlighted. Another aspect of this debate is that those arguing for imprisonment are seen to be "for action" and those arguing against imprisonment seem to be arguing "against action." It is important that the dynamics of this debate be transformed so that both parties are proposing an "action," and the two strategies are then compared side by side as to their value.

Imprisonment will no doubt retain its unique symbolic value for many people. The alternatives—such as early intervention and intervention with high risk youth—need to be promoted in terms of their capacity to prevent crime. Slogans such as *act smarter not tougher* may need to be used to capture succinctly the difference between prevention and punishment. A change of posture may also be engendered by going on the offensive and pointing to negative actions taken by politicians—the squandering of public funds on ineffective actions and the relative underfunding of effective crime prevention initiatives.

Our diagnosis of the factors underlying the drift to penal populism suggests several ways of applying a brake to the process. As we shall discuss below, there is some (albeit limited) scope for reducing the political payoffs in talking tough on crime. It may also be possible to achieve some changes in the way that the mass media cover crime and punishment. There is certainly much more that can be done to improve public understanding of the issues and to foster public acceptance of more effective (but also more complicated) solutions to complex problems. More intelligent measurement of attitudes to punishment would in itself help to interrupt the process.

Any attempt to render the penal debate "fireproof" against populism cannot be simply defensive. As noted, crime rates are declining in most jurisdictions at the present. However, if demographics or the economy are responsible for this decline, this trend may change in the future. Also, crime is still perceived to be a serious social problem, and one which is much more visible now than it was for the greater part of the twentieth century.[2] Politicians *have* to be able to respond to public concern about crime; they will listen to the message that Draconian sentencing is ineffective only when they are provided with positive and plausible suggestions for effective replacement strategies. If they are to achieve any impact, critics of penal populism need to offer politicians some persuasive alternatives.[3]

These alternatives must not be (and cannot be seen to be) ones which fail to hold offenders accountable for their actions or which fail to reflect understanding of the importance of the problem. Returning briefly to the events in August 2000 in England, immediately following the murder of Sarah Payne, it was clear that the populist response to the tragedy, of rounding up all allegedly dangerous pedophiles and creating life sentences, was seen by the public as "doing something" about the problem. Those who advocated a more reflective approach to sex offending were easily dismissed as not caring enough about the problem or being obstructionist in terms of effective solutions. Indeed, they were labeled as such. When one writer argued that "there are some abusers whose behavior, though indecent and vile, does not represent a homicidal threat to children," this was labeled by the leading Sunday newspaper as "typical of the liberal establishment's otherworldliness on this issue",[4] and so it must have struck millions of Britons.

It is beyond the scope of this book to discuss in detail the shape that such a program might take, and in any case, it will vary across jurisdictions and need to be responsive to local conditions and priorities. But in brief, it is helpful to think in terms of intervention at two levels. On the one hand, it is important to recognize the legitimacy of public frustration with the court process itself. Specific problems which need addressing in all five countries include

- procedural delays in court processing;
- disparities of outcome at the sentencing stage;
- a tendency to place the requirements of legal practitioners above those of victims and witnesses;
- a lack of adequate compensation for victims of crime;
- a perception that judges are "out of touch" with the general public.

It is equally necessary to offer politicians a coherent vision of crime control, in which the severity of sanctions and indeed, imprisonment itself, plays a less central role. Our prescription is for an approach that draws a much wider range of individuals and organizations into the effort to respond to crime. There should be a *preventive* duty on those whose activities create—or fail to close off—the opportunities for crime. To take a mundane example, manufacturers of new consumer products that are easy to steal need to incorporate ways of preventing theft. At the same time, there is a clear *restorative* duty on those who commit crime to repair the harm inflicted by their offending. Leaving aside the elaboration of such a large-scale and long-term enterprise, the rest of this chapter considers what specifically can be done to impede or slow the march of penal populism. [Against the Tide]

What is needed now is a new version of the classic *Honest Politician's Guide to Crime Control*, published by Norval Morris and Gordon Hawkins in 1970.

Against the Tide: Transnational Reform Movements

Although penal populism appears to have emerged as a consistent political feature in a number of Western countries in the 1990s, it is important to acknowledge the range of reform movements that have developed in response. These movements range from very local groups to international organizations. Some groups have developed considerable resources such as websites in the effort for law reform (see below). Such groups are vital in the public debate in order to deepen the level of understanding and draw attention to the effects of current crime and justice policies.

The groups that are attempting to counter populist crime policy include existing organizations such as Amnesty International, Human Rights Watch, and Prison Reform International, as well as new groups emerging in response to excessively punitive crime policies. The many organizations aligned against the death penalty are an example of this phenomenon. At a more general level, in the United States, there is a campaign for effective sentencing and an organization that represents families affected by mandatory sentencing policies. In Australia, various legal and political groups have joined forces to oppose mandatory sentencing (e.g., Territorians for Effective Sentencing). Payback is an unusual British campaigning body, which pays a great deal of attention to the packaging of its messages in attractive, engaging, and accessible formats; it is discussed in more detail later in this chapter.

Various academics, legal workers, human rights activists, and those concerned about prisons and prisoners have contributed to a growing "alternative" body of knowledge through their efforts to counter ineffective and unjust sentencing. These groups can often be effective by working with academics, who can alert them to, or provide them with, valuable research documents and other relevant material.

Examples of Organizations/Web sites on Sentencing and Criminal Justice

The Sentencing Project: www.sentencingproject.org
Campaign for an Effective Crime Policy: http://crimepolicy.org
Payback: www.payback.org.uk
Families against Mandatory Minimums: http://www.famm.org
Australian Human Rights and Equal Opportunity Commission site: http://www.hreoc.gov.au/human_rights/children/
National Center on Institutions and Alternatives: http://www.igc.org/ncia
National Coalition to Abolish the Death Penalty: www.ncadp.org
Amnesty International: http://www.amnesty.org
Territorians for Effective Sentencing: http://ms.dcls.org.au

That work contained a number of sagacious criminal policy suggestions, reflecting a knowledge of crime and justice at that time. A new edition should succinctly address the issue of penal populism. [The Honest Politician's Guide to Responding to Penal Populism]

Get the Facts about Crime and Justice to Politicians

This response consists of ensuring that the facts *do* stand in the way of a good story. It is predicated on the assumption that politicians promote and represent populist responses as a "remedy" to crime. There is, therefore, either the hidden

The Honest Politician's Guide to Responding to Penal Populism

These 10 points are designed as an aid for the honest politician wanting to respond to populist exploitation of crime as a policy issue:

1. Get the facts about crime and justice to politicians.
2. Improve the measurement of public attitudes
3. Improve the level of public knowledge of crime and criminal justice
4. Improve the quality of information available to the news media.
5. Ensure that the populist is required to explain the source of funds.
6. Require evaluation research for all reform legislation.
7. Punish penal populism.
8. Focus on effective punishment in the community.
9. Create a policy "buffer" between politicians and the criminal justice system.
10. Improve the public face of the criminal justice system.

or explicit assumption, hope, or belief that the penalties will work to somehow make the community safer. The role of those that know better and actually want to see a safer community is to continue to point out the flaws in the assumption. This involves drawing politicians' minds back to their responsibilities and the need for scientific evidence.

An important tool in the attempt to get the facts about crime and justice is an independent crime information and prevention agency.[5] This can be sold as an essential weapon in the fight against crime. No one would contemplate going to war without a sophisticated array of information and intelligence through which targets can be established and success or otherwise monitored. Why should it be different with crime? The research evidence about the crime strategies that work should be more widely disseminated. Information about the increasing or decreasing punitiveness of the courts could be provided, as well as the average sentences handed out for a range of offenses. This information would provide an effective counter to the exploitation of aberrant cases of sentencing that are used by the mass media and populist politicians to provoke community outrage. Because crime policy has been so highly politicized in the past, it is essential that good sources of information, carefully packaged to maximize access, be supported. This will form the basis of a rational crime policy and an essential component of any mechanism of accountability such as the community safety budget.

Improve the Measurement of Attitudes to Punishment

The political debate about penal policy needs to be much better serviced with information on people's opinions on the topic. Public opinion is far from unidimensional; members of the public have sophisticated views about punishment;

and many people are ambivalent about the appropriate response to offending. While the majority think that the courts are generally too soft, majorities also tend to recognize that prison is an expensive response to crime. One of the findings across our jurisdictions is that this group of offenders tends to be dealt with much more severely than people generally recognize. In short, polls can be doubly misleading. They tap into attitudes about a *minority* of court sentences, about which people tend to be systematically *misinformed.*

The frustration that people feel with the courts is real, and politicians' instincts about the need to respond to this frustration are understandable. However, they are unlikely to respond in the right way, unless the information they are given about public attitudes is valid. Those who assemble information about public opinion on this topic need to document concern about crime and punishment and also to explain fully what underlies the concern. The superficial measurement of public views is part of the process which sustains penal populism.

Improving the measurement of public attitudes requires closer adherence to best practices in designing polls. For example, it is bad practice to ask people questions when it is clear that the majority lack the information necessary to make a sensible response. It is bad practice to use loaded terms: for example, asking if the courts are "tough enough on persistent criminals" is guaranteed to elicit agreement from the vast majority of the population. Although these are obvious enough lessons, ones which could have been drawn 20 years ago, many surveys of the public continue to ignore them. All too often, opinion polling is a weapon used to bolster a specific penal policy, rather than a tool to establish the direction of public attitudes and the limits on particular positions. Better measurement of public attitudes also involves placing the results of an opinion poll in some context. This context would include information about what people know of the problem being explored in the poll, as well as the results of previous polls dealing with the same issue. Although for some issues the public is not cost-sensitive, for others costs are relevant and should be provided in any public survey of policy options. [Measuring Public Attitudes]

Improve the Level of Public Knowledge about Crime and Punishment

Penal populism feeds off public ignorance and misunderstanding about crime and punishment. The obvious remedies here are to improve the quality and availability of information on the subject. In doing so, there are issues to consider with respect to *allocating responsibility, targeting,* and *styles* of communication.

Measuring Public Attitudes toward Mandatory Sentencing

It is surprising, in light of the proliferation of mandatory sentencing laws in recent years, that so little attention has been paid to public knowledge of and attitudes toward mandatory sentencing. The few surveys that have been conducted have, like the New Zealand referendum question identified in chapter 2, approached the question in a highly leading manner.

An important weakness of surveys examining mandatory sentencing is that they do not take into account related public beliefs and stereotypes of offenders. Consider the specific wording of one U.S. question: *Do you favor or oppose mandatory prison sentences for people convicted of violent crime?* This formulation makes no mention of the specific kinds of offenders to whom the law applies. Respondents are likely to assume that it applies to the most serious crimes of violence. We also know from previous research that when people respond to sentencing questions, they have in mind a stereotypical image of an offender, and that this image does not correspond to reality (see, e.g., Brillon, Louis-Guerin & Lamarche, 1984; Doob and Roberts, 1988; Stalans, 1993). The public tend to think of the most serious offenses committed by offenders with considerable criminal histories.

With respect to the Canadian firearms mandatory minimum sentence of four years in prison, there are two ways of canvasing public opinion. The public could be asked a general question such as *"Are you in favor of or opposed to a mandatory sentence of imprisonment of four years for offenders convicted of violent crimes involving a firearm?"* A question of this kind would surely generate substantial public support for mandatory sentencing, not necessarily because the public supports the principle of such sentences, but because they have in mind the most serious kinds of violent crime committed by recidivists.

An alternative method would involve giving respondents summaries of actual cases. These should include the range of offenses and offenders affected by the mandatory sentence. For example, let us return to the following case which was appealed to the Canadian Supreme Court and described earlier:

> Marty Morrisey has pleaded guilty to criminal negligence causing death. He has no previous convictions. Marty is a woodsman who has had a drinking problem since he was 14. He stopped drinking for a while, but started again after the break-up of a relationship. One day, when he had been drinking heavily and had taken some prescription drugs for depression, Marty went into the woods with a friend. At some point, while holding a loaded gun, Marty tried to wake his sleeping friend. He slipped, and the gun fired, killing the other man. "Are you in favor of or opposed to a four-year term of imprisonment for this offender?"

If respondents were given this case to consider, in all likelihood, the percentage endorsing a mandatory sentence of imprisonment for four years would be quite low (see Roberts, 2003, for further discussion).

Responsibility for Communication

In our view, the main responsibility for informing people about court practices must lie with governments rather than with local courts, although the latter obviously have a role to play, the nature of which is discussed below. The anonymity of large cities means that local communication networks are ineffective in communicating information about who gets punished, in what manner, and for what kinds of crimes. The most pressing need is for information systems that can successfully summarize overall sentencing patterns while managing to communicate what the "going rate" is for specific sorts of crime. Criminal justice statisticians have usually managed the former but not the latter. It is relatively easy in all five countries to find out what proportion of convicted offenders get sent to prison; but it remains virtually impossible in these jurisdictions to find out what the risk of imprisonment is for a specific offender—a 25-year-old burglar, for example, with 10 previous convictions,[6] who stole goods worth $500 to feed a heroin habit. How can people assess whether punishments fit the crime in the absence of such information? Awareness of aggregate sentencing statistics (knowing, e.g., that 60% of burglars are sent to prison) then, is useful, but only up to a point.

Demands for harsher sentencing do not spring from a systematic study of sentencing patterns in trial courts. Members of the public never argue that the ninetieth percentile custodial sentence imposed in cases of burglary is too low; they read about a sentence which seems, in light of the summary of facts provided by the media, to be too lenient, and then conclude that we need to do something about sentencing. This leads us to suggest that there must be a way of calming public anxiety about specific sentencing decisions.

Necessity of Providing a Context for Public Evaluation of Sentences

The public need to have some frame of comparison within which to consider whether a particular sentence is appropriate. One important framework is the average penalty imposed or the range of sentence lengths for a particular offense. All too often the public spontaneously make (and are encouraged by the media to make) comparisons between the sentence handed down and the theoretical maximum penalty, which is almost never imposed in any of our five jurisdictions. This discrepancy between trial court practices and the maximum penalty structure simply feeds the desire for raising the tariff or instituting a mandatory penalty. Providing the news media with comprehensible, up-to-date sentencing statistics is therefore a priority. This may not ensure that the data will be provided to the reader or listener in some form when a sentencing story appears, but at least the news media will not have the excuse that these data are either unavailable or only available in an indigestible format. A necessary step then is to ensure that systematic sentencing statistics are available. At the present, such data do not exist; only the United States and the United Kingdom have comprehensive annual statistics on sentencing patterns.

Of course, some people will still be dissatisfied with sentencing patterns, and knowing that a particular sentence is consistent with other sentences imposed for the same offense will lead them to argue for harsher sentences generally. But that is a broader debate about what is and is not an appropriate sentence for a particular crime. It is not an uninformed opinion based on a selective newspaper article.

International comparisons might also be useful in this context. Members of the public in all our countries tend to assume that the situation is better elsewhere, and by "better," they mean "tougher." We can illustrate this point by reference to Canada. Most Canadians are unaware of the fact that the rate of incarceration in their country is high, relative to many other Western nations (Roberts, Nuffield, and Hann, 1999). Similarly, as noted in chapter 7, almost all Canadians feel that sentences imposed on young offenders in Canada are too lenient. If they knew that the use of incarceration for juvenile offenders is about the same in Canada as in the United States (see Sprott & Snyder, 1999), the acknowledged leader in incarceration, people in Canada might be more tolerant of the sentencing practices in their youth courts. Finally, many Canadians feel that offenders convicted of murder should never receive parole. A survey conducted in 1988 found that four out of five respondents thought that such prisoners should never be paroled (Roberts, 1988), although as noted earlier, this general attitude changes when they are in court reviewing applications for early review of parole. On average, offenders convicted of first degree murder in Canada spend almost 30 years in custody (Correctional Service of Canada, 1999). This is significantly longer than most other countries. The lesson seems clear: if Canadians knew (a) how much time convicted murderers actually spend in prison before being released on parole, and (b) how this statistic compares to other jurisdictions, they may be less critical of sentence lengths served by offenders convicted of murder.

Best Practices in Sentencing

There is also a degree of insularity that characterizes populist policies. Politicians tend not to learn from the experience of other countries, and the same mistakes tend to be repeated around the world. The problems created by mandatory sentencing have been well documented by sentencing scholars in the United States for some time now. As one leading scholar who reviewed the literature noted: "As instruments of public policy, they do little good and much harm" (Tonry, 1996, p. 164). Tonry's comment was made in the mid-1990s, since then mandatory minimum sentences of imprisonment have continued to attract the attention of populist politicians.

There is also a need to convey to the public much clearer information about crime trends. At the time of writing, crime rates were falling in most of our five jurisdictions and have been for almost a decade. Despite this, the majority view remains that crime rates are rising. In Canada, for example, the annual crime statistics were released in July 2000, showing a significant decline for all categories of crime over the previous year (Tremblay, 2000). Shortly after these data were released, a national survey of the public found that approximately two-thirds of the public believed that crime was increasing (Ekos Research, 2000). This misperception would be understandable if the decline in crime rates was very recent. However, as noted, the latest decline was the eighth consecutive annual decrease.[7] As long as members of the public continue to believe that crime is constantly increasing, there will be repeated calls for harsher sentencing.

One difficulty with news treatment of crime statistics is that there is differential reporting, depending on the direction of the trend. When there are increases in crime rates to report, these hit the headlines: crime "soars" or "surges," and the reader is denied any insight into the reliability of the data. When crime rates fall, this is usually reported by the media, but in terms of tabloid news values, a small fall in crime has little editorial allure.

The release of crime statistics is an infrequent event, and this undermines their impact. National crime figures generally appear once a year. As we have seen, the overall trend for our five jurisdictions is now downward. Thus, once a year, there may be good news to report about crime. However, that leaves 364 days in which there is a constant stream of reports of individual crimes, usually offenses involving serious personal injury. Crime statistics simply do not compel the same degree of public attention as serious crimes of violence; they do not appear as often; and they are much less memorable. The only way that crime statistics are likely to remain in the public mind is if the media place the incident in a statistical context. This is unlikely ever to happen for two reasons. First, contextual information is seldom provided by the news media; and second, reporting the details of, for example, a homicide while simultaneously noting that the homicide rates are at a 30-year low, is likely to be seen as insulting the relatives of the victim, for whom statistical trends with respect to murder are understandably totally irrelevant.

The same divorce between public opinion and reality exists with respect to punishment trends. The vast majority of the public see the system as being excessively lenient to offenders; imprisonment rates are always too low, and parole rates too high, although no one ever has an accurate idea of how many people are imprisoned, for how long, or how many of these prisoners are eventually granted parole. When asked to estimate statistics such as the incarceration rate, in general, or with respect to specific offenses, as noted in chapter 2, people underestimate the true severity of the system. Two recent examples illustrate the veracity of this summary. As described earlier, the British public greatly underestimates the use of imprisonment for burglars, muggers, and especially for rapists. Second, a national survey of Canadians asked people about the percentage of prisoners released on parole: over four-fifths of the sample overestimated the parole grant rate, most by a very significant margin (Roberts et al., 1999).

Clearly, ways have to be developed of presenting crime and justice statistics in a manner that both emphasizes their limitations and communicates the realities underlying the statistics. Ironically, the more heated the climate of debate about crime, the more difficulty governments have in presenting an accurate view of crime trends to the public. In England and Wales, for example, crime statistics published in July 2000 have shown an upturn after several years of decline; even though the probability is that the steepest rises are statistical artifacts, fear of appearing complacent in the face of rising crime has stopped any serious discussion of this possibility.[8]

Targeting Audiences

Whatever institutional arrangements exist for providing information about the penal process, it will always be essential to identify and target key subgroups of the population. General messages about the functioning of the system are unlikely to have much impact on specific groups with different needs. To use the jargon of market research, audiences need to be properly segmented, and messages properly constructed to address the needs of different audiences. While some progress can be made in reaching the general public, it is almost certainly more efficient to reach separate subgroups directly. Key groups are likely to include:

- Victims
- Offenders
- Young people
- Parents with adolescent children
- People from minority ethnic groups

Victims, offenders, and people between the ages of 12 and 25 comprise three overlapping groups forming the principal set of "clients" of the criminal process. Leaving aside the opportunity to reach people within this age bracket through schools, colleges, and universities, each contact with the courts provides an opportunity (usually ignored) to shape participants' expectations about the criminal justice system and to provide information about its true function and performance.

Styles of Communication

Once key audiences have been identified, they need to be provided with information in a way that is tailored to their specific needs and receptivity. Our experience is that few nonspecialists can find their way around the sentencing statistics of any of the five countries covered in this book. The statistical systems are comprehensive to differing degrees; the more comprehensive they are, the more incomprehensible they become. We can find no examples of initiatives whereby this information has been reduced to its essentials and packaged in different ways for specific sets of audiences. Part of the reason for this may be that departments of justice and the criminal justice systems that they run simply lack the skills for effective communication, and lack any tradition of acquiring these skills.

It is hardly an exaggeration to say that the court systems in our five countries collectively represent a public relations failure. The majority of the public lack confidence in the key decision-makers within these systems, namely, sentencers. Most people also express little confidence in other criminal justice professionals, with the notable exception of the police. In the absence of any accurate knowledge of the severity of typical sentences, they think that the judicial product—punishment—is totally inadequate. Any commercial organization facing such a crisis would not hesitate to contract the skills of communication experts. The crisis in public confidence in the courts and the parole system will not be resolved by communications alone, but such an initiative will have a positive influence.

Central and federal government is not the only sector with a patchy record in getting across messages about criminal justice. Groups campaigning for liberal criminal justice reform and criminologists who share their agenda appear to have had little impact in terms of restraining the development of penal populism. In their defense, one could perhaps argue that without their efforts we would now be faced with even more punitive penal policies. A harsher assessment is that academics have failed to engage effectively with this debate and have proved unable to develop persuasive alternatives to penal populism. As Brereton notes: "Talking to and with each other at academic conferences and through academic journals are enjoyable and worthwhile activities, but more can be done to communicate research findings to a wider audience" (1996, p. 87).

Scholars have too often developed an isolationist approach, preferring to criticize penal policies in recondite journals (with limited circulation) and at academic conferences, attended almost exclusively by like-minded peers. It is clear that once criminal policy gets politicized, politicians become deaf to arguments for penal reform. It is also clear that advocacy groups pressing for penal reform have—with rare exceptions—continued to advance these arguments and failed to adapt to the selective deafness of populist forces. [Payback: A "Tabloid" Campaigning Body]

Using New Technology

Until recently, the mass media enjoyed a near-monopoly on access to the general public. Messages of any complexity had to be presented via the media, and those who wished to reach the public inevitably had to surrender some control over the process. The IT revolution has changed all this. By the year 2000, approximately one North American adult in four had Internet access; the figure for Britain is one in 10. The proportion of the population with Internet access will obviously grow rapidly. There will be inevitable limits to the extent to which people seek out information about crime and punishment, but it is worth extending these limits as far as possible. Interactive websites constitute an ideal medium for rendering complex, detailed information about crime and punishment in an accessible way and for providing it in a manner that is at the convenience of the consumer. In addition, the sheer volume of information that can be made accessible in a website makes the Internet an ideal vehicle for communicating the results of research.[9]

Payback: A "Tabloid" Campaigning Body

One British campaigning body is of particular interest for its unusual style of operation. Payback was set up in 1998 as a small charity to promote the use of community penalties and to increase public understanding of crime and punishment. Its work is premised on the assumption that many penal reform bodies have assembled the information needed to counter penal populism but have failed to promote this information effectively. Payback thus places a premium on packaging its messages in attractive, engaging, and accessible formats, with a readiness to exploit the skills of advertising and communications specialists. It has an attractive Web site: www.payback.org.uk.

Payback often uses humor to get its points across, retaining the services of a professional cartoonist. It often uses whimsical methods of securing the attention of professional audiences. To our knowledge, it is the only criminal justice campaigning body that has inundated a country's criminal justice system with small tins of chocolates carrying messages about community penalties. It is prepared to simplify issues to a degree that makes them widely accessible.

Respond to the Media

As we discussed earlier in this volume, the mass media play a complex role in the development of penal populism. Television, radio, and newspapers—and the tabloid press in particular—simultaneously respond to and shape public opinion. Some of the distortions in public understanding about crime and punishment stem from the influence of commercial news values. We have seen how vulnerable the courts are to selective and exaggerated reporting. How far then can the media and the tabloid press, in particular, be encouraged to adopt a more responsible form of journalism? To be realistic, the most optimistic answer must be "not much." However, there are some things that can be done. Newspapers' editorial policies on the coverage of crime and punishment may be moderated a little if their unintended consequences are pointed out to editors.

There are some encouraging precedents in this respect. For example, in the 1980s, the British Home Office set up an independent committee to examine the media's role in exacerbating public fear of crime.[10] The committee's chairman and several members were influential media personalities. Their recommendations regarding the responsible reporting of crime were subsequently adopted by the broadcast media and may have exercised a *temporary* brake, at least, on the tendency of the tabloid press to sensationalize crime and undermine confidence in the criminal justice system. One can envisage equivalent initiatives to discourage the media from fostering undue cynicism about the penal process, in general, and about sentencers, in particular.

Often the way in which the media handle a crime story is less a function of news values than of lack of familiarity with the criminal justice system; crime reports are seldom written by reporters who specialize in criminal justice. Reporters work to tight deadlines, often without any expert knowledge. For example, they might report specific sentences in the context of the maximum penalty possible or make comparisons with another case which was unique in some respect. Sentencing stories (and editorials) frequently blame judges for sentences that appear lenient, without realizing that many sentences reflect joint submissions from the defense and the prosecution, and that in most jurisdictions, judges will not impose a sentence that differs from the joint submission.

Media personnel are prone to the same misunderstandings about crime and punishment as the layperson, and their reporting will reflect these misunderstandings. Those responsible for the management of the criminal process need to ensure that opinion-formers are properly supported with accurate information about criminal justice. Unfortunately, it can prove quite a demanding discipline for government departments to maintain an open information policy for journalists, when they are equally concerned to control the spin that the media place on their policies. Journalists tend to be wary of being "co-opted" into delivering the government's message. It is probably best in the long run that journalists have direct access to the statisticians and researchers who understand sentencing and crime statistics.

There are many things that could be done in most jurisdictions to improve the links between the media and the criminal justice process. These include appointing press officers (whether at central government, state, or local level), improving media access to specialist staff such as statisticians and academics, and striving for the better use of technology to communicate statistical information to the press.

Ensure That the Populist Is Required to Explain the Source of Funds

Typically, during federal elections in the United States, candidates must present a proposed budget and economists subsequently critique each candidate's proposals in terms of whether they can be implemented without provoking a deficit or requiring cuts in existing programs. Instead of rhetoric about "law and order," a new tradition could begin whereby parliamentary (or congressional) candidates as well as executive candidates could be required to submit proposals that include estimate spending in the area of criminal justice. Criminologists could provide an independent estimate of a specific proposal's impact on crime trends and correctional populations. Debates about crime and justice might then adopt a more rational tone.

Politicians should be required to identify the source of funds for specific proposals. For example, funding for prison construction should not be derived from crime prevention initiatives. This response to penal populism is part of a broader attempt to promote accountability. Most conservatives will see accountability as a virtue and a sign of responsible government; this means that they can be shamed if they refuse to be accountable for crime and the use of punishment. [The Community Safety Budget]

Scheingold argued that "If . . . it becomes increasingly less attractive, even for fiscal reasons, to campaign on get-tough, anti-crime platforms, the political climate may cool significantly. The ensuing de-politicization of crime will put policy back into the hands of criminal process professionals [who] can be expected to lead a retreat from the punitive drift of recent years" (1984, p. 231). He was discussing the wave of punitive policies that emerged in the late 1970s, but the argument is equally valid in the early years of the new millennium.

The Community Safety Budget

The strategy starts from a position of common agreement: we all want to live in a safer community and we would all support policies that will achieve this. The only disagreement surrounds the strategy—the best way to achieve this goal. The focus should be on evidence and evaluation, not rhetoric. The pursuit of public safety should be the aim, but it needs to be measured fairly against a baseline that is different in each jurisdiction.

Politicians tend to believe that "something" (in this case more prisons) is better than "nothing." But is it? Most populists believe that they are adding something or at least they are not making things worse. However, if the money spent on prisons was spent on good crime prevention, the benefits in terms of community safety would be much greater. It could then be argued that politicians deciding to spend public funds on prisons rather than crime prevention would be responsible for a certain reduction in public safety. To make this argument convincing, the comparative advantage of good crime prevention needs to be quantified. Increasing prison terms by five years may cost the government an extra $50 million. Examining the estimated benefits of $50 million spent on early intervention or other proven crime prevention strategies could be quantified in terms of numbers of burglaries, robberies, and assaults prevented. The true costs of spending on imprisonment would then be revealed.

All criminal justice practices should be included as part of a government budget that is rigorously and independently audited by a suitable authority in terms of public safety outcomes. The "community safety budget" could evolve to integrate what is learned worldwide in terms of more effective strategies for crime prevention, policing, and corrections. Effective practices would be slowly but systematically enhanced and developed, ineffective ones would be transformed or replaced. Funds would be diverted from ineffective areas to effective areas. Strategies to stem the flow of funds in ineffective areas like prisons may be developed such as the demarcation of a limited level of funding for custodial options. Each item of expenditure in terms of crime prevention and criminal justice should be justified. Inputs in terms of investment, outputs in terms of enhancements to community safety. One of the most significant advantages of the community safety budget is that if public safety is established as an explicit goal, debates about crime and punishment could become less political. This strategy will help to ensure that issues are resolved through recourse to investigation of the available evidence rather than the most emotive rhetoric.

Require Evaluation Research for All New Legislation

In general, we would argue (as have many others, seldom with much success), that criminal justice proposals should be evidence-based. The debate should be moved off the emotional wavelength that populists employ in their appeal to the public.

When proposals are directed at crime reduction initiatives, objective evaluation research should be mandatory. Indeed, every important statutory reform should include an evaluation requirement, the results of which would be reported back to the legislature within a specified period of time. This would shift attention to tangible results; if the proposed programs fail to achieve the goals ascribed to them, then the money allocated to the specific programs should be reallocated. For example, if the incidence of firearm-related crimes does not decline following the creation of a mandatory minimum sentence of imprisonment, the mandatory sentence should be revisited. Yet how many jurisdictions that have introduced mandatory sentences have subsequently evaluated their impacts?

This strategy draws on one of the characteristics of neoliberalism and its focus on accountability (see O'Malley, 1999). By ensuring a very clear accounting for all expenditures made to achieve the aim of public safety, the effectiveness of crime control policies will become more evident. The focus on costs and accountability should appeal to neoliberals and should have the effect of shifting the argument into a more evidence-based debate about how to enhance community safety. One of the best ways to achieve this is to include all criminal justice practices as part of a government budget that is rigorously and independently audited by a suitable authority in terms of public safety outcomes.

Punish Populism

The reactive nature of the populist response generates some hope that the political process can be disciplined into the pursuit of more rational penal policies. We have some sympathy for the dilemma of politicians who believe that they will lose electoral ground if they fail to match their opponents' penal rhetoric. It is naive to think that one can entirely remove the politics from criminal policy development. However, the growth in penal populism—as with any form of political opportunism—has been accompanied by an increasing public sensitivity to, and distaste for, populist posturing. For example, in the course of the 2001 general election in Britain, political commentators increasingly drew attention to the "unpopular populism" of the Conservatives. Indeed, this sensitivity to populism is probably one of the main factors that has prompted large sectors of the population to disengage from the electoral process in some industrialized democracies.

It is unlikely that politicians will voluntarily adopt a self-denying ordinance, choosing to replace simplistic rhetoric with a recognition of the complexities and difficulties of crime control. But it is possible to devise strategies to increase the chances that politicians are punished for engaging in penal populism. The electoral value of "talking tough" on crime would be considerably reduced if its insincerity were made more transparent. Ironically, the people best placed to punish populism are, of course, politicians themselves. They have much to gain if they can successfully expose and ridicule their opponents' policies as consisting of political spin rather than substance. For this to happen, it is essential that they should have ready access to the right information to enable them to do this quickly and definitively.

In the absence of counterbalancing pressure, political parties will probably continue to converge in pursuing populist solutions to crime problems. If pressure groups for penal reform—and associated criminal justice scholars—wish to undermine this populism, they may have to form broader alliances. Traditionally, the advocates of liberal reform have aligned themselves with politicians from the center or left of the political spectrum. An earlier chapter documented a process whereby the latter have been drawn progressively into penal populism in competition with more conventionally conservative political parties. The implication of this is that pressure groups may have to seek support across the full political spectrum, including those on the political right, when mobilizing opposition to populist initiatives. Given the international dimensions of penal populism, perhaps there is a need for national groups to coalesce to provide an international response, along the lines of the international movements to protect human rights, and work for the abolition of capital punishment.

Focus on Punishment in the Community

Most debates about criminal justice policy focus on the worst case scenario, the sexual predator, the teenage killer, the armed heroin dealer. One challenge is to shift the focus of public attention to prisoners serving sentences in the community, as these represent the vast majority of cases processed by the criminal justice system. Morever, it is here, among this population that the success stories are to be found, which provide a counterweight to the parole "failures." Of course, community penalties must be, and must be seen to be, tough enough to offer a realistic alternative to imprisonment. If all community punishments are seen as variants of probation, focusing on these alternative sanctions is likely to make matters worse, not better.

It is important as well to challenge the myth that prison is a solution because offenders can be locked away. This point can probably be brought home most poignantly by converting the populist pro-prison talk into the number of ex-cons that will be released onto our streets direct from prison. The image of an army of former prisoners returning to the street should help to promote better policies, as even those that are angry now need to share some responsibility for safety in the future. Most people intuitively understand that if you want to deal effectively with a problem, you have to address the root causes. By moving the discussion to the causes of crime, rather than the severity of punishments, it may be possible to increase support for less punitive criminal justice policies.

Create a Policy "Buffer" Between Politicians and the Criminal Justice System

The closer that politicians come to directly determining sentencing policies, the more likely it is that these policies will reflect the forces of blind populism. If there were any doubts about this assertion, they should be dispelled by examining private member's bills in the area of criminal justice in Canada, most of which are very uninformed and reflect blatantly populist sentiments (see chapter 3). They are usually drafted by back-bench politicians safe in the knowledge that the legislative agenda of Parliament is unlikely to review the proposed legislation beyond first reading. Nevertheless, getting this far permits the individual member to say that they "have tried to do something about the crime problem."

It is also noteworthy that many private member's bills are introduced by the sponsoring politician with reference to the popularity of the proposal. Popularity is seldom established by reference to careful analyses of public opinion along the lines we have suggested. Rather, the consistency of the proposal with public opinion is established by reference to letters from constituents, or specific polls tailored to elicit a particular response from respondents. A similar argument applies to opposition politicians who have no realistic prospect of imminent electoral success. This reality liberates them to devise and promote sentencing policies that they might shrink from if they were in office or about to form a government.

This analysis suggests that jurisdictions, in which there is a body with a mandate to develop criminal justice policy (independent of the political element), are less likely to develop populist policies. There is considerable variation in the extent to which such bodies exist. In the United States., the most visible policy-making bodies with respect to sentencing are, of course, the state and federal sentencing commissions that develop sentencing policies and prescribe sentencing ranges. The weakness with these commissions is that (as has been observed) the mandate, membership, and on-going activities of the commissions are frequently influenced by political considerations. The U.S. National Institute of Justice certainly *sounds* like it has the credentials to fill the buffer role we envisage, but functionally it is part of the Department of Justice, with a clear role in the development of federal criminal policy.

Canada has no permanent sentencing commission or even a Law Reform Commission to develop sentencing reform proposals for parliamentarians to consider.[11] Penal policy development is therefore left exclusively in the hands of the federal government departments responsible for criminal justice. These departments are subject to pressure from external groups, and internally from the minister's political staff. Conscientious civil servants charged with developing responsible criminal law policy have a lot to contend with. Parliamentary and congressional committees with responsibility for justice matters also provide some balance to the development of policy. However, at the end of the day, these committees are composed of elected representatives, who are themselves subject to populist pressures, and who are seldom specialists in criminal justice.

Turning to Britain, proposals for a sentencing council were advanced by the Labour Party when in opposition. To date, however, all that has been put in place is a Sentencing Advisory Panel, whose role is to advise the judiciary—in the shape of the Court of Appeal—on sentencing matters. In establishing this body, politicians did not delegate any of their own decision-making powers. However, a recent review of the sentencing framework in England and Wales (Home Office, 2001a) has suggested the establishment of a new sentencing commission as part of its fairly far-reaching proposals for a new sentencing system. The degree to which such a body would enjoy independence from political control is unclear, however. Indeed, we think it unlikely that politicians in any of our five jurisdictions will positively choose to place any aspects of penal policy beyond their own reach.

What this implies is that "policy buffers" are unlikely to emerge from the political process without a great deal of pressure from other parties. An associated development that may help would be the creation of special new institutions which draw upon expertise within the criminal justice system and elsewhere. These new institutions should be designed to provide authoritative nonpartisan information and evaluation advice on matters of crime and justice. There is a need for bodies with national visibility, that can speak with as much or more authority on penal matters than politicians. These bodies should be established to provide information on the critical issue of the cost effectiveness of penal measures. Part of this agenda should also be to advocate the development of effective policy development bureaus. They need to be politically independent and they also need to be independent of criminal justice agencies, while maintaining the confidence of all the main participants in the criminal justice system. If such independent "institutes of justice" are to emerge, they will—almost by definition—require arrangements for funding and management which place them beyond the reach of political pressure.

Estimating the Impact of Penal Reform Proposals

Another important contribution that a policy body of the kind described here could perform would be to conduct impact analyses or cost-benefit analyses of different sentencing reform scenarios. At present, this is accomplished in some jurisdictions, attempted in others, and ignored elsewhere. The North Carolina Sentencing and Policy Advisory Commission decided to link sentencing reforms to prison capacity, a strategy followed for years in some other states. In North Carolina, then, clear resource priorities are established for all to see. All reform proposals are then considered in terms of their effect on the prison population, and the financial impact is well known in advance.

In England and Wales, the Sentencing Reform Bill which introduced mandatory sentences carried a memorandum that estimated the cost of introducing the new mandatory terms of imprisonment. However, these figures carried a number of assumptions that were challenged by organizations external to the government. Divorcing the source of the legislation from the agency that carries out the impact evaluation research would be a superior option. Clearly, most jurisdictions can do better in this regard.

Improve the Public Face of the Criminal Justice System

While an understanding of the criminal process is generally poor, substantial minorities of the population have limited contact with the courts each year. Some people appear before the courts for sentencing; others are involved as witnesses, complainants, or jurors. Much more could be done to exploit these contacts—or at least to minimize the damage done to public confidence as a result of the contact. In part, this will be a question of making courts more responsive to the needs of the various participants. Many courts already run programs designed to make testifying more tolerable for victims and others to serve as witnesses, but the idea of a consumer or service orientation remains foreign to most justice systems.

However, it seems unlikely that courts will be able to manage their public face more effectively, unless those working within the system themselves have a better understanding both of the criminal process itself and of the ways in which the public think about it. Some will be poorly informed about their particular specialization; few will be well informed about other parts of the justice system. All are exposed to the same misinformation as the wider public. Possible strategies for sustaining or improving their confidence in the criminal justice system include the following:

- providing briefing material in a genuinely accessible form;
- providing information in eye-catching ways which take account of the limited attention span of busy professionals;
- designing Web sites to make them usable by nonspecialist professionals;
- marketing Web sites and targeting them at criminal justice system professionals;
- investing in the production of better professional journals;
- learning from successful analogous exercises in both private and public sectors.

It is also important to understand that public reaction to messages about criminal justice is going to vary enormously in impact, depending upon the credibility of the communicator. Surveys have shown that people place very little faith in criminal justice professionals, with the important exception of the police. Repeated administrations of the British Crime Survey, for example, found that ratings of the Crown Prosecution Service (CPS), probation officers, and judges were uniformly poor, with the judiciary attracting the poorest ratings (e.g., Hough and Roberts, 1998). Similar results emerge from surveys in other jurisdictions. A recent survey of the public in Canada asked respondents how much confidence they had in a number of professions, and lawyers attracted the lowest ratings. Finally, another Canadian survey provides a more precise response to the question of credibility with respect to criminal justice policies (Environics Research Group, 1998). Respondents were asked the following question: "*When it comes to crime and solutions to crime, how believable are the following?*" Results showed that government officials, those who traditionally carry responsibility for public legal education initiatives, received the lowest ratings: less than one-third of the sample described this group as believable in terms of crime and solutions to crime. On the other hand, over two-thirds of the sample found police chiefs and representatives of victims' rights groups to be believable. These results suggest that criminal justice professionals and representatives of the justice bureaucracy are far from the ideal group to convey information about the criminal justice system.

Role of the Judiciary

Finally, we add a word about the role of the judge. As noted, public dissatisfaction with sentencing reflects the perception of excessive leniency. Almost everyone, it seems, can cite cases in which a serious crime of violence resulted in the imposition of a sentence that appeared to be too lenient. In our collective experience, few judges are very lenient and particularly not when sentencing offenders convicted of crimes of violence. Seldom, if ever, have we seen a very lenient sentence imposed that did not have some precedent in the case law or characteristics which made the case exceptional in some respect. In addition, we have all seen cases where important mitigating factors existed, but which did not make it into the media account of the sentencing decision. It seems important, therefore, for judges to make a greater attempt to articulate the reasons for sentence, the mitigating and aggravating factors that influenced the sentence, and the range of disposition advocated by the counsel for the offender and the state. In Canada, one of the reforms passed in 1996 created an obligation on judges to state the reasons for their sentences. This reasonable requirement may help promote greater community acceptance of specific sentencing decisions.

Utility of a "Judicial Information Office"

Judges are understandably reluctant to enter the public arena to defend their sentencing decisions in individual cases. When the media turn on the heat with regard to a particular sentence, almost all judges elect to suffer in silence. Crown prosecutors are also quite reticent to comment publicly after a sentence is imposed, in part, because the decision may be appealed. Perhaps what is needed, therefore, is an office or an individual attached to the Chief Justice or head judge, who would not aggressively *defend* specific judges under attack for imposing lenient sentences, but who would be able at the very least to disseminate the reasons for sentence, to convey the recommendations for sentence that were made at the sentencing hearing, and perhaps to cite the precedents that guided the sentencing judge. This kind of information might help to reduce the community anger that is aroused by an apparently lenient sentence.

Conclusion

This book has analyzed the development of penal populism with using examples from five jurisdictions and has examined the pressures which impel politicians down the path of populist justice. At one level, penal populism is just one example of a tendency (which is afflicting many areas of political debate) to reduce complex issues to simplistic propositions that give rise to simple solutions. Popular disengagement from democratic institutions and processes leads politicians to pay increasing attention to the presentation of their policies and decreasing attention to the content. This strategy may buy short-term benefits at the ballot box, but in the longer term probably accelerates popular cynicism about politics. Finding ways of arresting this downward spiral is one of the major political challenges of the twenty-first century.

However, there are features of penal policy which render it uniquely vulnerable to populism. Anxieties about crime and personal safety are deep-seated and pervasive in industrialized democracies. There are structural reasons why the mass media should amplify these anxieties, both in the crime stories that they report and the way in which they do so. Political parties exploit these anxieties and can cause real damage to their opponents if they can expose them as being "soft on crime." Whatever broader trends there may be toward populism, it is this dynamic that tends to prompt the penal "arms races" which we have seen in all five countries studied here and have documented in this book.

If there is a single lesson to be learned from this survey of criminal justice policy development in recent years, it is that penal populism will dominate the reform landscape and determine the future of our criminal justice systems—unless and until a more vigorous and coordinated response is generated. We cannot expect this response to come from politicians themselves, however. Any minister of justice seeking an expeditious (but respectable) route to early retirement needs only insist that crime is a complex social problem for which there are no easy answers.

Toward the end of this book, we have sketched the shape of the counterweights which are needed to offset the pressures toward penal populism. In designing these counterweights, two key principles must be observed. First, the political costs of penal populism need to be increased. This implies a very different style of political advocacy than that traditionally pursued by liberal penal reformers. Second, politicians need to be offered cogent and compelling alternative models of crime control. This implies an agenda for reform which places as much emphasis on finding effective methods of crime reduction as it does on curtailing the worst excesses of the criminal process. If these two principles are to assume any practical reality, professionals within and around the criminal process need to think harder about the institutional arrangements needed to ensure that there are adequate buffers between penal practice and populist policy. We need more effective alliances between practitioners, academics, and reform groups that will allow rational penal policy to develop a coherent, audible, and authoritative voice. In the absence of such alliances, populism will continue to dominate sentencing reform; if this occurs, the public, victims, offenders, indeed, all of us will be worse off.

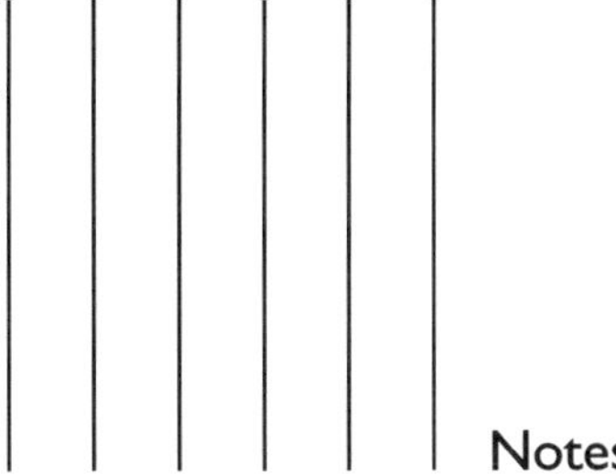

Notes

Chapter 1

1. The term populism has been subject to increasing critical scrutiny (e.g., Taggart, 2000) and theoretical exposition. It is not our intention here to summarize these debates; our use of the term "populism" will be explored in greater detail later in this volume. However, as Taggert (2000) and others note, populism is an elusive and complex phenomenon that carries important considerations for the criminal justice systems of most Western nations. Some of its core features are hostility to representative politics, an identification with an idealized heartland, authoritarianism, anti-elitism, and above all a mistrust of expert opinion.
2. Some scholars would disagree with this assertion; see, for example, Block and Twist (1994).
3. There are many reasons for this conclusion. First, only a small percentage of offenses results in the imposition of a sentence. This means that regardless of the severity of the disposition imposed, it will have little impact on the *overall* crime rate. Second, the only other mechanism by which the sentencing process can reduce crime rates is through general deterrence. The latest research evidence suggests that harsh sentencing, and in particular the use of imprisonment, does not serve as an effective general deterrent for potential offenders (see Von Hirsch, Bottoms, Burney, and Wikstrom, 1999.)
4. The police statistics derive from Maguire and Pastore (1998).
5. Canada does not have an annual victimization survey to provide information on crime trends independent of the police statistics. However, there is a periodic survey (the General Social Survey) which was conducted in 1988, 1993, and most recently in 1999. Comparative analyses based on the last two surveys generally confirmed the trends that emerged from the official criminal justice statistics (see Gartner and Doob, 1994; Besserer and Trainor, 2000). Overall rates of victimization were stable over the period 1993–1999. The offenses that increased in frequency of reporting tended to be the less serious crimes, with generally more labile rates at any point in time (e.g., theft, vandalism). Break and enter, an offense likely to be reported to the police or recalled by victimization survey respondents, declined 7% between 1988 and 1993 and a further 4% between 1993 and 1999 (Besserer and Trainor, 2000).
6. The general picture to emerge is that police statistics of recorded crime *overstated* the rate of increase until 1991 and *understated* it between 1991 and 1995. It is plausible, at least, that the police figures were deflated as a result of the introduction of performance indicators and a management regime which placed great emphasis on improving detection rates and reducing overall crime levels.
7. Making international comparisons of crime trends based on official, police-

recorded statistics is a notoriously tricky business. Victimization surveys provide a more uniform measure of crime. The only international victimization survey that included all five countries was the International Crime Victimization Survey in 1992. In 1992, New Zealand participated, for the first time, in the International Victimization Survey. The rate of overall victimization was 63%. This is comparable to the rate in Australia and the United Kingdom but is significantly higher than the rate reported for the United States or Canada (Harlan, 1995).

8. The irony is that people are so skeptical about crime statistics, even when they are derived from the criminal justice professionals in whom the public have the greatest degree of confidence: the police.
9. Scheingold quotes President Reagan describing crime as an "American epidemic," even though rates had leveled off by 1973.
10. *National Post*, Thursday, July 20, 2000.
11. We do not make comparisons between countries in terms of sentence lengths. The reason for this is that comparisons become complicated by the issue of time served and the question of release on parole.
12. The sentencing reform of 1996 contained a statement of purpose that urged judges to use imprisonment only when no other sanction was appropriate. In addition, the bill introduced a new (for Canada at least) noncustodial sentence (the conditional sentence), which was designed to reduce the number of prison terms (see Roberts and Cole, 1999).
13. Nor was the increase uniform: the rate of increase in imprisonment rates was considerably lower in Victoria (12%), Western Australia (16%), and the Northern Territory (9%) and much higher in South Australia and Queensland (70%).

Chapter 2

1. Public opinion is central to sentencing policy in general, not just "get tough" policies. The recent (2001) report of the Sentencing Review in England and Wales made it quite clear that public opinion was an important consideration in determining the future of sentencing policy in that jurisdiction (see Home Office, 2001a; Roberts, 2002a).
2. The BCS recorded a 14% decline in crime rates between 1995 and 1997, while approximately six respondents in 10 thought that crime rates had increased over this period.
3. The focus here is on attitudes toward sentence severity; we do not deal with the large and complex empirical literature on public support for different sentencing purposes (e.g., Innes, 1993; Applegate, Cullen, and Fisher, 1997; Cullen, Fisher, and Applegate, 2000).
4. Sometimes even this kind of research strategy is replaced with an "environmental scan" which involves no data at all, but which makes assertions about the likely tenor of public opinion.
5. The fit between public sentencing preferences and court practices was far from perfect. As the researchers note, there were areas "in which public opinion appears to be at odds with court practice, sometimes being more punitive, sometimes less" (Walker, Collins, and Wilson, 1987, p. 2).
6. Young and Brown (1993) discuss the comparative literature examining the reasons for different levels of public punitiveness and also consider the relationship between these levels of punitiveness and the nation's penal policy.

Chapter 3

1. The offenses and sentence length vary greatly across the states.
2. The states that incorporate resource matching into their sentencing guidelines are: Utah, Washington, Oregon, Tennessee, Virginia, Louisiana, Kansas, Arkansas, and North Carolina. Louisiana's guidelines were later rescinded, though the state still requires statements on how a proposed sentencing bill will affect resources. Five other states had guidelines under consideration that required resource matching: Massachusetts, Missouri, Ohio, Oklahoma, and South Carolina (see Frase, 1995).
3. In his influential book *Criminal Sentences: Law without Order*, Frankel described the pitfalls of indeterminate sentencing and proposed the creation of an executive sentencing commission insulated from politics to oversee penal policies and sentencing.
4. Under the truth in sentencing law, time served in prison is estimated to increase by 47 months for rape offenders, 26 months for robbery offenders, and 16 months for offenders convicted of assault.
5. The provinces have the responsibility for administering the criminal justice system.
6. The commission recommended a statutory statement of sentencing purpose and principle, according to which certain conditions would have to be fulfilled before a judge could impose a term of imprisonment (see Canadian Sentencing Commission, 1987, p. 154).
7. According to sections 718.2 (d) and (e) of the *Criminal Code*, "an offender should not be deprived of liberty, if less restrictive sanctions may be appropriate in the circumstances; and (e) all available sanctions other than imprisonment that are reasonable in the circumstances should be considered for all offenders, with particular attention to the circumstances of aboriginal offenders."
8. Approximately one-third of all robberies recorded by the police in Canada involve some kind of firearm (Leesti, 1997).
9. An earlier version of the bill would have removed judicial discretion and made the consecutive periods of parole ineligibility for offenders convicted of multiple murders mandatory. That provision was modified after consultation with officials from the Ministry of the Solicitor General.
10. The bill also created a presumption in favor of consecutive sentences for "sexual predators," although poor drafting resulted in this provision applying only to the least serious form of sexual assault.
11. However, the legislation gave the courts an unfettered power to *mitigate*, and a previous good record is an obvious mitigating factor. This subtlety was not appreciated by many commentators, and indeed, by some judges (see Ashworth and Hough, 1996).
12. While the dominant trend in British penal politics has been toward populist punitiveness, there are exceptions. The penal policies of Scotland and Northern Ireland, for example, have continued along a more reasonable trajectory since the early 1980s. The imperative to "out-tough" the opposition policies did not stretch beyond England and Wales. Policy toward drug offenses and drug-related crime also managed to escape the demands of populism to a significant extent (see Home Office, 1996). Though mandatory sentences were introduced for drug supply, harm reduction policies also formed an important part of government policy.

13. It is interesting to note that the Conservative leader made a number of recommendations for responding to pedophiles, some of which were quite reasonable (e.g., enhanced supervision of sex offenders serving sentences in the community), it is the life sentence that was picked up and made into a headline by the media (see *Sunday Times*, August 13, 2000).
14. Hogg and Brown (1998) calculate that prison sentences rose by 60% in the first three years following the introduction of the Sentencing Act.
15. Part of the anger with juvenile crime is directed toward young aboriginal offenders. Aboriginals are certainly overrepresented among juvenile offenders in Western Australia, typically making up over half the population of juveniles in detention, yet accounting for less than 5% of the general juvenile population. The anti-aboriginal sentiment peaked with the "good riddance to bad rubbish" comment by a radio-show host, following the deaths of a group of aboriginal offenders in a high speed car chase. High speed car chases had also been high on the media and political agenda for at least the previous two years.
16. Baseball is not followed to any large extent in Australia. The national ball and bat game cricket is extremely popular, making the use of the baseball term serve as a code that something tough, ruthless, and American will now be applied.
17. In November 1996, the Northern Territory Parliament passed the Sentencing Amendment Act (No. 2).
18. Ministerial Statement to the Northern Territory Legislative Assembly: "The criminal justice system and the victims of crime," 20th August 1996 (cited in Flynn, 1997).
19. Boot camps and their variants have been introduced (for maximum political advantage) in both Western Australia (WA) and the Northern Territory (NT). In WA, the boot camp was introduced against the weight of international evidence for advantage during an election campaign. Following various difficulties and a review, it was disbanded.
20. These are obligations under the International Covenant on Civil and Political Rights (ICCPR) which was ratified in 1980. This covenant prohibits arbitrary detention (article 9(1)) and provides that sentences must be reviewable by a higher tribunal (14 (5)).
21. These are listed in Senator Brown's Second Reading Speech. Generally, they concern poor young indigenous people sentenced for lengthy periods of imprisonment for trivial offenses, usually involving small items (cigarette lighters, cans of beer, etc). One case that received much attention concerned a 29-year-old homeless aboriginal man, who wandered into a backyard when he was drunk and stole a towel from the clothes line. It was his third minor property offense. He was imprisoned for one year.
22. The major qualification to this statement concerns the provisions in the Criminal Justice Act 1985. As Brown and Young (2000, p. 27) note, "There is a statutory provision in favor of full time custodial sentences for serious and repetitive violent and sexual offenders. This must be considered a very marginal curtailment of judicial discretion, and compared to the kinds of legislation introduced in Australia, much tamer."
23. This is shown in a detailed way by the analysis provided in Brown and Young (2000).

24. For a discussion see Indermaur (2000). The growing sensitivity to violence fits well within Elias's theory of changing sensibilities discussed by many scholars. For a contemporary and deep analysis of Elias to the crisis of modern punishment, see Vaughan (2000). The police figures in New Zealand do show rapid rises in violent crime, but this is exactly what one would expect as sensitivity to violence grows. Brown and Young (2000) note that much of the increase in recorded violence has occurred in domestic violence offending, and most of that at the lower end of the scale B, precisely the type of offending susceptible to increasing capture during a period of growing sensitivity to violence.

Chapter 4

1. Ellsworth and Ross (1983) report the findings from a U.S. survey, in which 79% of those who favored the death penalty said that they sometimes felt outraged when a murderer was sentenced to a penalty other than the death penalty.
2. See Herbst (1998). In a series of studies, Brooks (1985, 1987, 1990) has presented evidence indicating that there is little if any direct relationship between "mass public opinion" and government policy in Western democracies. Kennamer (1992) notes that "effective" public opinion is opinion that actually reaches decision makers and is perceived as representing public opinion.
3. Bottoms (1995, p. 40) defines "populist punitiveness" as "politicians tapping into, and using for their own purposes, what they believe to be the public's generally punitive stance."
4. There is an extensive literature on the tensions between good government, the maintenance of political consent, and the maintenance of political power—running from Thucydides' account of the development of Athenian populism in the late 4th century B.C. and Machiavelli's exposition in *The Prince*. There is not the scope here to discuss these ideas; however, it is important to note that the debate over the legitimacy of populism actually has a deep and rich history and principally concerns the nature of democracy and particularly the form of relationship between the populace and the government.
5. It is particularly hard to draw the dividing line between sincerely held views and manipulative reflection of popular thought in relation to inexperienced politicians. In Australia, a defining political phenomenon of the 1990s was the rapid rise—and fall—of a novice politician, who dared articulate the sentiments resonating with the newly disenfranchised lower middle class. Her campaign relied on a melange of undeveloped and unsophisticated positions which were anti-immigration, anti-affirmative action, and anti-welfare. Although her campaign eventually collapsed resoundingly, she nevertheless exposed an intense divide between the elites and the conservative lower middle class. The "One Nation" movement in Australia was just one form of late twentieth-century populism. Many others have subsequently arisen, finding support particularly in the lower middle class groups.
6. The Labour party in Australia (which does not have jurisdiction over sentencing) opposed mandatory sentencing.
7. As Beckett notes in regard to the Bush/Dukakis contest and the use of the Willie Horton case. Garland (2000) goes further in noting the "long shadow" that this bruising political encounter has cast over American politics. In fact, the use of

such "negative campaigning" in the United States has been picked up and employed throughout the English-speaking world.

8. Wilson (1977) argued that the rise of the Right was a function of the number of failures of social programs to make a difference. As Bayer (1981) notes, however, what is really important is the loss of faith in the ideal of being able to make society better. The rise of the New Right thus signaled the belief that the current social order is "as good as it gets."
9. "Framing" refers to the way that key individuals and institutions can depict and/or construct reality—making sense of it for the general public. Thus through what is selected, the way it is discussed, the meaning given to it by political leaders and the media can "frame" reality for the general public, promulgating an understanding of what reality is, how it will unfold, and what needs to be done about it. Without a means of having access to their own information and analysis most citizens, even if they may disagree with policy directions, will not question the selection of issues and the depicted reality of that issue and thus reality has been effectively "framed."
10. However, this thinking may be changing. According to the National Institute of Justice *Sourcebook of Criminal Justice Statistics 1998* (p. 116), the proportion of U.S. residents believing there is more crime than there was a year ago dropped from a high of 89% in 1992 down to 52% in 1998 (source: http://www.gallup.com/poll/indicators/indcrim.asp).
11. Examination of factors at this level is associated with the work of Giddens (1990, 2000) and criminologists such as Bottoms (1995), Garland (1996, 2000, 2001), Young (1999), and Garland and Sparks (2000).
12. Garland develops the notion of the "crime complex" as a phenomenon afflicting those Western countries where the crime issue has become so entrenched in personal and political thinking that it becomes much more than just real rates of risk. Garland discusses the situation in the United Kingdom and United States, but his description of "high crime" societies and the crime complex clearly applies to all five jurisdictions that are the subject of this book.
13. See Weisberg (1999, p. 65). See also Warr (1995) for a summary of findings which show the consistent trend in beliefs (in the U.S.) that crime is increasing from surveys conducted from 1965 to 1993. Wright (1985) has gone even further back to demonstrate that the "myth of rising crime" was common even at times of unprecedented low rates of official crime in the 1950s.
14. Tonry (1999) and Garland (2000). Similar themes emerge in many other writings. For example, van Swaaningnen (1997) in discussing the situation in continental Europe argues that the rise of actuarial justice coincided with the decline of the welfare state. Van Swaaningnen sees this decline as paradoxically a function of its own success in the 1970s. The welfare state, developed after the war to meet the harsh and poor social conditions existing then and to remedy the inequities existing prior to the war, has coincided with substantial economic growth and rising affluence for most of those at the middle and lower levels of society. With rising affluence has come an evaporation of concern and social compassion underlying the motivation for welfarism. Tonry (1999) argues that the current fashion for intolerance may be seen as part of a historical cyclical pattern moving away from the earlier period of tolerance. Van Swaaningnen's analysis is also important, however, because he alerts us to the fact that many of the social changes discussed in

this chapter are also occurring in Europe and producing hostility from the large majority that is both middle class and "aspirational" against a marginalized "poor" class that is both a minority and a source of social problems.

15. However, increasing socioeconomic inequality in countries of the English-speaking world is also likely to have had an effect in increasing the brittle flavor of the political culture in these countries. Furthermore, the European political structures are also under assault from a range of populist parties promising to make government simpler and more egalitarian.
16. For an example of how the adoption of American style inequality has been taken up to the detriment of social policy in two more welfare-oriented economies, see James (1995) for a discussion of the cultural change engendered in the United Kingdom under Thatcherism, and Polk and White (1999) for a discussion of the impact on youth unemployment in Australia.

Chapter 5

1. For an overview of the UK literature, see Reiner (1997), and for a spirited discussion of the effect of entertainment media, see Sparks (1992). A special supplementary issue of the *Australian and New Zealand Journal of Criminology* in 1995 contains two articles by Daly (1995) and Chan (1995); see also Grabosky and Wilson (1989) for an Australian study of the construction of crime news, and Hogg and Brown (1998) for a discussion of Australian media campaigns on "law and order" in the 1990s. In Canada, see also the work of Ericson (1991, 1995) and Ericson, Baranek, and Chan (1987, 1989, 1991).
2. For Canada, see the Canadian Sentencing Commission (1987). For Australia, see Broadhurst and Indermaur (1982).
3. See Iyengar (1991).
4. An overview of this literature is found in Reiner (1997) and a collection of essays in Ericson (1995).
5. See Marsh (1991) and Graber (1980). It has been argued that these measures of crime—particularly police-recorded crime—do not report the "reality" of crime but simply represent another construction of crime. It is suggested that these measures come much closer to an accurate picture of the extent of the nature and trends in crime. From a purely pragmatic point of view, they would constitute a much better guide to the actual risks that a citizen may face than the picture derived from the media, and thus it would be misleading to dismiss them as flawed to the same extent as the media construction of crime.
6. These findings have been documented for all our countries apart from New Zealand, see Roberts and Stalans (1997) for a comprehensive description and analysis.
7. For example, see O'Connell and Whelan (1996) who, in analyzing Irish newspapers, found that newspapers identified as containing the most crime news also had readers with the highest estimates of crime prevalence.
8. Chiricos et al. used information from Dialog Information Service for coverage of 26 major newspapers in the United States and another source for the analysis of three TV networks (CBS, NBC, and Fox). Their analysis covered the period from January 1992 to March 1994. The number of news stories about violence actually remained quite stable until July 1993 and then increased sharply until January 1994 before falling.

9. The Center for Media and Public Affairs presents itself as a nonpartisan research and educational organization which studies news and entertainment media. Available at: http://www.cmpa.com/index.htm
10. *Media Monitor* 15, no. 1 (Jan./Feb. 2001), published by The Center for Media and Public Affairs.
11. Marsh (1991) provides the most comprehensive overview of the content analyses. Williams and Dickinson (1993) provides a more up-to-date analysis of the extent and differences in British newspapers.
12. This theory was originally proposed by behavioral psychologists (Dollard et al., 1939), has been subject to much criticism, and has been through many revisions.
13. See Doob and Roberts (1983); Indermaur (1987).
14. It was the result of some of these concerns that led to the establishment of the *Cultural Indicators Project* in 1967. The project was developed and is maintained by scholars mainly in the field of media studies to monitor the on crime policy of media representations of crime, Gerbner (1995), cited in Reiner (1997).
15. Potter and Chang (1990) developed a range of measures that are useful in measuring these kind of factors. See Reiner (1997) for a discussion of the question as to whether exposure to entertainment crime media has increased.
16. For example, see Signorelli and Gerbner (1988), and Signorelli (1990).
17. See Heath and Gilbert (1996) for a general review of the effect of mass media on the fear of crime.
18. See Gunter (1987) for a review of the British experience in light of cultivation analysis.
19. Sparks (1996) points to the exaggerated forms of masculinities displayed in Hollywood "Blockbusters," featuring stars like Stallone (Rambo series) and Schwarzenegger (Terminator series), which he argues develop in reaction to current instabilities in the masculine identity. This kind of reactive masculinity, where the hero is depicted as a victim of the current social order that he defies through transcendent, magical, and stunning acts of force, may also reflect this anti-bureaucratic frustration.
20. See Fishman and Cavender (1998) for a good collection of articles on reality crime TV programs such as "Cops" and "True Stories of the Highway Patrol" (U.S.) and "Crimewatch" (UK). Australia regularly screens the American reality crime TV shows and occasionally has attempted "fly on the wall" documentaries of Australian police operations. When one such program actually displayed a range of ugly behavior by the police, it sparked a heated debate about police misconduct.
21. See Donovan, (1998). On military manipulation of the media, see the collection in Bennett and Palatz (1994).
22. See, for example, Baer and Chambliss (1997) citing the work of Gans (1995), who points out that the consequences of the new punitiveness, based on distorted media treatments, far exceeds just penal policy and creates an intractable form of classism. "The perpetuation of the image of crime out of control justifies as well the elimination of support systems such as welfare and job creation programs as [Black] residents increasingly come to be defined as "the inherently criminal dangerous classes" and therefore "undeserving" (p. 104).
23. See Cullen, Fisher, and Applegate (2000) for a comprehensive review of studies

looking not only at alternatives to the death penalty and imprisonment but also for wider crime prevention programs such as early intervention.

24. Lewis (2001) argues that the media use public opinion polls selectively to create certain views of public opinion. See also Herman and Chomsky (1988).
25. See Rubin (1999) and Elias (1993). A number of studies (e.g., Connor, 1972; Broadhurst and Indermaur, 1982; Taylor, 1981) examine processes by which the seriousness of certain crimes can be exacerbated by media campaigns.
26. One example of this comes from Western Australia (Indermaur, 1995a, p. 74), where even at the Court of Appeal in that state, judges in one case cited burglary offenses as reaching "epidemic proportions," despite the fact that the trend in burglary offenses was relatively stable, measured in terms of police reports or victimizations.
27. See Taggart (2000).
28. See Cullen et al. (2000).
29. See Taggart (2000). An example of this can be found in the statements of Australian politicians in the furor that followed the suicide of an aboriginal boy incarcerated under mandatory sentencing laws. Rather than defending the laws on their merits, the premier of Western Australia defended them by claiming that his government simply enacted the "will" of the people. Similarly, Margaret Thatcher argued that it was not her but "the people of Britain who are going to make crime an issue" (van Swaaningnen, 1997, p. 178).
30. Orcutt and Turner (1993) and others have critiqued and analyzed the way that the media used the drug problem to create sensational stories, aided and abetted in this endeavor by a conservative administration benefiting from the crisis surrounding the "war on drugs."
31. Had the interest been in trying to prevent such crimes, other details would have been more useful for the reader (Rubin, 1999). For example, Davis (the offender) drove his car into a ditch several hours after the abduction and hid Polly Klaas bound but alive in a nearby woods. Two police officers then helped Davis pull his car out of the ditch unaware that he was a suspect—the bulletins had not reached them or they had not accessed them by this time. The media might also have focused on the offender's background (clearly a causative factor) in the interests of trying to prevent more such crimes. Instead, the focus was on the fact that this offender had been released from prison.
32. Cleveland (in the UK) was the site of a major scandal and subsequent inquiry into the overzealous intervention into families on the basis of allegations of child sexual abuse (see Nava, 1988).

Chapter 6

1. Diamond (1990) explains this finding by suggesting that the part-time lay magistrates focused on changing the behavior of individual defendants, whereas the full-time professional magistrates placed more emphasis on deterring others from committing crimes.
2. Although lay magistrates often reflect public views about sentencing more accurately than legally trained magistrates, this may bring its own problems. The experience in remote areas of Australia, which have relied on the lay magistracy largely out of necessity, has been mixed. Concerns have been expressed that lay

magistrates, who serve as justices of the peace, have been too willing to imprison offenders for relatively minor offenses when they are considered disruptive to a local community. Recently, lay magistrates in aboriginal communities have bowed to community pressure to jail "petrol sniffers" that have exasperated community resources. Some professionals believe that imprisonment for these offenders is inappropriate, and there is a need to continually monitor and restrict the tendency of magistrates to resort to prison.

3. The Crown prosecutor in Canada has a right to appeal an acquittal if the jury was not properly instructed on the law (Vidmar, 1996). Juries do not have the right to decide cases based on conscience and to nullify the letter of the law. The Supreme Court decided in 1895 in the case of *Sparf and Hansen v. United States* that juries did not have the right to base decisions on conscience. Only two states, Indiana and Maryland, instruct juries that they have the role and right to be both triers of facts and triers of the law; these states, however, have restricted juries' rights to nullify and do not inform all juries of their power to nullify the law (Creagan, 1993).
4. Judges typically oppose jury nullification and have taken several steps to limit juries to a fact-finding role based on the evidence. For example, jurors can be excused for cause if it can be shown that they are intentionally attempting to base their verdict on conscience rather than on evidence (*U.S. v. Grady Thomas*). Also, judges are not obliged to inform juries of their power to nullify or allow defense attorneys to make arguments supporting nullification (*U.S. v. Dougherty*).
5. Criminal justice professionals are so opposed to juries basing their decisions on conscience that some individuals who distribute leaflets at courthouses have been charged with jury tampering. In these cases, the defendants have often been acquitted and jurors have been suspected of basing their verdicts on their consciences rather than on objective evaluation of the evidence.
6. Over the course of one year, 10 patients received legal prescriptions for an overdose and 8 patients actually used these prescriptions (Farrenkopf & Bryan, 1999).
7. Based on opinion poll data, support for assisted suicide among physicians has increased over time with only approximately 35% endorsing assisted suicide in 1935 to over 50% endorsing suicide in the 1990s (Chochinov & Wilson, 1995).
8. A federal jury subsequently found the Los Angeles police officers guilty of violating Rodney King's civil rights.
9. Offenders sentenced to life imprisonment for first degree murder must spend 25 years in prison before becoming eligible for parole. Cases of second degree murder result in a minimum of 10 and a maximum of 25 years prior to parole eligibility, with the exact number between these limits being determined by the trial judge.
10. The jurors apparently wanted Latimer to be sentenced to at most a year in prison.
11. Research on the effect of the severity of a penalty on mock jurors' verdict decisions has generated inconsistent results. Studies using cases of robbery, assault, and murder that presented a straightforward scenario of the offender committing the act with full intention and without extenuating circumstances have found that knowledge of the severity of penalty does not affect verdict decisions (see Freedman, Krismer, MacDonald, and Cunningham, 1994). Mock jury studies have found that severe unjust penalties produce a significantly higher percentage of ac-

quittals when the evidence is weak or extenuating circumstances exist (see Kaplan, 1994 for a summary of this literature and a critique of the Freedman et al., 1994 studies; see also Hester and Smith, 1975 for empirical findings).

12. The United States has executed about 19,200 offenders since 1608, and of these 540 executions occurred between1973 and 1999 (Streib, 1999). From 1973 to 1999, juries have imposed 6,600 death sentences, and of these 6,600 death sentences, 540 were imposed on juvenile offenders (Streib, 1999).

Chapter 7

1. Barry Feld writes that "citizens and politicians perceive a significant and frightening increase in youth crime and violence. A desire to 'get tough' . . . provides political impetus to transfer some young offenders to criminal courts for prosecution as adults and to strengthen the sanctioning powers of juvenile courts" (Feld, 1995, p. 966).
2. Part of the current wave of public criticism of youth can be explained by "old fogeyism." Thus, in June 2000, the British Home Secretary lamented the excessive and conspicuous consumption of alcohol by the younger generation of Britons and suggested that his generation had been more circumspect in its consumption of alcohol. Anyone who lived through the 1950s and 1960s in England will recall similar criticisms being leveled at the first postwar generation. And once again, members of the generation that preceded the postwar generation had been held up as paragons of industry and restraint.
3. Several justifications exist for imposing mitigated punishments on juvenile offenders. Juveniles may have less understanding of the full consequences of their behavior or the wrongfulness of their behavior and/or may not fully be able to control their behavior. Immaturity is a justified excuse that reduces the offender's degree of responsibility and moral blameworthiness. This diminished responsibility means that such offenders are less culpable than adults and accordingly should be treated with greater leniency.
4. Covell and Howe used five different cases, so the differences between experimental conditions could not be attributed to specific features of a single case history.
5. The peak in the number of youth accused of violent crime occurred in 1993. This figure has been stable or more recently declining (see Savoie, 1999, figure 1).
6. Data from the annual crime statistics release show that property crimes accounted for half of all youth charged with an offense, but only one-third of adults charged (Tremblay, 2000).
7. It is sometimes argued that the official crime statistics fail to capture certain trends in crime. Perhaps the British public detected increases in juvenile offending not finding their way into official statistics. For this reason, Mattinson and Mirlees-Black (1999) examined shoplifting statistics from the British Retail Consortium. They report an even greater decline in thefts at a time when the volume of retail trading was presumably high as a function of the flourishing economy.
8. Only for the offense of robbery were custodial sentences of equivalent length for adults and juveniles. One qualification to this finding is that the sentences include open and closed custody for juveniles, whereas this distinction does not exist at the adult level.
9. Interestingly, many young people share this view. A Canadian study of juveniles found that the older respondents (those above 14 and under 18) also regarded

youth court sentences as too lenient, although younger participants (under 14) did not hold this perception. The authors of this survey attributed this age difference in perceptions of youth court sentencing to the fact that the older teenagers were more likely to be exposed to the sources of information that have also shaped adult perceptions.

10. The sample consisted of a random sample of 1,000 adults living in Ohio, U.S.
11. Results are based on a telephone survey of a random sample of adults living in the Winnipeg, Manitoba area.
12. The breakdown was 43% violent offenses, 37% property offenses, 14% drug offenses and 6% public order offenses (Gainsborough & Young, 2000).
13. Research has also found no difference in the public's recommendations of sentences for young and older juveniles who commit a heinous act of premeditated murder, where the offender set his brother on fire (Robinson & Darley, 1995).
14. The case of *Jahnke v. Wyoming* provides an example of public outcry about the severity of a sentence imposed on a juvenile who killed his abusive father. Jahnke was tried in adult court for first-degree murder of his physically abusive father. The jury convicted Jahnke of voluntary manslaughter. During his trial, expert testimony about how childhood abuse distorts perceptions of danger was ruled inadmissible. After Jahnke received a sentence of 5 to 15 years in adult prison, the public was very critical and demanded a less severe sentence for Jahnke. After the Wyoming Supreme Court upheld the sentence, the governor commuted the sentence to three years on the basis of compassion. This case provides another illustration of the injustices created by mandatory rules applied to all offenders falling within a certain category.
15. For example, a 15-year-old offender found guilty of criminal sexual assault in juvenile court may receive an incarceration sentence of 12 years. His sentence would initially be served in juvenile detention until he surpassed the court's extended jurisdiction, at which time he would serve the remaining time in adult prison. Another alternative available to both juvenile and adult court judges is to give a juvenile offender both a juvenile sanction and an adult sanction. The judge can decide to hold the adult sanction and use it as the sanction if the juvenile fails to comply during the period of the juvenile sanction.
16. The Youth Criminal Justice Act permits publication of the names of juvenile offenders who receive an adult sentence, juveniles sentenced for a number of serious offenses or repeat violent offenses, juveniles at large, or young persons considered by a judge to be dangerous.
17. Not all policy changes involving juvenile offenders, however, have been punitive. There is increasing emphasis on prevention and early-intervention community-based programs. In Britain, policymakers at the beginning of the 1990s realized that creating tougher sanctions for serious juvenile crime would not reduce juvenile crime rates. Community-based programs that emphasized addressing the social problems underlying juvenile crime were implemented on an experimental basis (Pitts, 1996). Similar restorative justice and early-intervention community-based programs are now being more widely implemented in the United States.
18. It is interesting to note that a major review of the boot camp experience in the United States found that "the only positive effects on recidivism that were found were found in programs that included a strong rehabilitative component . . . Programs designed only to provide physical training, hard labor, and military disci-

pline did not reduce recidivism and may have a negative impact" (MacKenzie, 1994, p. 17).

19. One potential weakness of this kind of legislation is that it may undermine the extent to which young people are held responsible for their actions.
20. Only one Secure Training Centre was actually in service by the time the STO was abolished by the 1998 Crime and Disorder Act, and only a handful of STOs were ever imposed.
21. It rose from 12 to 24 months.

Chapter 8

1. Canada also considered a lifetime confinement sentence after the murder of a boy by a paroled molester with a long history of sexual offending, but did not enact a law due to concerns about whether it was constitutional (Jenkins, 1998). Pratt (1998a) notes that the sexual predator laws are similar to the sexual psychopath laws enacted between 1937 and 1960 in all five countries. Both sets of laws were enacted in a climate of public anxiety about sex offenses committed by strangers against children and had as their primary objective to protect public safety through the indefinite incarceration of sexual offenders.
2. The U.S. Supreme Court has not received any case challenging the constitutionality of this law, though the U.S. Supreme Court ruled in *Coker v. Georgia* that the death penalty for rape of an adult was cruel and unusual punishment (Schaaf, 2000).
3. These probation and parole programs attempt to increase the monitoring of offenders to manage their risk of recidivism while in the community. Most programs are modeled after the containment approach that includes three key components: (a) enhanced supervision through more frequent contacts with offenders, including regular searches of the offender's home and arrest checks; (b) specialized treatment for sex offenders, which usually consists of cognitive-behavioral group therapy supplemented with individual behavioral or counseling therapy; and (c) a team approach involving probation officers, therapists, and polygraphers to share information and lower the risk of reoffending (English et al., 1996).
4. Only the category of drug offenders experienced a higher annual growth rate in terms of prison population, with an average increase of 18% (Greenfeld, 1997).
5. The question stated "sexual abuse of a child when the offender did this for the first time. Would you say society should choose the death penalty, life without parole, prison for a limited time or some other consequences like treatment programs, fines or a few days in jail?" (Alabama Poll, 1994).
6. Sex offenders who are also fathers and stepfathers often claim that they were encouraged and had not hurt the victim: indeed, sex offender therapy is designed to replace these dysfunctional, inaccurate perceptions with a more appropriate view of the crime. Thus, surveys that pose such misleading scenarios have (unintentionally) presented a view that is uninformative and potentially destructive by blaming the child victim and thereby diminishing the moral blameworthiness of the offender.
7. In Canada, if the offender has sexually assaulted his child, this is recognized in the *Criminal Code* as a statutory aggravating factor that should result in a harsher penalty (s. 718.2(a)(ii)).

8. Full details on restorative justice experiments in Australia, including Kathleen Daly's papers on the SAJJ project in South Australia that deals with sex offenders, can be found on the Australian Institute of Criminology website: www.aic.gov.au under restorative justice.

Chapter 9

1. Queensland introduced mandatory life sentences for certain categories of drug dealers in 1986, but the legislation, widely criticized as being much too severe, was repealed in 1989.
2. Indermaur and Ferrante (1998) calculated that offenses involving the "use" of drugs made up 80% of all charges in Western Australia in 1996 and 1997, and the drug involved in 90% of all charges in both years was cannabis.
3. The American public continues to be concerned about drug use among teenagers. Over half of the adults surveyed in 1997 believed that drugs constituted the biggest problem facing children (Maguire & Pastore, 1998). In 1997, one-quarter of American parents and over one-third of American teenagers identified drugs as the most important problem facing people their age. Only one-quarter of the teenagers, however, would report to authorities someone selling illegal drugs at school (Sourcebook of Criminal Justice Statistics, 1997). In 1998, 39% of American teenagers held the view that drugs were the biggest problem facing people their age and no other problem was mentioned as often. Teenagers' concern is not driven only by imagination: 65% of 17-year-olds say they can buy marijuana within a day; one-third have witnessed the sale of illegal drugs in their neighborhood; and half know someone fairly well who has used acid, cocaine, or heroin (Sourcebook of Criminal Justice Statistics, 1997).
4. For example, it is now understood that not only were the media "driven" by an enhanced effort on the part of public officials, but also that as more media focused attention on the drug problem, it gained more legitimacy as a news story (see Brownstein, 1991).
5. Punitive drug policies also have been enacted with some tinges of racism. For example, criminal laws against the possession of opiates, heroin, and marijuana occurred first in the United States in those states that had a large population of immigrant minorities and occurred in Canada to reduce the influx of Asian immigrants (See Jensen and Gerber, 1998 and Tonry, 1995 for discussion of the differential policy in the US in regard to powder and "crack" cocaine that had the effect of selectively targeting poor inner city blacks.)
6. The U.S. National Drug Control Strategy of 1999 states that "drug trafficking and violence go hand in hand" (p. 24). It also asserts that marijuana use is associated with violent crime, using the percentage of male arrestees for violent crimes testing positive for marijuana in 1997; however, these data do not establish a relationship between marijuana use and violence because the sample does not include a group that was not violent. Using self-report data from youth, the report correlates the number of days that youth report smoking marijuana with anti-social behaviors (e.g., cutting class and stealing) and with violence (physically attacking someone or destruction of property). The report overstates the association and claims "aggressive anti-social behavior is clearly linked to marijuana use" (p. 19).
7. The media appear to be responsible for public concern over the harmfulness of drugs. In November 1998, 77% of adult respondents had seen a government ad-

vertisement to discourage drug use among children. National surveys of seniors in the United States reveal that the majority believes that trying crack cocaine or heroin even once carries great risks for the consumer. Only a small minority (15%) believed that trying marijuana once or twice carries a great risk, although over half believed that regular use of marijuana carries health risks. Similar patterns with respect to perceptions of harm are found in national samples of younger Americans (Sourcebook of Criminal Justice Statistics, 1997).

8. The public's skepticism seems well founded and echoes US state drug coordinators' dissatisfaction with federal drug initiatives (see Koven and Shelley, 1993). Research now suggests that countries with more severe legal sanctions do not have lower drug use rates than countries with less severe sanctions. Glass notes that "there is no evidence that measures designed to deter drug use have any effect whatsoever on the prevalence of drug use" (Glass, 2001, p. 698).
9. Possession of small amounts of marijuana for personal use are very rarely prosecuted in Vancouver (Cohen, 2001).
10. Support for legalizing marijuana possession has attracted only a minority of U.S. adults during the period from 1985 to 1999 (Sourcebook of Criminal Justice Statistics Online, 1999). When voters in Alaska in 2000 were given the opportunity to pass a referendum making marijuana possession legal for individuals 18 years and older, the majority rejected this measure (Facts.com, 2000). From 1993 to 2000, one-third of Australians supported legalization (Roy Morgan Research Center, 2000). Less than half of the Australian respondents between the ages of 18 to 34 supported legalization (Roy Morgan Research Center, 2000). Thus, even among the young, legalization does not have the support of the majority. In the United States, a third of the college students in 2000 and approximately a quarter of high school students in 1999 endorsed legalization (Sourcebook of Criminal Justice Statistics Online, 1999).
11. Data from Focus Group studies also suggest that the public see possession of small amounts of marijuana as requiring either no sanctions or alternatives to imprisonment (Begasse, 1997).
12. Only four states (Alaska, California, Oregon, and Washington) have actually implemented medical marijuana programs.

Chapter 10

1. Young persons in custody, particularly when they are incarcerated for the first time, carry the highest risk of suicide. This tragic finding has been witnessed in several of our jurisdictions, particularly Britain and Australia (see discussion in Liebling, 1992).
2. It is important to recall that although crime rates have been declining for years in some countries such as Canada, they are still much higher than thirty years earlier. For example, in Canada, the crime rate in 1999 declined for the eighth straight year, but was still twice as high as in 1969 (see Tremblay, 2000).
3. The "New Labour" slogan of "Tough on crime; tough on the causes of crime" is a good example, to which we have already referred, of a more rational penal policy that nevertheless appeals to centrist sentiment (which explains its cogency during the British election).
4. See editorial in the *Sunday Times*, August 13, 2000.
5. Several states in the United States have such organizations (e.g., Illinois Criminal

Justice Information Authority). These organizations obtain federal funds to implement community-based treatment or supervision programs and also fund an independent evaluation of the programs. The findings from these evaluations are then disseminated to criminal justice personnel and media sources via condensed and "reader-friendly" reports.

6. In Canada, for example, sentencing statistics do not include the number or seriousness of the offender's previous convictions or any indication of the seriousness of the crime (e.g., the amount of money stolen, the value of the property damaged, or the extent of the injury in a crime of violence). Since the seriousness of the crime and criminal record are the most important determinants of the nature and severity of the sentence imposed, this makes the statistics rather crude and uninformative.
7. It is also curious that the public believe that all categories of crime are increasing, not just violent crime, which clearly receives disproportionate attention from the news media. This finding suggests that it is not the sheer volume of media coverage that creates the public view that crime rates are constantly increasing.
8. The "counting rules" were changed in 1998, the main change being to include assaults without injury within the category of violent crime. Over a two-year period, the police have progressively improved their recording of such crimes, triggering serious public concern about soaring levels of violence.
9. An additional advantage of web-based dissemination of information is that this method attracts a disproportionate number of younger individuals, who have more malleable attitudes toward criminal justice. Accordingly, the potential for movement is greater than with more traditional print-based methods.
10. The committee was chaired by Michael Grade.
11. There was a sentencing commission in the mid-1980s, and one of its recommendations was the creation of a permanent sentencing commission. This recommendation was never adopted. In the early 1990s, the Law Reform Commission of Canada was abolished. Its successor, created in 1998, is called the Law Commission of Canada, but it does not address substantive criminal law reform issues.

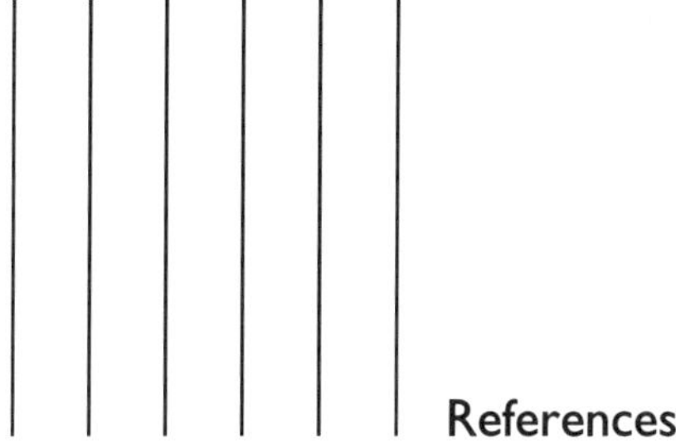

References

AAP (May 15, 2001). NSW to proceed with cannabis trial. www.smh.com.au/breaking/2001/05/15/ffxw5520rmc.html.

Abel, G. G., et al. (1987). Self-reported sex crimes of nonincarcerated paraphilics. *Journal of Interpersonal Violence, 2,* 3–25.

Abramson, J. (1994). *We the jury: The jury system and the ideal of democracy.* New York: Basic Books.

Adams, D. B. (1999). *Summary of state sex offender registry dissemination procedures.* U.S. Department of Justice: Bureau of Justice Statistics Clearinghouse. Available at: http://www.ojp.usdoj.gov/bjs/pub/ascii/sssordp.txt.

AIHW (1999). *1998 National Drug Strategy Household Survey: First results.* Australian Institute of Health and Welfare Catalogue No. PHE 15 (Drug Statistics Series). Canberra: Australian Institute of Health and Welfare.

Alabama Poll (1994). Question 160. Capstone poll survey for Institute for Social Science Research. University of Alabama. Available at: http://www.irss.unc.edu/tempdocs.

——— (1995). Capstone poll survey for Institute for Social Science Research. University of Alabama. Available at: http://www.irss.unc.edu/pub/search_resu/.

Albonetti, C. A. (1997). Sentencing under the federal sentencing guidelines: Effects of defendant characteristics, guilty pleas, and departures on sentence outcomes for drug offenses, 1991–1992. *Law and Society Review* 31 (4): 789–822.

American Bar Association (1999). *Perceptions of the U.S. justice system.* Available at: www.wisbar.org/bar/ptc/ptca4.html.

Anderson, D. (1995). *Crime and the politics of hysteria.* New York: Random House.

Angus Reid Research. (1997). *Attitudes to the Young Offenders Act.* Ottawa: Angus Reid Research.

Angus Reid Group, Inc. (1998). *Canadians' attitudes toward the Young Offenders Act.* Ottawa: Angus Reid Group, Inc.

Applegate, B. K., F. T. Cullen, and B. S. Fisher (1997). Public support for correctional treatment: The continuing appeal of the rehabilitative ideal. *The Prison Journal* 77 (3): 237–258.

Arizona Poll (1998). Questions 22, 24. Howard W. Odum Institute for Research in Social Science (IRSS study number: NNSP-AZ-NA-011A).

Ashworth, A. (1995). *Sentencing and criminal justice.* London: Butterworths.

——— (1997). English sentencing since the Criminal Justice Act 1991. In M. Tonry and K. Hatlestad, eds., *Sentencing reform in overcrowded times: A comparative perspective* (pp. 146–148). New York: Oxford University Press.

——— (2000). *Sentencing and criminal justice.* 3d ed. London: Butterworths.

Ashworth, A., and M. Hough (1996). Sentencing and the climate of opinion. *Criminal Law Review*: 1–12.

Associated Press. (March 21, 2001). *Pew poll on drug war.* Pew Research Center for the People and the Press.

——— (May 7, 2001). Church-run drug injecting center opens in Australia. Available at: www.foxnews.com/story/0,2933,23039,00.html.

Atmore, C. (1996). Cross-cultural mediations: Media coverage of two child sexual abuse controversies in New Zealand/Aotearoa. *Child Abuse Review* 5: 334–345.

Attitudes on Substance Abuse and Addiction Survey (1995). Public opinion online (Question Number 62). Roper Center at the University of Connecticut, New Haven.

Austin, J., J. Clark, P. Hardyman, and D. A. Henry (1999). The impact of "three strikes and you're out." *Punishment and Society* 1 (2): 131–162.

Baer, J., and W. Chambliss (1997). Generating fear: The politics of crime reporting. *Crime, Law and Social Change* 27: 87–107.

Baker, J. (1998). Are the courts becoming more lenient? Recent trends in convictions and penalties in NSW Higher and Local Courts. *Crime and Justice Bulletin: Contemporary Issues in Crime and Justice* 40. NSW Bureau of Crime and Statistics and Research.

Balogh, S. (1999). Jury returns acquittal on Said Morgan case. *The Australian News*, Available at: www.theaustralian.news.com.au.

Barak, G. (1994). Newsmaking criminology: Reflections on the media, intellectuals and crime. In G. Barak, ed., *Media, process and the social construction of crime: Studies in newsmaking criminology*. New York: Garland.

Barclay, G., and C. Tavares (2000). *International comparisons of criminal justice statistics.* Home Office Statistical Bulletin 4/00. London: Home Office.

Barkan, S. E. (1983). Jury nullification in political trials. *Social Problems* 31 (1): 28–44.

Barlow, M. H., D. E. Barlow, and T. G. Chiricos (1995). Economic conditions and ideologies of crime in the media: A content analysis of crime news. *Crime and Delinquency* 41: 3–19.

Baron, S., and T. Hartnagel (1996). It's time to get serious: Public attitudes toward juvenile justice in Canada. In J. H. Creechan and R. A. Silverman, eds., *Canadian Delinquency*. Scarborough, Ont.: Prentice-Hall.

Bayer, R. (1981). Crime, punishment and the decline of the liberal optimism. *Crime and Delinquency* 27: 169–190.

Beck, A. J., and J. C. Karberg (2001). *Prison and jail inmates at midyear 2000.* Bureau of Justice Statistics Bulletin NCJ 185989. U.S. Department of Justice.

Beckett, K. (1997). *Making crime pay: Law and order in contemporary American politics.* New York: Oxford University Press.

Beckett, K., and T. Sasson (2000). *The politics of injustice: Crime and punishment in America.* Thousand Oaks, CA: Pine Forge Press.

Begasse, J. K. (1997). Oregonians support alternatives for nonviolent offenders. In M. Tonry and K. Hatlestad, eds., *Sentencing reform in overcrowded times: A comparative perspective* (pp. 270–275). New York: Oxford University Press.

Belden, Russonello, and Stewart Research and Communications (April 1997). *Report of existing public opinion data on juvenile justice issues.* Washington, DC: Belden & Russonello.

Bennett, L., and D. Palatz, eds., (1994). *Taken by storm: The media, public opinion and U.S. foreign policy in the Gulf War.* Chicago: University of Chicago Press.

Berliner, L., D. Schram, L. L. Miller, and C. D. Milloy (1995). A sentencing alternative for sex offenders: A study of decision making and recidivism. *Journal of Interpersonal Violence* 10 (4): 487–502.

Besserer, S., and C. Trainor (2000). Criminal victimization in Canada, 1999. *Juristat* 20 (10).

Best, J. (1999). *Random violence: How we talk about new crimes and new victims.* Berkeley: UCLA Press.

Bishop, D., and C. Fraizer (1997). The transfer of juveniles to criminal court: Does it make a difference? *Crime and Delinquency* 42: 111–143.

Blendon, R. J., and J. T. Young (1998). The public and the war on illicit drugs. *Journal of the American Medical Association* 279 (11): 827–832.

Block, M. K. (1996). Supply side imprisonment policy. National Institute of Justice. Available at: http://www.ncjrs.org.

Blumstein, A., and A. J. Beck (1999). Population growth in U.S. prisons, 1980–1996. In M. Tonry, and J. Petersilia, eds., *Crime and justice: A review of the research.* Vol. 26, *Prisons.* Chicago: University of Chicago Press.

Bonczar, T. P., and A. J. Beck (1997). *Lifetime likelihood of going to state or federal prison.* Washington, D.C.: U.S. Bureau of Justice Statistics.

Bottoms, A. E. (1995). The philosophy and politics of punishment and sentencing. In C. Clarkson and R. Morgan, eds., *The politics of sentencing reform.* Oxford: Clarendon Press.

Bourque, L. B. (1989). *Defining rape.* Durham, NC: Duke University Press.

Bowdy, M. A. (1999). Needle exchanges: Prevention or problem. *State Government News* Jan/Feb: 26–28.

Bowers, W., M. Vandiver, and P. Dugan (1994). A new look at public opinion on capital punishment: What citizens and legislators prefer. *American Journal of Criminal Law* 22: 77–150.

Bowman, J., and R. Sanson-Fisher (1994). Public perceptions of cannabis legislation. *National Drug Strategy Monograph Series No. 28.* Canberra: Australian Government Printing Service.

Bradley, T. (1999). Crime prevention and the politics of law and order. *Criminology Aotearoa/New Zealand* 11. Wellington, New Zealand: Institute of Criminology, Victoria, University of Wellington.

Braithwaite, J. (1999). Restorative justice: Assessing optimistic and pessimistic accounts. In M. Tonry, ed., *Crime and justice: A review of research.* Chicago: University of Chicago Press.

Braithwaite, J., and K. Daly (1998). Masculinities, violence, and communitarian control. In S. L. Miller, ed., *Crime control and women: Feminist implications of criminal justice policy* (pp. 151–180). Newbury Park, CA: Sage.

Brereton, D. (1996). Does criminology matter? Crime, politics and the policy process. *Current Issues in Criminal Justice* 8 (1): 82–88.

Brillon, Y., C. Louis-Guerin, and M. Lamarche. (1984). *Attitudes of the Canadian public toward crime policies.* Ottawa: Ministry of the Solicitor General Canada.

Broadhurst, R., and D. Indermaur (1982). Crime seriousness ratings: The relationship of information accuracy and general attitudes in Western Australia. *Australian and New Zealand Journal of Criminology* 15: 219–234.

Brooks, J. (1985). Democratic frustration in Anglo-American politics: A quantification of inconsistency between mass public opinion and public policy. *Western Political Quarterly* 38: 250–261.

——— (1987). The opinion-policy nexus in France: Do institutions and ideology make a difference? *Journal of Politics* 49: 465–480.

——— (1990). The opinion-policy nexus in Germany. *Public Opinion Quarterly* 54: 508–529.

Brown, S. (1999). Public attitudes toward the treatment of sex offenders. *Legal and Criminological Psychology* 4: 239–252.

Brown, J., and P. Langan (1999). *Felony sentences in the United States, 1996*. Bureau of Justice Statistics Bulletin. Washington, D.C.: U.S. Department of Justice.

Brown, M., and W. Young (2000). Recent trends in sentencing and penal policy in New Zealand. *International Criminal Justice Review* 10: 1–31.

Brownstein, H. (1991). The media and the construction of random drug violence. *Social Justice* 18 (4): 85–103.

Burke, D. (March 8, 2000). *Press Release: Australians support NT laws.*

Butler, P. (1997). Racially based jury nullification: Black power in the criminal justice system. *Yale Law Journal* 105: 677–725.

California Poll (1986). Field Institute (9102) (IRSS Study Number NNAP-CA-066). Available at: http://www.irss.unc.edu.

——— (1988). Question number 47f. Howard W. Odum Institute for Research in Social Science (IRSS study number NNSP-CA-052). Available at: http://www.irss.unc.edu.

Campbell, M. (1999). *An analysis of private member bills*. Ottawa: Ministry of the Solicitor General.

Canadian Sentencing Commission (1987). *Sentencing reform: A Canadian approach*. Ottawa: Supply and Services Canada.

Capps, S. A. (September 18, 1996). Chemical castration law signed by Wilson. *San Francisco Examiner*, p. A7.

Carcach, C., and A. Grant (1999). Imprisonment in Australia: Trends in prison populations and imprisonment rates, 1982–1998. *Trends and Issues in Crime and Criminal Justice* No. 130. Canberra: Australian Institute of Criminology.

Carmody, D. (1998). Mixed messages: Images of domestic violence on "reality" television. In M. Fishman and G. Cavender, eds., *Entertaining crime—television reality programs*. New York: Aldine De Gruyter.

Carriere, D. (2000). Youth court statistics, 1998/99. *Juristat* 20 (2).

Carrington, P. (1999). Trends in youth crime in Canada, 1977–1996. *Canadian Journal of Criminology* 41: 1–33.

Castellano, T., and E. McGarell (1991). Politics of law and order: Case study evidence for a conflict model of the criminal law formation process. *Journal of Research in Crime and Delinquency* 28: 304–329.

Cavender, G., and M. Fishman (1998). Television reality crime programs: Context and history. In M. Fishman and G. Cavender, eds., *Entertaining crime—television reality programs*. New York: Aldine De Gruyter.

Chambliss, W. (1999). *Power, politics and crime*. Boulder, CO: Westview Press.

Chan, J. (1995). Systematically distorted communication? Criminological knowledge, media representation, and public policy. *Australian and New Zealand Journal of Criminology* (Special Suppl.): 23–30.

Chapin, L. A. (1997). Out of control? The uses and abuses of parental liability laws to control juvenile delinquency in the United States. *Santa Clara Law Review* 37: 621–672.

Chiricos, T., S. Eschholz, and M. Gertz (1997). Crime news and fear of crime: Toward an identification of audience effects. *Social Problems* 44: 342–355.

Chiricos, T., K. Padgett, and M. Gertz (2000). Fear, TV news, and the reality of crime. *Criminology* 38 (3): 755–786.

Chochinov, H. M., and K. G. Wilson (1995). The euthanasia debate: Attitudes, practices, and psychiatric considerations. *Canadian Journal of Psychiatry* 40: 593–602.

Christie, S. (1998). Trial by media: Politics, policy and public opinion, the case of the ACT heroin trial. *Current Issues in Criminal Justice* 10 (1): 37–50.

Cintron, M., and W. Johnson (1996). The modern plague: Controlling substance abuse. In T. J. Flanagan and D. R. Longmire, eds., *Americans view crime and justice: A national public opinion survey*. Thousand Oaks, CA: Sage.

Clark, J., J. Austin, and D. A. Henry (1997). Three strikes and you're out: A review of state legislation. *National Institute of Justice: Research in Brief* (NCJ 165369). Washington, D.C.: U.S. Department of Justice.

Cohen, J. (May 31, 2001). Getting dot-bombed in Vancouver. *Culture*. Wired Digital Inc. Available at: www.wired.com/news/culture/0,1284,42655,00.html.

Connor, W. (1972). The manufacture of deviance: The case of the Soviet purge, 1936–1938. *American Sociological Review* 37: 403–413.

Conrad, C. S. (1999). *Jury nullification: The evolution of a doctrine*. Durham, NC: Carolina Academic Press.

Corpus Christi (May 20, 2001). Sex offender signs hailed and faulted: Most reader responses oppose Banales' orders. Corpus Christi Caller Times. Available at: www.caller.com/2001/may/20/today/localnew/568.html.

Correctional Service of Canada (1999). *Comparison of time served in prison by life prisoners in western nations*. Ottawa: Correctional Service of Canada.

Covell, K., and R. Howe (1996). Public attitudes and juvenile justice in Canada. *The International Journal of Children's Rights* 4: 345–355.

Cowan, R. (April 4, 1998). More on UK jury acquittal of man on cultivation charges: Vows to keep giving cannabis to wife with MS. Available at: http://www.marijuananews.com/more_on_uk_jury_acquittal_of_man.htm.

——— (Aug. 8, 2000). Founder of New Zealand NORML calls for rational debate of marijuana laws. Available at: www.marijuananews.com/news.

Creagan, K. (1993). Jury Nullification: Assessing recent legislative developments. *Case Western Reserve Law Review* 43: 1101–1150.

Crutcher, N. (2001). Mandatory minimum penalties of imprisonment: An historical analysis. *Criminal Law Quarterly* 44: 279–291.

Cullen, F. T., B. S. Fisher, and B. K. Applegate (2000). Public opinion about punishment and corrections. In M. Tonry, ed., *Crime and justice: A review of the research*. Vol. 27, Chicago: University of Chicago Press.

Cullen, F. T., J. Wright, S. Brown, M. Moon, M. Blankenship, and B. Applegate (1998). Public support for early intervention programs: Implications for a progressive policy agenda. *Crime & Delinquency* 44: 187–204.

Currie, E. (1998). *Crime and punishment in America*. New York: Henry Holt.

D'Anjou, L. J., C. Cozijn, L. V. Toorn, and C. M. Verkoegn (1978). Demanding more severe punishment: Outline of a theory. *British Journal of Criminology* 18 (4): 326–347.

Daly, K. (1995). Celebrated crime cases and the public's imagination: From bad press to bad policy. *Australian and New Zealand Journal of Criminology* (Suppl. Issue): 6–22.

——— (2000). Revisiting the relationship between retributive and restorative justice. In H. Strang and J. Braithwaite, eds., *Restorative justice: From philosophy to practice*. Aldershot: Dartmouth.

——— (2002). Restorative justice in theory and practice. In A. von Hirsch et al., eds., *Restorative justice and criminal justice*. Oxford: Hart.

Davis, T., and C. Lee (1996). Sexual assault: Myths and stereotypes among Australian adolescents. *Sex Roles* 34 (11/12): 787–803.

DEA (2001). Overview of drug use in the United States. Washington, D.C.: U.S. Department of Justice Drug Enforcement Administration. Available at: www.usdoj.gov/dea/stats/overview.htm.

Dean, M. (2000). Tabloid campaign forces UK to reconsider sex offence laws. *The Lancet* 356 (923): 745–749.

Decima Research (1993). *Canadians and the Young Offenders Act*. Ottawa: Decima Research Limited.

Diamond, S. S. (1990). Revising images of public punitiveness: Sentencing by lay and professional English magistrates. *Law & Social Inquiry* 15 (2): 191–221.

Diamond, S. S., and L. J. Stalans (1989). The myth of judicial leniency in sentencing. *Behavioral Science and the Law* 7: 73–89.

DiMascio, W. M. (1997). *Seeking justice: Crime and punishment in America*. New York: Edna McConnell Clark Foundation.

Ditton, P. M., and D. J. Wilson (1999). Truth in sentencing in state prisons. *Bureau of Justice Statistics: Special Report* (NCJ 170032). Washington, D.C.: U.S. Department of Justice.

Doble, J. (1995). *Crime and corrections: The views of the people of North Carolina*. Englewood Cliffs, NJ: Doble Research Associates.

——— (1997). Survey shows Alabamians support alternatives. In M. Tonry and K. Hatlestad, eds., *Sentencing reform in overcrowded times: A comparative perspective* (pp. 255–258). New York: Oxford University Press.

Doble, J., S. Immerwahr, and A. Richardson (1991). *Punishing criminals*. Philadelphia: The Public Agenda Foundation.

Doble, J., and J. Klein (1989). *Punishing criminals. The public's view*. New York: Edna McConnell Clark Foundation.

Dodge, L. (1998). Fully informed juries: The secret silver bullet. Available at: http://nowscape.com/fija/_idessa.htm.

Doherty, L. (May 16, 2001). Premier prescribes marijuana for pain. Available at: www.smh.com.au/news/0105/16/pageone/pageone6.html.

Dollard, J., L. W. Doob, N. E. Miller, O. H. Mowrer, and R. R. Sears (1939). *Frustration and aggression*. New Haven, CT: Yale University Press.

Donovan, P. (1998). Armed with the power of television: Reality crime programming and the reconstruction of law and order in the United States. In M. Fishman and G. Cavender, eds., *Entertaining crime—television reality programs*. New York: Aldine De Gruyter.

Doob, A. (1979). Public's view of the criminal jury trial. *Studies on the jury*. Ottawa: Law Reform Commission of Canada.

Doob, A. N. (2000). Transforming the punishment environment: Understanding public

views of what should be accomplished at sentencing. *Canadian Journal of Criminology* 42: 323–340.
Doob, A. N., and V. Marinos (1995). Reconceptualizing punishment: Understanding the limitations on the use of intermediate punishments. *University of Chicago Law School Roundtable* 2: 413–433.
Doob, A., and J. V. Roberts (1983). *An analysis of the public view of sentencing.* Ottawa: Department of Justice Canada.
Doob, A., and J. V. Roberts (1988). Public punitiveness and public knowledge of the facts: Some Canadian surveys. In N. Walker and M. Hough, eds., *Public attitudes to sentencing: Surveys from five countries.* Aldershot: Gower.
Doob, A. N., and J. Sprott (1998). Is the "quality" of youth violence becoming more serious? *Canadian Journal of Criminology* 40: 185–194.
Doob, A., and J. Sprott (1999). Changes in youth sentencing in Canada. *Federal Sentencing Reporter* 11: 262–268.
Dopplet, J. (1992). Marching to the police and court beats. In J. Kennamer, ed., *Public opinion, the press and public policy.* Westport, CT: Praeger.
Dopplet, J. C., and P. M. Manikas (1990). Mass media and criminal justice decision making. In J. R. Surrette, ed. *Media and criminal justice policy.* Springfield, IL: Charles C. Thomas.
Dorfman, L., and V. Schiraldi (2001). Off balance: Youth, race & crime in the news. Justice Policy Institute. Available at: www.buildingblocksforyouth.org/media/media.html.
Dowds, L. (1994). *The long-eyed view of law and order: A decade of British social attitudes survey results.* London: Home Office.
Doyle, A. (1998). "Cops": Television policing as policing reality. In M. Fishman and G. Cavender, eds., *Entertaining crime—television reality programs.* New York: Aldine De Gruyter.
Drell, A. (May 13, 1999). Dr. Death's crusade lives on. *Chicago Sun-Times, Late Sports Final,* p. 6.
Drug Policy Expert Committee (2001). Heroin facing the issue. Available at: www.dhs.vic.gov.au/phd/dpec/index.htm.
Drug Strategies Survey (1994). Public Opinion Online (Question Numbers 14, 18). Roper Center at the University of Connecticut, New Haven. (Accession Number 0215614)
Drugs and Crime Facts (2000). Public opinion about drugs. Available at: www.ojp.usdoj.gov/bjs/dcf/poad.htm.
Drugs and Crime Facts (2001). Public opinion about drugs. Available at: www.ojp.usdoj.gov/dcf.
Eisenberg, N., R. G. Owens, and M. E. Dewey (1987). Attitudes of health professionals to child sexual abuse and incest. *Child Abuse & Neglect* 11(1): 109–116.
Ekos Research (2000). *Canadian attitudes toward youth crime.* Ottawa: Ekos Research.
Elias, R. (1993). *Victims still: The political manipulation of crime victims.* Newbury Park, CA: Sage.
Ellsworth, P. C., and L. Ross (1983). Public opinion and capital punishment: A close examination of the views of abolitionists and retentionists. *Crime and Delinquency* 29 (1): 116–169.
Elrod, P., and M. Brown (1996). Predicting public support for electronic house arrest: Results from a New York county survey. *American Behavioural Scientist* 39: 461–473.

English, K., S. Pullen, and L. Jones (1996). *Managing adult sex offenders: A containment approach.* Lexington, KY: American Probation and Parole Association.

Environics Research Group (1998). *Environics focus on crime and justice.* National Opinion Survey. Ottawa: Environics Research Group.

Erickson, P. G. (2000). The harm minimization option for cannabis: History and prospects in Canadian drug policy. In J. E. Inciardi and L. D. Harrison, eds., *Harm reduction: National and international perspectives.* Thousand Oaks, CA: Sage.

Ericson, R. (1991). Mass media, crime, law and justice. *British Journal of Criminology* 31(3): 219–249.

———, ed. (1995). *Crime and the media.* Aldershot: Dartmouth.

Ericson, R. V., P. M. Baranek, and J. B. Chan (1987). *Visualising deviance: A study of news organizations.* Toronto: University of Toronto Press.

——— (1989). *Negotiating control: A study of news sources.* Toronto: University of Toronto Press.

——— (1991). *Representing order: Crime, law and justice in the news media.* Toronto: University of Toronto Press.

Evening Post (April 7, 2001). Available at: www.nzdf.org.nz/update/.

Fabianic, D. (1997). Television dramas and homicide causation. *Journal of Criminal Justice* 25 (3): 195–203.

Facts.com (September 23, 1999). Politics: D.C.: 1998 Marijuana Vote Tallied. Available at: www.2facts.com/stories/index/199914960.asp.

Facts.com (March 29, 2000). Australia: U.N. criticizes treatment of aborigines. Available at: www.2facts.com/stories/index/2000170680.asp.

Facts.com (April 19, 2000). Australia: Mandatory sentencing deal reached. Available at: www.2facts.com/stories/index/2000172650.asp.

Facts.com (November 1, 2001). Great Britain: Marijuana law relaxation announced. Available at: http://www.2facts.com/stories/index/2001230030.asp.

Farkas, S. (1997). Pennsylvanians prefer alternatives to prison. In M. Tonry and K. Hatlestad, eds., *Sentencing reform in overcrowded times: A comparative perspective* (pp. 265–270). New York: Oxford University Press.

Farrenkopf, T., and J. Bryan (1999). Psychological consultation under Oregon's 1994 Death with Dignity Act: Ethics and procedures. *Professional Psychology: Research and Practice* 30 (3): 245–249.

Fedorowycz, O. (2000). Homicide in Canada—1999. *Juristat* 20 (9).

Feld, B. (1995). Violent youth and public policy: A case study of juvenile justice law reform. *Minnesota Law Review* 79: 965–1128.

Finckenauer, J. O. (1978). Crime as national political issues, 1964–76. *Crime & Deliquency* 24 (1): 13–27.

Field, A., and S. Casswell (1998). Drugs in New Zealand National Survey, 1998. Available at: http://www.aphru.ac.nz/projects/drugsns.htm.

Finkel, N. J. (1990). Capital felony-murder, objective indica, and community sentiment. *Arizona Law Review* 34(A) 819–920.

——— (1995). *Commonsense justice.* Cambridge, MA: Harvard University Press.

Finkel, N. J., and K. B. Duff (1991). Felony-murder and community sentiment: Testing the Supreme Court's assertions. *Law and Human Behavior* 15: 405–423.

Finkel, N. J., and S. F. Smith (1993). Principals and accessories in capital felony-murder: The proportionality principle reigns supreme. *Law and Society Review* 27 (1): 129–156.

Finn, P. (1997). *Sex offender community notification* (NCJ 162364). Washington, D.C.: U.S. Department of Justice.

Fischer, B. (1998). Prohibition as the art of political diplomacy: The benign guises of the War on Drugs in Canada. In E. L. Jensen and J. Gerber, eds., 157–176, *The new War on Drugs: Symbolic politics and criminal justice policy.* Cincinnati, OH: Anderson.

Fishkin, J. (1995). *The voice of the people: Public opinion and democracy.* New Haven, CT: Yale University Press.

Fishman, M. (1981). Police news: Constructing an image of crime. *Urban Life* 9: 371–394.

Fishman, M., and G. Cavender, eds. (1998). *Entertaining crime—television reality programs.* New York: Aldine De Gruyter.

Fitzmaurice, C., and K. Pease (1986). *The psychology of judicial sentencing.* Manchester: Manchester University Press.

Flanagan, T. J., and D. R. Longmire (1996). *Americans view crime and justice: A national public opinion survey.* Thousands Oaks, CA: Sage.

Flynn, M. (1997). One strike and you're out! *Alternative Law Journal* 22 (2): 72–76.

Focus Canada (1987). *Attitudes toward capital punishment.* Focus Canada Report.

Focus Canada (1998). *Public attitudes to sentencing in Canada.* Ottawa: Focus Canada.

Frase, R. S. (1995). State sentencing guidelines: Still going strong. *Judicature* 78 (4): 173–179.

Freedman, J. L., K. Krismer, J. E. MacDonald, and J. A. Cunningham (1994). Severity of penalty, seriousness of charge, and mock jurors' verdicts. *Law and Human Behavior* 18 (2) 189–202.

Freiberg, A. (1997a). Sentencing reform in Victoria. In M. Tonry and K. Hatlestad, eds., *Sentencing reform in overcrowded times: A comparative perspective* (pp. 148–151). New York: Oxford University Press.

——— (1997b). Sentencing and punishment in Australia in the 1990s. In M. Tonry and K. Hatlestad, eds., *Sentencing reform in overcrowded times: A comparative perspective* (pp. 156–162). New York: Oxford University Press.

——— (1998). Prison populations up, sentencing policy harsher in Australia. *Overcrowded Times* 9 (1): 9–11.

——— (1999). Explaining increases in imprisonment rates. Paper presented at 3rd National Outlook Symposium on Crime in Australia, sponsored by the Australian Institute of Criminology, Canberra.

——— (2001). Affective versus effective justice: Instrumentalism and emotionalism in criminal justice. *Punishment and Society* 3 (2): 265–278.

Freiberg, A., and S. Ross (1999). *Sentencing reform and penal change: The Victorian experience.* Sydney: Federation Press.

Gallup Canada. (1994). *Canadians favor a stricter Young Offenders Act.* Toronto: Author.

——— (1999). Canadians want a strict Young Offenders Act. *The Gallup Poll* 59 (23).

Gallup Poll (1999). Office of National Drug Control Policy Consultation with America: A look at how Americans view the country's drug problem. Princeton, NJ: The Gallup Organization. Available at: www.whitehousedrugpolicy.gov/pubs/gallup.

Gans, H. J. (1995). *The war against the poor: The underclass and antipoverty policy.* New York: Basic Books.

Garland, D. (1990). *Punishment and modern society: A study in social theory.* Chicago: University of Chicago Press.

——— (1996). The limits of the sovereign state: Strategies of crime control in contemporary society. *British Journal of Criminology* 36 (4): 445–471.

——— (2000). The culture of high crime societies: Some preconditions of recent "Law and Order" policies. *British Journal of Criminology* 40 (3): 347–375.

——— (2001). *The culture of control: Crime and social order in contemporary society.* Chicago: University of Chicago Press.

Garland, D., and R. Sparks (2000). Criminology, social theory, and the challenge of our times. *British Journal of Criminology* 40 (2): 189–204.

Gartner, R., and A. N. Doob (1994). Trends in criminal victimization: 1988–1993. *Juristat* 14 (13).

Geis, G., and A. Binder (1991). Sins of their children: Parental responsibility for juvenile delinquency. *Notre Dame Journal of Law, Ethics & Public Policy* 5: 303–322.

Georgia Poll (1991). Archival Study NNSP-GA-020. Howard W. Odum Institute for Research in Social Science. University of North Carolina at Chapel Hill. Available at: ftp://vance.irss.unc.edu/pub/.

Giddens, A. (1990). *The consequences of modernity.* Oxford: Polity Press.

——— (2000). *The third way and its critics.* Cambridge: Polity Press.

Glass, N. (2001). Council of Europe proposes new approach to tackling drug abuse. *Lancet* 357 (9257): 698.

Global Illicit Drug Trends (2000). United Nations Office for Drug Control and Crime Prevention. Available at: www.undcp.org/report_2000-09-21_1.html.

Gordon, D. (1998). Keeping sex offenders off the streets. *State Legislatures*: 32–33.

Graber, D. (1980). *Crime, news and the public.* New York: Praeger.

Grabosky, P., and P. Wilson (1989). *Journalism and justice: How crime is reported.* Sydney: Pluto Press.

Green, T. A. (1985). *Verdict according to conscience: Perspectives on the English criminal trial jury, 1200–1800.* Chicago: University of Chicago Press.

Greenfeld, L. A. (1997). Sex offenses and offenders. Washington, D.C.: U.S. Department of Justice (NCJ-163392), Bureau of Justice Statistics.

Gunter, B. (1987). *Television and the fear of crime.* London: John Libbey.

Haghigh, B., and J. Sorenson (1996). America's fear of crime. In T. Flanagan and D. Longmire, eds., *Americans view crime and justice: A national public opinion survey.* Thousand Oaks, CA: Sage.

Hague, W. (Aug. 13, 2000). Life for paedophiles must be an option. *Sunday Times.*

Hall, S. (1979). *Drifting into a law and order society.* London: Cobden Press.

Hans, V. P., and N. Vidmar (1986). *Judging the jury.* New York: Plenum Press.

Harding, R. (1995). Problems, responses and evaluations: A conspectus of this report. In A. Harlan, *Victimization in New Zealand as measured by the 1992 International Crime Survey.* Wellington: New Zealand Ministry of Justice.

Harlan, A. (1995). *Victimization in New Zealand as measured by the 1992 International Crime Survey.* Wellington: New Zealand Ministry of Justice.

Harris & Associates (1990). Question J3. Harris study no. 892049.

Harris Poll (1994). Question H4. Howard W. Odum Institute for Research in Social Science (IRSS Study Number S941107). Available at: http://www.irss.unc.edu

Heath, L., and K. Gilbert (1996). Mass media and the fear of crime. *American Behavioral Scientist* 39 (4): 379–386.

Henry, S. (1994). Newsmaking criminology as replacement discourse. In G. Barak, ed.,

Media, process and the social construction of crime: Studies in newsmaking criminology. New York: Garland.
Herbst, S. (1998). *Reading public opinion*. Chicago: University of Chicago Press.
Herman, E., and N. Chomsky (1988). *Manufacturing consent*. New York: Pantheon.
Hester, R. K., and R. E. Smith (1975). Effects of a mandatory death penalty on the decisions of simulated jurors as a function of heinousness of the crime. *Journal of Criminal Justice* 1:319–326.
Higgins, D., and R. Snyder (1996). North Carolinians want alternative sentences for nonviolent offenders. *Overcrowded Times 7*: 12–15.
Hilton, N. Z. (1993). Police intervention and public opinion. In N. Z. Hilton, ed., *Legal responses to wife assault: Current trends and evaluation*. Newbury Park, CA: Sage.
Hogg, R., and D. Brown (1998). *Rethinking law and order*. Sydney: Pluto Press.
Home Office (1990a). *Crime, justice and protecting the public*. (Cm 965). London: Home Office.
——— (1990b). *Supervision and punishment in the community: A framework for action*. London: Home Office.
——— (1996). *Protecting the public: The government's strategy on crime in England and Wales*. (Cm 3190). London: Home Office.
——— (1999). *Prison statistics, England and Wales 1998*. Cm 4430. London: Stationery Office.
——— (2001a). *Making punishments work. Report of a review of the sentencing framework for England and Wales*. London: Home Office.
——— (2001b). *Criminal statistics, England and Wales, 2000*. London: Home Office.
——— (2001c). Recorded crime in England and Wales to September 2000. *Home Office Statistical Bulletin* 1/01. London: Home Office.
Horowitz, I. A. (1988). Jury nullification: The impact of judicial instructions, arguments, and challenges on jury decision making. *Law & Human Behavior* 12 (4): 439–453.
Horowitz, I. A., and T. E. Willging (1991). Changing views of jury power: The nullification debate, 1787–1988. *Law & Human Behavior* 15 (2): 165–182.
Hough, M. (1996). People talking about punishment. *The Howard Journal* 35: 191–214.
——— (1998). Attitudes to punishment: Findings from the 1992 British Crime Survey. Social Science Research Paper No. 7. London: South Bank University.
Hough, M., and J. V. Roberts (1998). Attitudes toward punishment: Findings from the British Crime Survey. Home Office Research Study no. 179. London: Home Office, Research and Statistics Directorate.
——— (1999). Sentencing trends in Britain: Public knowledge and public opinion. *Punishment & Society* 1 (1): 11–26.
Hough, M., H. Lewis, and N. Walker (1988). Factors associated with punitiveness in England and Wales. In N. Walker and M. Hough, eds., *Public attitudes to sentencing: Surveys from five countries*. Aldershot, England: Gower.
Howitt, D., ed. (1998). *Crime, the media and the law*. Chichester: John Wiley and Sons.
Illinois Poll (1997). Question 96. Howard W. Odum Institute for Research in Social Science. The University of North Carolina at Chapel Hill.
Illinois Policy Survey (1997). Archival Study NNSP-IL-015. Howard W. Odum Insti-

tute for Research in Social Science. University of North Carolina Institute for Research in Social Science. Available at: ftp://vance.irss.unc.edu/pub/.

Indermaur, D. (1987). Public perceptions of sentencing in Perth, Western Australia. *Australian and New Zealand Journal of Criminology* 20: 163–83.

——— (1990). *Perceptions of crime seriousness and sentencing: A comparison of court practice and the perceptions of the public and judges.* Report to the Criminology Research Council. Canberra: Australian Institute of Criminology.

——— (1995a). Are we becoming more violent? A comparison of trends in violent and property offences in Australia and Western Australia. *Journal of Quantitative Criminology* 11: 247–270.

——— (1995b). *Violent property crime.* Sydney: Federation Press.

——— (2000). Patterns of violence: An Australian perspective. *Australian and New Zealand Journal of Criminology* 33 (3): 287–299.

Indermaur, D., and A. Ferrante (1998). The drug crime picture in Western Australia: Policing the prohibition at the frontier. Keynote address at the 13th Mandurah Addiction Symposium.

Innes, C. (1993). Recent public opinion in the United States toward punishment and corrections. *Prison Journal* 73: 222–236.

Insight Canada (1994). *Perspectives Canada.* Toronto: Insight Canada Research.

Iyengar, S. (1991). *Is anyone responsible? How television frames political issues.* Chicago: University of Chicago Press.

Jacobs, J. (Dec. 4, 2000). Public wises up to bad drug policies. *San Jose (CA) Mercury News.*

James, O. (1995). *Juvenile violence in a winner-loser culture: Socio-economic and familial origins of the rise of violence against the person.* London: Free Association Books.

Jenkins, P. (1998). *Moral panic: Changing concepts of the child molester in modern America.* New Haven, CT: Yale University Press.

Jensen, E., and J. Gerber (1998). *The new war on drugs: Symbolic politics and criminal justice policy.* Cincinnati, OH: Anderson.

Johnson, M. T., and S. A. Gilbert (1997). *The U.S. Sentencing Guidelines: Results of the Federal Judicial Center's 1996 survey.* Washington, D.C.: Federal Judicial Center.

Johnson, P. A., R. G. Owens, M. E. Dewey, and N. E. Eisenberg (1990). Professionals' attributions of censure in father-daughter incest. *Child Abuse & Neglect* 14 (3): 419–428.

Kalven, H., and H. Zeisel (1966). *The American jury.* Chicago: University of Chicago Press.

Kaplan, M. F. (1994). Setting the record straight (again) on severity of penalty: A comment on Freedman et al. *Law & Human Behavior* 18 (6): 697–699.

Kaplan, M. F., and S. Krupa (1986). Severe penalties under the control of others can reduce guilt verdicts. *Law & Psychology Review* 10: 1–18.

Kappeler, V. E., M. Blumberg, and G. W. Potter (1993). *The mythology of crime and criminal justice.* Prospect Heights, IL: Waveland Press.

Katz, J. (1987). What makes crime news? *Media, Culture and Society* 9: 47–75.

Kennamer, J. (1992). Public opinion, the press and public policy: An introduction. In J. Kennamer ed., *Public opinion, the press and public policy.* Westport, CT: Praeger.

Kentucky Poll (1992). Howard W. Odum Institute for Research in Social Science. University of North Carolina at Chapel Hill. Available at: http://vance.irss.unc.edu.

Kershaw, C., T. Budd, G. Kinshott, J. Mattinson, P. Mayhew, and A. Myhill (2000). The 2000 British Crime Survey. *Home Office Statistical Bulletin* 18/00. London: Home Office.

King, N. J. (1998). Silencing nullification advocacy inside the jury room and outside the courtroom. *University of Chicago Law Review* 65 (2): 433–500.

Knowles, J. J. (1987). *Ohio citizen attitudes concerning crime and criminal justice.* Columbus: Governor's Office of Criminal Justice Services.

Kooistra, P. G., J. S. Mahoney, and S. D. Westervelt (1998). The world of crime according to "Cops." In M. Fishman and G. Cavender, eds., *Entertaining crime—television reality programs.* New York: Aldine De Gruyter.

Kopel, D. (1999). I, the jury. *American Enterprise* 10 (3): 83–84.

Koven, S. G. and M. C. Shelley (1993). No consensus on fighting the drug war: Differences between state policy elites and the mass public. *International Journal of the Addictions* 28 (14): 1531–1548.

Kury, H., and T. Ferdinand (1999). Public opinion and punitivity. *International Journal of Law and Psychiatry* 22: 373–392.

La Fond, J. Q. (1998). The costs of enacting a sexual predator law. *Psychology, Public Policy, and Law* 4 (1/2): 468–504.

Lane, S. D., P. Lurie, B. Bowser, J. Kahn, and D. Chen (2000). The coming of age of needle exchange: A history through 1993. In James A. Inciardi and Lana D. Harrison, eds., 47–68, *Harm reduction: National and international perspectives.* Thousand Oaks, CA: Sage.

Langan, P. A., and D. P. Farrington (1998). *Crime and justice in the United States and in England and Wales (1981–1996).* Washington, D.C.: Bureau of Justice Statistics, U.S. Department of Justice. Available at: www.ojp.usdoj.gov/bjs/pub/html/cjusew96/contents.

Lawrence, C. (Sept. 7, 1999). Juvenile offenders need tough love: Poll. *Chicago Sun Times*, p. 14 (Metro Section).

Lee, D. R., and C. Wellford (1997). Crime and sentencing: A public opinion survey of the people of Maryland. Baltimore: Maryland Justice Analysis Center. Available at: http://www.gov.state.md.us/sentencing/homepage/html/survey.html.

Leesti, T. (1992). Sentencing in youth courts, 1986–87 to 1990–91. *Juristat* 12 (4).

——— (1997). Weapons and violent crime. *Juristat*, 17 (7).

Lenton, S., D. McDonald, R. Ali, and T. Moore (1999). Laws applying to minor cannabis offences in Australia and their evaluation. *International Journal of Drug Policy* 10 (4) 299–303.

Levesque, Roger J. R. (2000). Sentencing sex crimes against children: An empirical and policy analysis. *Behavioral Sciences and the Law* 18: 331–341.

Lewis, J. (2001). *Constructing public opinion: How political elites do what they like and why we seem to go along with it.* New York: Columbia University Press.

Liebling, A. (1992) *Suicides in prison.* London: Routledge.

Liss, M. B., N.J. Finkel, and V. R. Moran (1994). Equal justice for accessories? Young pearls of proportionate wisdom. Paper presented at the American Psychology-Law Society's mid-year meeting.

Logan, R. (2001). Crime statistics in Canada, 2000. *Juristat* 21, (8).

Los, M., and S. E. Chamard (1997). Selling newspapers or educating the public? Sexual violence in the media. *Canadian Journal of Criminology* 39: 293–328.

Lurigio, A. J., M. Jones, and B. E. Smith (1995). "Up to speed"—Child sexual abuse:

Its causes, consequences, and implications for probation practice. *Federal Probation 59:* 69–76.

MacKenzie, D. (1994). Boot camps: A national assessment. *Overcrowded Times* 5 (4): 14–18.

Maguire, K., and A. Pastore, eds. (1997). *Sourcebook of criminal justice statistics.* Washington, D.C.: Bureau of Justice Statistics, U.S. Department of Justice.

——— (1998). *Sourcebook of criminal justice statistics.* Washington, D.C.: U.S. Department of Justice.

——— (1999). *Sourcebook of criminal justice statistics.* Washington, D.C.: U.S. Department of Justice.

——— (2000). *Sourcebook of criminal justice statistics.* Washington, D.C.: U.S. Department of Justice.

Makkai, T. (1994). *Patterns of drug use in Australian society.* Canberra: Australian Government Printing Service.

——— (2000). Harm reduction in Australia: Politics, policy, and public opinion. In J. E. Inciardi and L. D. Harrison, eds. *Harm reduction: National and international perspectives.* Thousand Oaks, CA: Sage.

Makkai, T., and I. McAllister (1993). Public opinion and the legal status of marijuana in Australia. *Journal of Drug Issues* 23 (3): 409–427.

——— (1998). *Patterns of drug use in Australia, 1985–95.* Canberra: Commonwealth Department of Health and Family Services.

Marsh, H. L. (1991). A comparative analysis of crime coverage in newspapers in the United States and other countries from 1960–1989: A review of the literature. *Journal of Criminal Justice* 19 (1): 67–80.

Maryland Poll (1992). Question 7. Odum Institute for Research in Social Science. The University of North Carolina at Chapel Hill.

——— (1997). Questions 1a, 1b, 11a. Odum Institute for Research in Social Science. The University of North Carolina at Chapel Hill. Available at: www.vance.irss.unc.edu.

Mattinson, J., and C. Mirrlees-Black (2000). *Attitudes to crime and criminal justice: Findings from the 1998 British Crime Survey.* London: Home Office.

——— (2001). *Confidence in the criminal justice system: Findings from the 2000 British Crime Survey.* Research Findings No. 137. London: Home Office.

Mayhew, P., and P. White (1997). *The 1996 International Crime Victimization Survey.* Home Office Research and Statistics Directorate. Research Findings No. 57. Available at: www.homeoffice.gov.uk/rds/pdfs/r57.pdf.

Maynard, C., and M. Wiederman (1997). Undergraduate students' perceptions of child sexual abuse—effects of age, sex, and gender role attitudes. *Child Abuse & Neglect* 21 (9): 833–844.

McCoombs, M. E., and D. E. Shaw (1972). The agenda setting function of the mass media. *Public Opinion Quarterly* 36: 176–187.

McGarrell, E. F., and M. Sandys (1996). The misperception of public opinion toward capital punishment: Examining the spuriousness explanation of death penalty support. *American Behavioral Scientist* 39 (4):500–513.

McNulty, J. (Aug. 9, 2000). Ottawa's archaic marijuana law goes to pot. *The Vancouver Province.* Available at: www.vancouverprovince.com.

Meek, J. (1995). The revival of preventive detention in New Zealand 1986–93. *Australian and New Zealand Journal of Criminology* 28 (3):225–257.

Meredith, C., B. Steinke, and S. Palmer (1994). *Research on the application of Section 85 of the Criminal Code of Canada.* Ottawa: Department of Justice Canada.

Miller, J. G. (1996). *Search and destroy: African-American males in the criminal justice system.* New York: Cambridge University Press.

Miller, J. G., D. M. Bersoff, and R. L. Harwood (1990). Perceptions of social responsibility in India and in the United States: Moral imperatives or personal decisions? *Journal of Personality and Social Psychology* 58: 33–47.

Miller, R. D. (1998). Forced administration of sex-drive reducing medications to sex offenders: Treatment or punishment? *Psychology, Public Policy, and Law* 4: 175–199.

Monmaney, T. (June 27, 1997). Suicide issue now in court of public opinion. *Los Angeles Times*, p. A-1.

Moon, M. M., J. L. Sundt, F. T. Cullen, and J. Wright (2000). Is child saving dead? Public support for juvenile rehabilitation. *Crime and Delinquency* 46 (1): 38–60.

Morgan, N. (1999). Accountability, transparency and justice: Do we need a sentencing matrix? *University of Western Australia Law Review* 28: 259–292.

Morgan Poll (Oct. 17, 2000). Majority of Australians disapprove of legalised heroin injecting rooms. Available at: www.roymorgan.com/polls

——— (July 11, 2000). Most Australians believe smoking marijuana should remain illegal. Finding No. 3315. The Roy Morgan Research Center. Available at: www.roymorgan.com/polls.

National Drug Control Strategy (1999). Washington, D.C.: Office of National Drug Control Policy.

National Post (July 20, 2000). Inside the crime stats.

National Public Radio (NPR). (October 16, 1995, 4:30 p.m. ET). All things considered: Simpson case focuses attention on jury nullification. Available at: http://www.primenet.com/slack/fija/butler3.txt.

Nava, M. (1988). Cleveland and the press: Outrage and anxiety in the reporting of child sexual abuse. *Feminist Review* 28: 103–121.

New South Wales (1996). *Sentencing Law Reform Commission of NSW.* Discussion Paper 33. Sydney: Law Reform Commission of NSW.

New Zealand Country Report (March 2001). *Report prepared for the 44th session of the Commission on Narcotic Drugs in Vienna.* Wellington, New Zealand: Ministry of Health (ISBN 478-24328-6).

New Zealand Ministry of Justice (1998a). *Crime to sentence: Trends in criminal justice 1986–1996.* Wellington: New Zealand Ministry of Justice.

——— (1998b). *The use of imprisonment in New Zealand.* Wellington: New Zealand Ministry of Justice.

Niedermeier, K. E., I. A. Horowitz, and N. L. Kerr (1999). Informing jurors of their nullification power: A route to a just verdict or judicial chaos? *Law & Human Behavior* 23 (3): 331–351.

NORML (December 13, 2001). DEA okays first medical marijuana trials in nearly two decades. Available at: http://www.norml.org/news/index,shtml.

O'Connell, M., and A. Whelan (1996). The public perception of crime prevalence, newspaper readership and "mean world" attitudes. *Legal and Criminological Psychology* 1: 179–195.

Oliver, M. B., and G. B. Armstrong (1998). The colour of crime: Perceptions of Caucasians' and African-Americans' involvement in crime. In M. Fishman and G. Cavender, eds., *Entertaining crime—television reality programs.* New York: Aldine De Gruyter.

O'Malley, P. (1994). Neo-liberal crime control: Political agendas and the future of crime prevention in Australia. In D. Chappell and P. Wilson, eds., *The Australian criminal justice system: The mid 1990s.* Sydney: Butterworths.

——— (1999). Volatile and contradictory punishment. *Theoretical Criminology* 3: 175–196.

ONDCP (March 2001). *Drug treatment in the criminal justice system.* Drug Policy Information Clearinghouse Fact Sheet. NCJ-181857.

Orcutt, J. D., and J. B. Turner (1993). Shocking numbers and graphic accounts: Quantified images of drug problems in the print media. *Social Problems* 40 (2): 190–206.

Payne, B., and R. Gainey (1999) Attitudes toward electronic monitoring among monitored offenders and criminal justice students. *Journal of Offender Rehabilitation* 29: 195–208.

Pithers, W. D., and A. Gray (1998). The other half of the story: Children with sexual behavior problems. *Psychology, Public Policy, and Law* 4 (1–2): 200–217.

Pitts, J. (1996). Juvenile-justice policy in England and Wales. In J. C. Coleman and C. Warren-Anderson, eds., *Youth policy in the 1990's: The way forward.* London: Routledge.

Plotnikoff, J., and R. Wolfson (2000). *Where are they Now? An evaluation of sex offender registration in England and Wales.* Police Research Series Paper 126. London: Home Office.

Polk, K., and R. White (1999). Economic adversity and criminal behavior: Rethinking youth unemployment and crime. *Australian and New Zealand Journal of Criminology* 32: 284–302.

Potter, W. J., and I. C. Chang, (1990). Television exposure measures and the cultivation hypothesis. *Journal of Broadcasting and Electronic Media* 34 (3): 313–333.

Pratt, J. (1998a). The rise and fall of homophobia and sexual psychopath legislation in postwar society. *Psychology, Public Policy, and Law* 4: 25–49.

——— (1998b). Towards the "decivilizing" of punishment? *Social and Legal Studies* 7: 487–515.

Queensland Criminal Justice Commission (2000). *Prisoner numbers in Queensland: An examination of population trends in Queensland's correctional institutions.* Toowong, Queensland: Research and Prevention Division of the Queensland Criminal Justice Commission.

Radzinowicz, L. (1948–86). *A History of the English criminal law and its administration from 1750.* Vol. 5, *The Emergence of Penal Policy in Victorian and Edwardian England.* London: Stevens and Sons.

Ramsay, M., and S. Partridge (1999). *Drug misuse declared in 1998: Results from the British Crime Survey.* London: Home Office.

Reichel, P., and A. Gauthier (1990) Boot camp corrections: A public reaction. In R. Muraskin, ed., *Issues in justice: Explaining policy issues in the criminal justice system.* Bristol, IN: Wyndham Hall.

Reidy, T. J., and N. J. Hochstadt (1993). Attribution of blame in incest cases: A comparison of mental health professionals. *Child Abuse & Neglect* 17(3): 371–381.

Reiner, R. (1997). Media made criminality: The representation of crime in the mass media. In M. Maguire, R. Morgan, and R. Reiner, eds., *The Oxford handbook of criminology*. New York: Oxford University Press.

Riley, P. and V. Rose (1980). Public vs. elite opinion on correctional reform: Implications for social policy. *Journal of Criminal Justice* 8: 345–356.

Roach, K. (1999). *Due process and victims' rights. The new law and politics of criminal justice*. Toronto: University of Toronto Press.

Roberts, J. V. (1988). Early release: What do the Canadian public really think? *Canadian Journal of Criminology* 30: 231–239.

——— (1992). Public opinion, crime and criminal justice. In M. Tonry, ed., *Crime and justice: A review of research*. Vol. 16. Chicago: University of Chicago Press.

——— (1994). *Public knowledge of crime and justice: An inventory of Canadian findings*. Ottawa: Department of Justice Canada.

——— (1997). Paying for the past: The role of criminal record in the sentencing process. In M. Tonry, ed., *Crime and justice: A review of the research*. Vol. 22. Chicago: University of Chicago Press.

——— (2001). The evolution and consequences of sentencing reform in Canada. *Sociologie et Societes* 33: 67–83.

——— (2002a). Alchemy in sentencing: An analysis of sentencing reform proposals in England and Wales. *Punishment and Society*, 4(4): 445–462.

——— (2002b). Mandatory sentences for firearms offences: Explaining the consequences for the sentencing process. *Osgoode Hall Law Journal*, in press.

——— (2002c). Determining parole eligibility dates for life prisoners: Lessons from jury hearings in Canada. *Punishment and Society* 4:103–114.

——— (2003). Public opinion and mandatory sentences of imprisonment: A review of international findings. *Criminal Justice and Behavior* (in press).

Roberts, J. V., and D. Cole (1999). Sentencing and parole arrangements for cases of murder. In J. V. Roberts and D. Cole, eds., *Making sense of sentencing*. Toronto: University of Toronto Press.

Roberts, J. V., and A. N. Doob (1983). *Sentencing: An analysis of the public's view*. Ottawa: Department of Justice Canada.

——— (1988). Public punitiveness and public knowledge of the facts: Some Canadian surveys. In N. Walker and M. Hough, eds., *Public attitudes to sentencing*. Cambridge Studies in Criminology 49. Aldershot, England: Gower.

——— (1989). Sentencing and public opinion: Taking false shadows for true substances. *Osgoode Hall Law Journal* 27: 491–515.

——— (1997). Race, ethnicity and criminal justice in Canada. In M. Tonry, ed., *Crime and justice*. Vol. 21, *Ethnicity, crime and immigration: Comparative and cross-national perspectives*. Chicago: University of Chicago Press.

Roberts, J. V., A. N. Doob, and V. Marinos (2000). Judicial attitudes towards conditional sentences of imprisonment: Results of a national survey. Ottawa: Department of Justice Canada.

Roberts, J. V., and C. Grimes (2000). Adult criminal court statistics, 1998–99. *Juristat* 20 (1).

Roberts, J. V., J. Nuffield, and R. Hann (1999). Parole and the public: Attitudinal and behavioural responses. *Empirical and Applied Criminal Justice Research* 1.

Roberts, J. V. and L. S. Stalans (1997). *Public opinion, crime and criminal justice*. Boulder, CO: Westview Press.

Roberts, J. V., and M. Hough, eds. (2002). *Changing public attitudes to sentencing.* Cullompton, Devon: Willan Publishing.

Robinson, P. H., and J. M. Darley (1995). *Justice, liability, and blame: Community views and the criminal law.* Boulder, CO: Westview Press.

Rock, P. (1986). *A view from the shadows.* Oxford: Clarendon Press.

Rossetti, J. (1995). The mark of Cain: Reintegrating pedophiles. *America* 173 (6): 9–17.

Rossi, P. H., and R. A. Berk (1997). *Just punishments : Federal guidelines and public views compared.* New York: Aldine De Gruyter.

Roy Morgan Research (2000). Majority of Australians disapprove of legalized heroin injecting rooms. Bulletin, Finding No. 3341. New Zealand Herald. Available at: http://www.mapinc.org/drugnews/v01/n482/a09.htm.

Rubin, E. L. (1999). Introduction: Minimizing harm as a solution to the crime policy conundrum. In E. L. Rubin, ed., *Minimizing harm: A new crime policy for modern America.* Boulder, CO: Westview Press.

Sallmann, P., and J. Willis (1984). *Criminal justice in Australia.* Melbourne: Oxford University Press.

Sanders, T. (2000). Sentencing of young offenders in Canada, 1998/99. *Juristat* 20 (7).

Sanders, T., and J. V. Roberts (2000). Public attitudes toward conditional sentencing: Results of a national survey. *Canadian Journal of Behavioural Science* 32: 199–207.

Saney, P. (1986). *Crime and culture in America.* Westport: Greenwood Press.

Sauer, K. K. (1995). Informed conviction: Instructing the jury about mandatory sentencing consequences. *Columbia Law Review* 95: 1232–1256.

Savelsberg, J. (1994). Knowledge, domination and criminal punishment. *American Journal of Sociology* 99: 911–43.

Savelsberg, J. (1999). Knowledge, domination and criminal punishment revisited: Incorporating state socialism. *Punishment and Society* 1: 45–70.

Savoie, J. (1999). Youth violent crime. *Juristat* 19 (13).

Schaaf, D. W. (2000). Note: What if the victim is a child? Examining the constitutionality of Louisiana's challenge to *Coker v. Georgia. University of Illinois Law Review,* 347.

Scheflin, A. W. (1972). Jury nullification: The right to say no. *Southern California Law Review* 45: 168–226.

Scheflin, A., and J. V. Dyke (1980). Jury nullification: The contours of a controversy. *Law and Contemporary Problems* 43 (4): 52–115.

——— (1991). Merciful juries: The resilience of jury nullification. *Washington and Lee Law Review* 48 (1): 165–183.

Scheingold, S. (1984). *The politics of law and order.* New York: Longman.

Schiraldi, V., and M. Soler (1998). *Will of the people? The public's opinion of the Violent and Repeat Juvenile Offender Act of 1997.* Washington, D.C.: Youth Law Center, The Justice Policy Institute.

Schwartz, I. (1989). The facts and myths of juvenile crime. Chapter 2 in *Justice for Juveniles.* Lexington, MA: Lexington Books.

——— (1992). Juvenile crime-fighting policies: What the public really wants. In I. M. Schwartz, ed., *Juvenile justice and public policy.* New York: Lexington Books.

Scott, D. (1995). The social construction of child sexual abuse: Debates about definitions and the politics of prevalence. *Psychiatry, Psychology and Law* 2: 117–126.

Senese, J. (1992). Intensive supervision probation and public opinion: Perceptions of community correctional policy and practice. *American Journal of Criminal Justice* 16: 33–56.

Shepherd, R. E., Jr. (1998). Juvenile justice: How the media misrepresents juvenile policies. *Criminal Justice: American Bar Association Magazine* 12 (4): 37–39.

Sickmund, M., H. N. Snyder, and E. Poe-Yamagata (1997). *Juvenile offenders and victims: 1997 update on violence statistics summary.* Pittsburgh: National Center for Juvenile Justice.

Sigler, R. T. (1995). Preferred labels and penalties for forced sexual intercourse. *International Journal of the Sociology of Law* 23: 171–187.

Signorelli, N. (1990). Television's mean and dangerous world: A continuation of the cultural indicators perspective. In N. Signorelli, and M. Morgan, eds., *Cultivation analysis: New directions in media effects research.* Newbury Park, CA: Sage.

Signorelli, N., and G. Gerbner (1988). *Violence and terror in the mass media.* New York: Greenwood.

Simon, J. (1998). Managing the monstrous: Sex offenders and the new penology. *Psychology, Public Policy, and Law* 4 (1/2): 452–467.

Simon, L. M. J. (1996). The effect of victim-offender relationship on the sentence length of violent offenders. *Journal of Crime & Justice* 19: 129–148.

Singer, P. A., S. Choudhry, J. Armstrong, E. M. Meslin, and F. H. Lowy (1995). Public opinion regarding end-of-life decisions: Influence of prognosis, practice, and process. *Social Science Medicine* 41 (11): 1517–1521.

Skibinski, G. J., and J. E. Esser-Stuart (1993). Public sentiment toward innovative child sexual abuse intervention strategies: Consensus and conflict. *Juvenile & Family Court Journal* 44 (3): 17–26.

Smith, B. L., and E. H. Stevens (1984). Sentence disparity and the judge-jury sentencing debate: An analysis of robbery sentences in six southern states. *Criminal Justice Review* 9 (1): 1–7.

Snyder, H. (2000). *Sexual assaults of young children as reported to law enforcement: Victim, incident, and offender characteristics.* Washington, D.C.: U.S. Department of Justice (NCJ 182990).

Snyder, H., and M. Sickmund (1999). *Juvenile offenders and victims: 1999 National Report.* Washington, D.C.: U.S. Office of Juvenile Justice and Delinquency Prevention.

Sourcebook of Criminal Justice Statistics Online (1999). Table 2.2, Attitudes toward important issues for the government to address. Available at: www.albany.edu/sourcebook/.

Sourcebook of Criminal Justice Statistics Online (2002). Table 2.1, Attitudes toward the most important problem facing the country, United States, 1982–2002. Available at: www.albany.edu/sourcebook/.

Southern Focus Poll (1997). Questions 99, 101. Howard W. Odum Institute for Research in Social Science. University of North Carolina at Chapel Hill. Available at: www.irss.unc.edu.

Sparks, R. (1992). *Television and the drama of crime: Moral tales and the place of crime in public life.* Philadelphia: Open University Press.

——— (1996). Masculinity and heroism in the Hollywood "blockbuster": The culture industry and contemporary images of crime and law enforcement. *British Journal of Criminology* 36: 348–360.

Speir, P. (1999). *Conviction and sentencing of offenders in New Zealand: 1989 to 1998.* Wellington: Ministry of Justice.

Spohn, C., and D. Holleran (2000). The imprisonment penalty paid by young, unemployed black and Hispanic male offenders. *Criminology* 38 (1): 281–306.

Sprott, J. (1996). Understanding public views of youth crime and the youth justice system. *Canadian Journal of Criminology* 38 (3): 271–290.

——— (1998). Understanding public opposition to a separate youth justice system. *Crime and Delinquency* 44: 399–411.

Sprott, J., and A. Doob (1997). Fear, victimization, and attitudes to sentencing, the courts, and the police. *Canadian Journal of Criminology* 39 (3): 275–291.

Sprott, J., and H. D. Snyder (1999). A comparison of juvenile delinquency in Canada and the United States. *Criminologie* 32 (2): 55–82.

St. John, R. (1997). License to nullify: The democratic and constitutional deficiencies of authorized jury lawmaking. *Yale Law Journal* 106 (8): 2563–2597.

Stalans, L. (1993). Citizens' crime stereotypes, biased recall, and punishment preferences in abstract cases: The educative role of interpersonal sources. *Law and Human Behavior* 17 (4): 451–470.

Stalans, L. and G. T. Henry (1994). Societal views of justice for adolescents accused of murder. *Law and Human Behavior* 18 (6): 675–696.

Stalans, L., M. J. Seng, and P. R. Yarnold (2001). *Long-term impact evaluation of specialized sex offender probation programs in three counties.* Chicago: Illinois Criminal Justice Information Authority.

Stein, K. (1999). *Review of Canadian attitudes towards crime and criminal justice.* Ottawa: Department of Justice Canada, Research and Statistics Division.

Steiner, B. D., W. J. Bowers, and A. Sarat (1999). Folk knowledge as legal action: Death penalty judgments and the tenet of early release in a culture of mistrust and punitiveness. *Law & Society Review* 33 (2): 461–505.

Straus, M. (1992). Sociological research and social policy: The case of family violence. *Sociological Forum* 7: 211–237.

Streib, V. L. (1999). The Juvenile Death Penalty Today: Death Sentences and Executions for Juvenile Crimes, January 1973–June 1999. Available at: http://www.law.onu.edu/faculty/streib/juvdeath.htm.

Stroud, D., S. L. Martens, and J. Barker, J. (2000). Criminal investigation of child sexual abuse: A comparison of cases referred to the prosecutor to those not referred. *Child Abuse & Neglect* 24 (5): 689–700.

Sundt, J., F. Cullen, B. Applegate, and M. Turner, (1998) The tenacity of the rehabilitative ideal revisited: Have attitudes toward offender treatment changed? *Criminal Justice and Behavior* 25 (4): 426–442.

Surette, R. (1994). Predator criminals as media icons. In G. Barak, ed., *Media, process and the social construction of crime.* New York: Garland.

Survey Research Laboratory (1995). *Public opinion regarding the juvenile justice system.* Richmond: Virginia Commonwealth University Press. Available at: http://www.vcu.edu/cppweb/srlweb/press/cp28yout.htm.

Tabachnick, J., F. H. Haydenville, and L. Denny (1997). Perceptions of child sexual abuse as a public health problem—Vermont. *Morbidity & Mortality Weekly Report* 46 (34): 801–804.

Taggart, P. (2000). *Populism.* Buckingham, England: Open University Press.

Taylor, B., and T. Bennett (1999). *Comparing drug use rates of detained arrestees in the United States and England.* NCJ 175052. Washington, D.C.: Office of Justice Programs, National Institute of Justice. Available at: www.ncjrs.org/txtfiles1/175052.txt.

Taylor, I. (1981). Crime waves in post-war Britain. *Contemporary Crises* 5: 43–62.

Tennessee Poll (1990). Question nos. 45, 47, 48. Howard W. Odum Institute for Research in Social Science. University of North Carolina at Chapel Hill.

Thomas, J. (2000). Adult correctional services in Canada, 1998–99. *Juristat* 20 (3).

Thorp, T. M. (1997). Sentencing and punishment in New Zealand, 1981–1993. In M. Tonry and K. Hatlestad, eds., *Sentencing reform in overcrowded times: A comparative perspective* (pp. 163–168). New York: Oxford University Press.

Threlkeld, M. (April 24, 1993). Jury Acquits Two in Deprogramming Case. Available at: http://www.rickross.com/reference/deprogramming1.html.

Tjaden, P., and N. Thoennes (1998). Prevalence, incidence, and consequences of violence against women: Findings from the National Violence against Women Survey. *National Institute of Justice Centers for Disease Control and Prevention Research in Brief.* Washington, D.C.: U.S. Department of Justice, Office of Justice Programs.

Toby, J. (1957). Social disorganization and stake in conformity: Complementary factors in the predatory behavior of hoodlums. *Journal of Criminal Law, Criminology and Police Science* 48: 12–17.

Tonry, M. (1995). Twenty years of sentencing reform: Steps forward, steps backward. *Judicature* 78 (4): 169–179.

——— (1996). *Sentencing matters.* New York: Oxford University Press.

——— (1999). The fragmentation of sentencing and corrections in America. *National Institute of Justice: Research in Brief.* NCJ 175721. Washington, DC: U.S. Department of Justice.

——— (2001). Symbol, substance, and severity in western penal policies. *Punishment and Society* 3: 517–536.

Tonry, M., and K. Hatlestad, eds. (1997). *Sentencing reform in overcrowded times: A comparative perspective.* New York: Oxford University Press.

Tremblay, S. (2000). Crime statistics in Canada, 1999. *Juristat* 20 (5).

Triggs, S. (1997). *Crime to sentence: Trends in criminal justice, 1986 to 1996.* Wellington: New Zealand Ministry of Justice.

Tufts, J., and J. V. Roberts (2002). Sentencing juvenile offenders: Public preferences and judicial practice. *Criminal Justice Policy Review* 13: 46–64.

Turner, C. F., L. Ku, S. M. Rogers, and L. D. Lindberg (1998). Adolescent sexual behavior, drug use, and violence: Increased reporting with computer survey technology. *Science* 28: 867–873.

Turner, M., F. Cullen, J. Sundt, and B. Applegate (1997). Public tolerance for community-based sanctions. *Prison Journal* 77: 6–26.

Tyler, T. R., and R. J. Boeckmann (1997). Three strikes and you are out, but why? The psychology of public support for punishing rule breakers. *Law and Society Review* 31 (2): 237–264.

United Nations Information Service (January 22, 2001). UN Drug Report Sees Hope on Horizon. Available at: www.undcp.org/press_release_2001-01-22_1.html.

United States v. Dougherty. 473 F2d 1113, 1130 (D.C. Cir 1972).

United States v. Thomas. 116 F3d 606, 617 (2d Cir 1997).

U.S. Sentencing Commission (1998). *1997 Sourcebook of federal sentencing statistics.* p. 56. Washington, D.C.: United States Sentencing Commission.

Vallient, P. M., C. J. Furac, and D. H. Antonowicz (1994). Attitudes toward sex offenders by female undergraduate university students enrolled in a psychology program. *Social Behaviour & Personality* 22 (2): 247–259.

Van Swaaningnen, R. (1997). *Critical criminology: Visions from Europe.* London: Sage.

Vaughan, B. (2000). The civilizing process and the Janus face of modern punishment. *Theoretical Criminology* 4: 71–91.

Venters, G. (1999). UK Physicians Call for Legalization of Marijuana. News Briefs. Available at: www.ndsn.org/Summer99/MEDMJ3.html.

Vidmar, N. (1996). Pretrial prejudice in Canada: A comparative perspective on the criminal jury. *Judicature* 79 (5):249–255.

Vidmar, N., S. S. Beale, M. Rose, and L. F. Donnelly (1997). Should we rush to reform the criminal jury? Consider conviction rate data. *Judicature* 80 (6): 286–290.

Von Hirsch, A. (1993). *Censure and sanctions.* New York: Oxford University Press.

Von Hirsch, A., A. E. Bottoms, E. Burney, and P. Wikstrom (1999). *Criminal deterrence and sentence severity: An analysis of recent research.* Oxford: Hart Publishing.

Walker, J., M. Collins, and P. Wilson (1987). How the public sees sentencing: An Australian survey. *Trends and Issues* no. 4. Australian Institute of Criminology.

Wall Street Journal (Oct. 4, 1995). Race seems to play an increasing role in many jury verdicts, p. 1.

Walmsley, R. (2000). *World prison population list.* Research Findings Number 116. London: Home Office.

Warr, M. (1995). Public opinion on crime and punishment. *Public Opinion Quarterly* 59: 296–310.

Waterman, C. K., and D. Foss-Goodman (1984). Child molesting: Variables relating to attribution of fault to victims, offenders, and non-participating parents. *Journal of Sex Research* 20: 329–349.

Weikopf, C. (Dec. 3, 2000). Court, Bush best hopes for medical pot. *Daily News of Los Angeles.* Available at: www.dailynews.com

Weisberg, R. (1999). Comment: Crime, violence and public mythology. In E. Rubin, ed., *Minimizing harm: A new crime policy for modern America.* Boulder, CO: Westview Press.

Wells, C. E., and E. E. Motley (2001). Reinforcing the myth of the crazed rapist: A feminist critique of recent rape legislation. *Boston University Law Review* 81 (127): 1–69.

Wilk, R. J., and C. R. McCarthy (1986). Intervention in child sexual abuse: A survey of attitudes. *Social Casework* 67 (1): 20–26.

Wilkins, L. (1991). *Punishment, crime, and market forces.* Aldershot, England: Dartmouth.

Wilkins, L.T., and K. Pease (1987). Public demand for punishment. *International Journal of Sociology and Social Policy* 7 (3): 16–29.

Williams, P., and J. Dickinson (1993). Fear of crime: Read all about it? The relationship between newspaper crime reporting and the fear of crime. *British Journal of Criminology* 33 (1): 33–56.

Williams, J. E., and K. A. Holmes (1981). *The second assault: Rape and public attitudes.* Westport, CT: Greenwood Press.

World Drug Report (2000). Oxford: Oxford University Press.
Wright, K. (1985). *The great American crime myth.* Westport, CT: Greenwood Press.
Wyoming Election Year Survey (1998). Archival Study NNSP-WY-003. Howard W. Odum Institute for Research in Social Science. University of North Carolina at Chapel Hill. Available at: ftp://vance.irss.unc.edu/pub/
Yankelovich, Skelly & White. (1983). Public Opinion Online (Question no. 90). Roper Center at the University of Connecticut, New Haven.
Yankelovich, D. (1991). *Coming to public judgment: Making democracy work in a complex world.* Syracuse, NY: Syracuse University Press.
Young, J. (1999). *The exclusive society.* London: Sage.
Young, M., and J. Gainsborough (2000). Prosecuting juveniles in adult court: An assessment of trends and consequences. The Sentencing Project. Report available at: www.sentencingproject.org.
Young, W., and M. Brown (1993). Cross-national comparisons of imprisonment. In M. Tonry, ed., *Crime and justice: A review of the research.* Vol. 17. Chicago: University of Chicago Press.
Young, W., N. Cameron, and Y. Tinsley (1999). *Juries in criminal trials: Part 2, A summary of the research findings.* Preliminary paper 37—vol. 2. Wellington: New Zealand Law Commission.
Zamble, E., and K. Kalm (1990). General and specific measures of public attitudes toward sentencing. *Canadian Journal of Behavioural Science* 22: 327–337.
Zedner, L. (1995). In pursuit of the vernacular: Comparing law and order discourse in Britain and Germany. *Social and Legal Studies* 4:517–534.
Zimring, F. (1998). *American youth violence.* New York: Oxford University Press.
——— (1999). The 1990s assault on juvenile justice: Notes from an ideological battleground. *Federal Sentencing Reporter* 11: 260–261.
Zimring, F., and G. Hawkins (1992). *Prison population and criminal justice policy in California.* Berkeley, CA: Institute of Governmental Studies.
——— (1999). Public attitudes toward crime: Is American violence a crime problem? In E. L. Rubin, ed., *Minimizing harm: A new crime policy for modern America.* Boulder, CO: Westview Press.

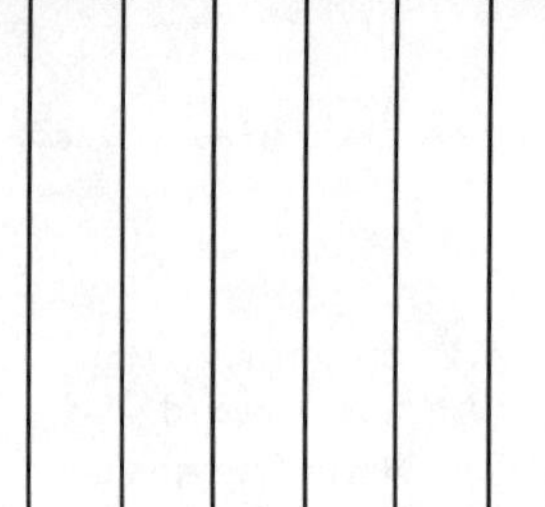

Index